DELETED

Bloom's Modern Critical Interpretations

The Adventures of
  Huckleberry Finn
The Age of Innocence
Alice's Adventures in
  Wonderland
All Quiet on the
  Western Front
Animal Farm
The Ballad of the Sad
  Café
Beloved
Beowulf
Black Boy
The Bluest Eye
The Canterbury Tales
Cat on a Hot Tin
  Roof
Catch-22
The Catcher in the
  Rye
The Chronicles of
  Narnia
The Color Purple
Crime and
  Punishment
The Crucible
Cry, the Beloved
  Country
Darkness at Noon
Death of a Salesman
The Death of Artemio
  Cruz
The Diary of Anne
  Frank
Don Quixote
Emerson's Essays
Emma
Fahrenheit 451
A Farewell to Arms
Frankenstein
The Glass Menagerie
The Grapes of Wrath

Great Expectations
The Great Gatsby
Gulliver's Travels
Hamlet
Heart of Darkness
The House on Mango
  Street
I Know Why the
  Caged Bird Sings
The Iliad
Invisible Man
Jane Eyre
The Joy Luck Club
Julius Caesar
The Jungle
King Lear
Long Day's Journey
  into Night
Lord of the Flies
The Lord of the Rings
Love in the Time of
  Cholera
Macbeth
The Man Without
  Qualities
The Merchant of
  Venice
The Metamorphosis
A Midsummer Night's
  Dream
Miss Lonelyhearts
Moby-Dick
My Ántonia
Native Son
Night
1984
The Odyssey
Oedipus Rex
The Old Man and the
  Sea
On the Road

One Flew over the
  Cuckoo's Nest
One Hundred Years of
  Solitude
Othello
Persuasion
Portnoy's Complaint
Pride and Prejudice
Ragtime
The Red Badge of
  Courage
Romeo and Juliet
The Rubáiyát of Omar
  Khayyám
The Scarlet Letter
A Separate Peace
Silas Marner
Slaughterhouse-Five
Song of Solomon
The Sound and the
  Fury
The Stranger
A Streetcar Named
  Desire
Sula
The Sun Also Rises
The Tale of Genji
A Tale of Two Cities
"The Tell-Tale Heart"
  and Other Stories
Their Eyes Were
  Watching God
Things Fall Apart
The Things They
  Carried
To Kill a Mockingbird
Ulysses
Waiting for Godot
The Waste Land
Wuthering Heights
Young Goodman
  Brown

Bloom's Modern Critical Interpretations

William Shakespeare's
The Merchant of Venice
New Edition

Edited and with an introduction by
Harold Bloom
Sterling Professor of the Humanities
Yale University

BLOOM'S
LITERARY CRITICISM
An imprint of Infobase Publishing

Bloom's Modern Critical Interpretations: The Merchant of Venice—New Edition

Copyright © 2010 by Infobase Publishing

Introduction © 2010 by Harold Bloom

All rights reserved. No part of this publication may be reproduced or utilized in any form or by any means, electronic or mechanical, including photocopying, recording, or by any information storage or retrieval systems, without permission in writing from the publisher. For more information contact:

Bloom's Literary Criticism

An imprint of Infobase Publishing

132 West 31st Street

New York NY 10001

Library of Congress Cataloging-in-Publication Data

William Shakespeare's The merchant of Venice / edited and with an introduction by Harold Bloom. — New ed.

    p. cm. — (Bloom's modern critical interpretations)

  Includes bibliographical references and index.

  ISBN 978-1-60413-885-6 (hardcover)

  1. Shakespeare, William, 1564–1616. Merchant of Venice. 2. Shylock (Fictitious character) 3. Jews in literature. I. Bloom, Harold.

  PR2825.W56 2010

  822.3'3—dc22

                            2010006132

Bloom's Literary Criticism books are available at special discounts when purchased in bulk quantities for businesses, associations, institutions, or sales promotions. Please call our Special Sales Department in New York at (212)967-8800 or (800)322-8755.

You can find Bloom's Literary Criticism on the World Wide Web at http://www.chelseahouse.com

Contributing editor: Pamela Loos

Cover design by Takeshi Takahashi

Composition by IBT Global, Troy NY

Cover printed by IBT Global, Troy NY

Book printed and bound by IBT Global, Troy NY

Date printed: July 2010

Printed in the United States of America

10 9 8 7 6 5 4 3 2 1

This book is printed on acid-free paper.

All links and Web addresses were checked and verified to be correct at the time of publication. Because of the dynamic nature of the Web, some addresses and links may have changed since publication and may no longer be valid.

Contents

Editor's Note

My introduction dwells on Shylock's conversion, a critique of Marlowe that costs the play dearly, destroying the plausibility of Shakespeare's comic villain as a character.

Harry Berger Jr. revisits the casket scene in discerning Portia's divine powers of mercifixion, after which Coppélia Kahn explores male friendship and betrayal in the play.

Richard A. Levin traces how the misfortunes of Venice follow the characters to idyllic Belmont, the setting of Portia's villa. Robert Ornstein locates the work's climactic resolution in the fourth act, which clears the way for the delusions of the play's ending.

Harry Levin returns us to the concord of Belmont and the play's final act, followed by Tony Tanner's parsing of Portia's telling question, upon entering court, "Which is the merchant here? and which the Jew?"

W. H. Auden suggests that a society built on speculative trade encourages frivolity and impulsiveness in the personal affairs of its citizens, after which Peter D. Holland also meditates on the ducat-mad world of the play. Grace Tiffany concludes the volume exploring the ways self-interest and the law intersect in *The Merchant of Venice*.

HAROLD BLOOM

Introduction

Of Shakespeare's displaced spirits, those enigmatic figures who sometimes seem to have wandered into the wrong play, Shylock clearly remains the most problematical. We need always to keep reminding ourselves that he is a comic villain, partly derived from the grandest of Marlovian scoundrels, Barabas, Jew of Malta. In some sense, that should place Shylock in the Machiavellian company of two villains of tragedy, Edmund and Iago, yet none of us wishes to see Shylock there. Edmund and Iago are apocalyptic humorists; self-purged of pathos, they frighten us because continually they invent themselves while manipulating others. Shylock's pathos is weirdly heroic; he was meant to frighten us, to be seen as a nightmare made into flesh and blood, while seeking the audience's flesh and blood. It seems clear to me that if Shakespeare himself were to be resurrected, in order to direct a production of *The Merchant of Venice* on a contemporary stage in New York City, there would be a riot, quite without the assistance of the Jewish Defense League. The play is both a superb romantic comedy and a marvelously adequate version of a perfectly Christian, altogether murderous anti-Semitism, of a kind fused into Christianity by the Gospel of John in particular.

In that latter assertion, or parts of it, I follow after the formidable E. E. Stoll, who observed that Shylock's penalty was the heaviest to be discovered in all the pound-of-flesh stories. As Stoll said, in none of them "does the money-lender suffer like Shylock—impoverishment, sentence of death, and an outrage done to his faith from which Jews were guarded even by decrees of German Emperors and Roman pontiffs." Of all the enigmas presented by

1

The Merchant of Venice, to me the most baffling is Shylock's broken acceptance of forced conversion. Is it persuasive? Surely not, since Shakespeare's Shylock, proud and fierce Jew, scarcely would have preferred Christianity to death. Consistency of character in Shylock admittedly might have cost Shakespeare the comedy of his comedy; a Shylock put to death might have shadowed the ecstasy of Belmont in act 5. But so does the forced conversion, for us, though clearly not for Shakespeare and his contemporary audience. The difficult but crucial question becomes: Why did Shakespeare inflict the cruelty of the false conversion, knowing he could not allow Shylock the tragic dignity of dying for his people's faith?

I find it astonishing that this question has never been asked anywhere in the published criticism of *The Merchant of Venice*. No other Shakespearean character who has anything like Shylock's representational force is handled so strangely by Shakespeare and ultimately so inadequately. That Shylock should agree to become a Christian is more absurd than would be the conversion of Coriolanus to the popular party or Cleopatra's consent to become a vestal virgin at Rome. We sooner could see Falstaff as a monk than we can contemplate Shylock as a Christian. Shakespeare notoriously possessed the powers both of preternatural irony and of imbuing a character with more vitality than a play's context could sustain. I cannot better the judgment on Christian conversion that Launcelot Gobbo makes in his dialogue with the charmingly insufferable Jessica, that Jewish Venetian princess:

Jessica: I shall be sav'd by my husband, he hath made me a
Christian!
Launcelot: Truly, the more to blame he; we were Christians
enow before, e'en as many as could well live one by another. This
making of Christians will raise the price of hogs. If we grow all
to be pork-eaters, we shall not shortly have a rasher on the coals
for money.

But Shakespeare takes care to distance this irony from the play's comic catastrophe, when the Jew is undone by Christian mercy. It is Antonio, the pious Jew baiter, who adds to the Duke's pardon the requirement that Shylock immediately become a Christian, after which Shakespeare seems a touch anxious to get Shylock offstage as quietly and quickly as possible:

Duke: He shall do this, or else I do recant
The pardon that I late pronounced here.
Portia: Art thou contented, Jew? what dost thou say?
Shylock: I am content.

Portia: Clerk, draw a deed of gift.
Shylock: I pray you give me leave to go from hence.
I am not well. Send the deed after me,
And I will sign it.

And in a moment, Shylock walks out of the play, to the discord of what must seem to us Gratiano's Nazilike jeers and threats. In our post-Holocaust universe, how can we accommodate Shylock's "I am content," too broken for irony, too strong for any play whatsoever? That question, I think, is unanswerable and does not belong to literary criticism anyway. What is essential for criticism is to ask and answer the double question: Why did Shakespeare so represent his stage Jew as to make possible the romantic interpretation that has proceeded from Hazlitt and Henry Irving right through to Harold C. Goddard and innumerable actors in our century, and having done so, why did the playwright then shatter the character's consistency by imposing on him the acceptance of the humiliating forced conversion to that religion of mercy, the Christianity of Venice?

In his lively essay on the play, W. H. Auden remarks on a different kind of implausibility that Shakespeare confers on Shylock:

After Portia has trapped Shylock through his own insistence upon the letter of the law of Contract, she produces another law by which any alien who conspires against the life of a Venetian citizen forfeits his goods and places his life at the Doge's mercy. Even in the rush of a stage performance, the audience cannot help reflecting that a man as interested in legal subtleties as Shylock, would, surely, have been aware of the existence of this law and that, if by any chance he had overlooked it, the Doge surely would very soon have drawn his attention to it. Shakespeare, it seems to me, was willing to introduce what is an absurd implausibility for the sake of an effect which he could not secure without it.

Auden is very shrewd here, but I cite him primarily to help suggest that Shylock's acceptance of enforced Christianity is a far more severe implausibility and one that distracts from dramatic or even theatrical effect. Indeed, as drama Shylock's "I am content" is necessarily a puzzle, not akin, say, to Iago's "From this time forth I never will speak word." Iago will die, under torture, in absolute silence: a dramatic death. We anticipate that Shylock the broken new Christian will live in silence: not a dramatic life. Is it that Shakespeare wished to repeal Shylock, as it were, and so cut away the enormous pathos of the character? We have seen no weaknesses in Shylock's will, no signs indeed that he can serve the function of a comic villain, a new Barabas. No red wig and giant nose will transform the speaker of Shylock's 360 dark lines into a two-dimensional character. Shylock, however monstrous his contemplated revenge, is all spirit, malign and concentrated, indifferent to the world and the flesh, unless Antonio be taken to represent both for him. Displaced spirit and so villain as he is, Shylock confronts in the heroically Christian merchant of Venice his tormentor and his double, the play's best Christian, who demonstrates the authenticity of his religious and moral zeal by his prowess in spitting at and cursing Shylock. I intend no irony there, and I fear that I read Shakespeare as he meant to *be* read. And yet every time I teach *The Merchant of Venice*, my students rebel at my insistence that Shylock is not there to be sympathized with, whereas Antonio is to be admired, if we are to read the play that Shakespeare wrote. One had best state this matter very plainly: To recover the comic splendor of *The Merchant of Venice* now, you need to be either a scholar or an anti-Semite, or best of all an anti-Semitic scholar.

E. E. Stoll sensibly said that if you sympathize with Shylock, then you must turn against Portia, a lesson that modern directors refuse to learn, preferring to have it both ways: a Shylock of sublime pathos and a Portia triumphant and wholly delightful. What is a serious reader to do with the more severe difference that is confronted when Goddard and C. L. Barber, two of the handful of great critics of Shakespeare in our time, are juxtaposed on the question of Shylock? Barber deftly improves on Stoll, first by noting that we never encounter Shylock alone, which denies the villain his inwardness and makes him subject to a group perspective. Second, Barber goes on:

> This perspective on him does not exclude a potential pathos. There is always potential pathos, behind, when drama makes fun of isolating, anti-social qualities. Indeed, the process of *making fun of* a person often works by exhibiting pretensions to humanity so as to show that they are inhuman, mechanical, not validly appropriate for sympathy.

Barber's persuasive view cannot be reconciled with Goddard's grand sentence: "Shylock's conviction that Christianity and revenge are synonyms is confirmed." For Goddard, Portia becomes one with the golden casket and fails her own inner self. On that reading, we return to a Shylock of tragic pathos and hardly to Barber's comic butt. René Girard, our contemporary authority on scapegoating, attempts to solve contradictory readings by ironizing Shakespeare:

Ultimately we do not have to choose between a favorable and an unfavorable image of Shylock. The old critics have concentrated on Shylock as a separate entity, an individual substance that would be merely juxtaposed to other individual substances and remain unaffected by them. The ironic depth in *The Merchant of Venice* results from a tension not between two static images of Shylock, but between those textual features that strengthen and those features that undermine the popular idea of an insurmountable difference between Christian and Jew.

I am myself a survivor of those "old critics" whom Girard scorns, and, like them, I do not speak of entities, substances, textual features, and ironic differences. One learns from Shakespeare to speak of characters, and the issue remains: Why did Shakespeare ultimately refuse consistency to his Jew, whether viewed as comic or as a figure of profound pathos? I cannot find more than a few aesthetic flaws in Shakespeare, and Shylock's acceptance of conversion seems to me much the most egregious, surpassing the peculiar final scene of *Measure for Measure* and even the brutal treatment of Malvolio at the end of *Twelfth Night*. Since act 5 of *The Merchant of Venice* is a triumphal ecstasy, the collapse of Shylock's pride in his Jewishness perhaps becomes an artistic blemish only when I brood on it in my study, but then I have never seen, will never see, and could not bear seeing a production of the play that is consonant with the play's own values.

Shylock is one of Shakespeare's displaced spirits, together with Barnardine, Lear's Fool, Malvolio, in some sense even Caliban, perhaps even an aspect of Sir John Falstaff, perhaps even the outcast Edgar, who is so slow to abandon his mask as poor Tom o'Bedlam. We do not know who wrote the great lyric "Tom o'Bedlam" found in a manuscript commonplace that scholars date about 1620, but being very unscholarly I always cheerfully assume that it was Shakespeare because it is too good to be by anyone else. I cite its final stanza here because it sums up, for me, the ethos of the ultimately displaced spirit, the Shakespearean outsider who needs a context less alien than Shakespeare will provide for him:

With an host of furious fancies
Whereof I am commander,
With a burning spear and a horse of air,
To the wilderness I wander.
By a knight of ghosts and shadows
I summoned am to a tourney

Ten leagues beyond the wide world's end:
Methinks it is no journey.
Yet will I sing, Any food, any feeding,
Feeding, drink, or clothing;
Come dame or maid, be not afraid,
Poor Tom will injure nothing.

One can hardly say that poor Shylock, incessantly demanding that he will have his bond, will injure nothing, and even I would hesitate at speaking of "poor Shylock" had not Shakespeare invented the monstrosity of the forced conversion. But the great Tom o'Bedlam song, whoever wrote it, manifests the same mixture of unbearable pathos and visionary intensity that I find in all of Shakespeare's displaced spirits: Shylock, Barnardine, Lear's Fool, Malvolio, and in a weird mode, Caliban. Ambivalence emanates from all of these, as it does from the alienated Edgar, and ambivalence is part of our response to them also. Oddly the least original of these, Shylock is too much the Belial figure of Christian tradition, and one wonders why Shakespeare could accept so much crudity of stock representation, even as he allowed the apparent pathos in Shylock that continues to divide critics. I suspect that the enigmas concerning Shylock can be resolved only if we return Shakespeare's Jew to his agonistic context, the Shakespearean need to compete with and overgo Marlowe's superb villain, Barabas, the Jew of Malta. Barabas is a farcical hero-villain, while Shylock is a comic villain, yet the contrast between them tends to abolish such distinctions. Could we conceive of Barabas accepting an imposed conversion? The question's absurdity turns on Marlowe's dramatic art, which works here as the purest caricature, excluding any possibilities of pathos. Barabas could no more say "If you prick us, do we not bleed? If you tickle us, do we not laugh?" than Shylock could roar out the parodic outrageousness and exuberance of Marlowe's Jew:

As for myself, I walk abroad a-nights,
And kill sick people groaning under walls;
Sometimes I go about and poison wells.

Marlowe, subverting every established order and tradition, loathes Christians, Muslims, and Jews with admirable impartiality, and so he is happy to have Barabas satirize the Christian myth of the Jewish sport of poisoning wells. Shakespeare hardly could have missed the jest, but for him Marlowe always represented, in art as in life, the way down and out, the way not to go. The savage gusto of Barabas is deliberately lacking in the rugged Shylock, whose only exuberance is his will to revenge himself, and his people, on that sincere Christian, the noble Antonio. Antonio's superior goodness is shown to us by his righteous contempt for Shylock. Splendid as this must have been for Shakespeare's audience, it is now our largest burden, I sometimes think, in reading *The Merchant of Venice*. Antonio is a Jew baiter, plain and simple. Marlowe gives us no such figure in *The Jew of Malta*, yet I suspect that Marlowe provoked Shakespeare into the ambivalence of our having to accept Antonio and Portia as angels, and Shylock as the Devil, albeit a Devil with strong feelings, akin to Marlowe's Mephistopheles in *Doctor Faustus*.

Though Barabas seems to me Shakespeare's prime model for Richard III and even for Aaron the Moor in *Titus Andronicus*, Barabas has nothing Shakespearean about him. There is a mad zest in Barabas, a kind of antic ferocity, that Shakespeare rejected as too raw, a rejection of great consequence, since it spurred Shakespeare into the creation of Edmund and Iago. That Marlovian parody, Ancient Pistol, is Shakespeare's sardonic commentary on Marlowe's exaltation of self-celebratory and exuberant ferocity. "I'll show you a Jew!" Shakespeare says to us by Shylock, thus implying that Barabas is no Jew but simply is Kit Marlowe. Barabas, of course, is a superbly outrageous representation of a Jew; he is no more Jewish than Marlowe's Christians are Christians or his Muslims are Muslims. Is there a more vivid, a more memorable representation of a Jew in postbiblical literature than Shakespeare's Shylock? Well, there is the Fagin of Charles Dickens, clearly more memorable than George Eliot's Daniel Deronda but about as acceptable to a post-Holocaust sensibility as Shylock. Jewish novelists from Disraeli to the present hardly have given us a being as intense as Shylock or as eloquent, though Shylock's eloquence is somber, even so rancid:

> You'll ask me why I rather choose to have
> A weight of carrion flesh than to receive
> Three thousand ducats. I'll not answer that,
> But say it is my humor. Is it answered?
> What if my house be troubled with a rat,
> And I be pleased to give ten thousand ducats
> To have it baned? What, are you answered yet?
> Some men there are love not a gaping pig,
> Some that are mad if they behold a cat,
> And others, when the bagpipe sings i' th' nose,
> Cannot contain their wine; for affection,
> Master of passion, sways it to the mood
> Of what it likes or loathes.

Extraordinary psychologist as Shakespeare has made him (akin in this to Edmund and Iago), Shylock is totally unable to achieve self-understanding. If "affection" (innate antipathy) totally dominates "passion" (any authentic emotion) in him, that is because he wills such domination. But thus he plays the Christian's game, and unlike Barabas he can only lose. Barabas goes down in pained but clamorous triumph, cursing Christians and Muslims with his final burst of spirit. Shylock, as Shakespeare deftly creates him, defeats himself, as Iago will, and ends in the terrible humiliation of being "content" to become a Christian, when in some sense (the Venetian one) he has been Christianized already, by accepting their exaltation of antipathy governing emotion, as in the good Antonio. Is this Shakespeare's irony, or does it not belong instead to a commonplace older than Shakespeare, as old as the Talmud? If, as Blake grimly insisted, we become what we behold, it is an ancient lesson, far older even than Hebraic morality. Shakespeare's comic villain undoes himself, as Barabas does not, in a critique of Marlowe that nevertheless was expensive for the play, *The Merchant of Venice*, since it ultimately destroys Shylock's heretofore strong plausibility as a character.

A displaced spirit, in Shakespeare, never ceases to be spirit, and though it is warped by displacement, such a spirit contaminates the drama through which it passes and of necessity contaminates the audience as well. To stage the play of Antonio, Portia, and Shylock now is to attempt what is virtually impossible, since only an audience at ease with its own anti-Semitism could tolerate a responsible and authentic presentation of what Shakespeare actually wrote. In this one play alone, Shakespeare was very much of his age and not for all time.

HARRY BERGER JR.

Marriage and Mercifixion in The Merchant of Venice: The Casket Scene Revisited

If fathers and children know that the world must be peopled, property handed down, and the status quo perpetuated, they also know that the price of this investment in the future is the acceptance of death. As Alexander Welch has put it, in a fine essay on Shakespeare's problem comedies, "sexuality has constrained the husband to give life to the son, but when he married he also acceded to the passing of his generation and his death."[1] Old fathers like Lear and Gloucester look back to the birth of an heir as their first step in prescribing their power, a step that binds them in service to their children's future lordship. The plague of custom and the curiosity of nations assign upbringing and inheritance to children as a right, not a privilege. Gloucester suspects that the rightful heir, born of the dull, stale, tired marriage bed by the order of law, may have more claims on him, may be more dangerous as, enemy and competitor, than the child of nature to whom nothing is owed. Edgar's appearance prophesies death, and the legitimate heir may be imagined to grow up waiting for his father to die so that he can rightfully claim what his father has kept from him all those years, and what his father finally loses: no less than all.

Against this liability the father balances the major asset provided by the begetting of children. In the *Republic*, Socrates remarks that "just as poets are fond of their poems, and fathers of their children, so money-makers too are

From *Shakespeare Quarterly* 32, no. 2 (Summer 1981): 155–62. Copyright © 1981 by The Folger Shakespeare Library.

serious about money—as their own product; and they are also serious about it . . . because it's useful." Moneymakers and money; poets and poems; fathers and children: these three pairs can easily converge, or change partners. Fathers can use children as money, for example, to pay back their debts, and also as poems, to guarantee their immortality—to preserve themselves against the very death toward which marriage is the first step. Gloucester says that his son by the order of law "is no dearer in my account" than the bastard. When we let the two senses of that phrase play over each other, they tell us that what the father chiefly values in his children is his investment in them—the shares of pleasure, shame, trouble, sacrifice, and legal tenderness he has deposited in their characters.

This naturally causes special problems for daughters who find themselves assigned the role of commodity in the alliance market, and in the present essay I shall examine Portia's response to this predicament in *The Merchant of Venice*. That response is summed up in an ambiguous remark she utters during the casket scene. As Bassanio approaches the caskets to make his choice, Portia compares him to Hercules about to save the Trojan maiden, Hesione, whose father, Laomedon, had offered her as a divine sacrifice to a sea monster. Bassanio (says Portia) goes

> With no less presence, but with much more love,
> Than young Alcides [Hercules], when he did redeem
> The virgin tribute paid by howling Troy
> To the sea monster. I stand for sacrifice.
>   (III.ii.54–57)[2]

I stand for sacrifice: either (1) I am placed here to be sacrificed, on the verge of being captured and destroyed in order to save my father's kingdom; or (2) I represent sacrifice, stand for the principle of self-giving as I prepare to surrender myself to whatever risks lie ahead (a subsequent remark by Portia inadvertently throws its beams on this sense of the phrase: "So shines a good deed in a naughty world," V.i.91); or finally (3) I advocate, I *demand*, sacrifice, expecting you to give and hazard all you have. This third sense is evoked by the inscription on the lead casket, "Who chooseth me must give and hazard all he hath," and for this reason it contributes to the evidence cited by those (including myself) who think Portia could conceivably be seen to help Bassanio choose the right casket.

The movement from sense 1 to sense 3 is a movement from weakness to strength, the third sense shining with more brilliance because set in, and set off by, the second. The force of this movement adds sharpness to an allusion which already has a certain bite to it. Superficially the analogy between

Bassanio's venturing for Portia and Hercules' saving Laomedon's daughter from the sea monster must be flattering to Bassanio. It confers on him the role of conquering hero. This may appear both tactful and self-canceling to those who construe the phrase "I stand for sacrifice" as pointing Bassanio toward the lead casket, since the words would then negate the very heroism they seem to call for. What makes this construal psychologically not improbable is the danger she is in, a danger anamorphically portrayed in the masculine marking of the myth she alludes to.

Hercules answers the father's summons in order to win, not his daughter, but his Trojan horses. It is as if Portia has guessed that Bassanio had earlier described himself to Antonio as one of the many Jasons questing for "the sunny locks" that hang on Portia's temples "like a golden fleece" (I.ii.169). Perhaps the keys that will open those locks are in her father's gift, like those to the caskets in one of which Portia is locked. The paternal lock is an emblem of wariness and apprehensiveness, of the father's refusal to trust his daughter's discretion in handling his property (i.e., herself). It is, then—if we displace the father's distrust and wariness to the lock itself—a shy lock. If, as is likely in Venice, Bassanio is another Jason for whom daughter and ducats, person and purse, are indistinguishable, then her passion for him will expose her to Medea's doom. Like Medea, who also betrayed her father's secret and helped her lover to the fleece, she may betray herself. She knows fathers are in league with monsters that venture on the deep in search of prey, and perhaps she suspects that monster and hero are one. Caught in the male conspiracy, Portia may feel that she can only win her freedom from the father by accepting captivity to the husband, moving from one prison or watery deathbed, one set of sunny locks, to another.

Lawrence Hyman has argued that "the main action of the play is centered on the struggle between Portia and Antonio for Bassanio's love."[3] This action, if analyzed, may be broken down into the following elements. (1) Antonio uses Shylock to put himself in jeopardy so as to bind Bassanio to him just when Bassanio, through his assistance, is about to embark on the venture that will set him free. (2) Portia uses Shylock to save Antonio in order to break his hold on Bassanio. (3) She therefore uses Antonio to complete her conquest of Bassanio, and in that way she perfects the control—over herself, her husband, and her property—which her desire placed in jeopardy in the casket scene. Hyman's argument is persuasive as far as it goes, and is especially to be commended for its careful avoidance of the temptation to convert the powerful *mono*sexual attachment of Antonio for Bassanio into a *homo*sexual attachment.[4] But it does not sufficiently account for other equally important aspects of the play: the centrality of the father–child theme and the consequent overlapping of family politics with sexual politics; the dilemma posed for Portia by the conflict within herself between the claims of desire and those of fear; and the deep structure of latent or tacit action which characterizes the various power struggles. For the most part the struggles are by no means *practices* in the straightforward sense exemplified by Don Pedro's stratagems in *Much Ado*. It would not be accurate to call them *plots* or *scenarios*, because they unfold at a less conscious level than that which we normally associate with the construction of plots and scenarios. This tacit quality is what makes *The Merchant of Venice* so haunting and tantalizing a play. A closer look at the casket scene will suggest how this quality is conveyed, and will at the same time link Portia's struggle with her father and Bassanio to the conflict within herself.

The famous problem about the casket scene provides us with a logical point of entry. Critics go astray when they insist that Portia either did or did not offer Bassanio clues to the right casket. Certainly "I stand for sacrifice" and the song's terminal syllables (rhyming with *lead*) provide at least the makings of clues. Portia may or may not have intended them; Bassanio may or may not have missed them. The point is rather that the script encourages us to wonder about, and even to debate, the possibility. The dialogue preceding Portia's "I stand for sacrifice" speech is full of hints that Portia knows the secret and that her desire makes her half-willing to sin against her father's will. These hints are countered—or rather covered, and therefore enabled—by formal protestations of her unwillingness to be forsworn. But the point is also that, having encouraged us to wonder, the script never gives us enough evidence to resolve the issue with confidence. It is never made clear to us whether or not Portia actually intends the clues that lie inertly in the scene. Nor are we able to determine whether Bassanio intuits the clues and acts on them, whether he betrays at any time a sense of Portia's complicity, and—most important—whether Portia is any less in the dark about these two questions than we are. This is important because if she feels he has recognized her contribution to the choice she may decide that either (1) he is in her debt for the assistance or (2) she is in his power for having compromised herself. The question of power is thus as ambiguous as the question of knowledge. If there is anything at all to these speculations, the result is to make us feel that Portia must still be concerned to resolve her doubts by increasing his obligation and binding him more securely to her. She knows and fears enough to second Gratiano's opinion that (at least in Venice) "All things that are, / Are with more spirit chased than enjoyed" (II.vi.12–13).

From the beginning of the scene Portia shows herself divided between desire and apprehension. She "betrays" to Bassanio her love for him by being conspicuously coy; she lets him see her difficulty in maintaining maidenly decorum: "There's something tells me, but it is not love, / I would not lose you"

(III.ii.4–5). She would detain him, first for a day or two, and then, a few lines later, for a month or two, and she makes it clear that she knows her father's secret: "I could teach you / How to choose right, but then I am forsworn" (III. ii.10–11). On the other hand, she would detain him "before you *venture* for me." *Venture* strikes a different note because it implies some apprehensiveness about his interest in her golden fleece. This adds an undertone to her previous words; i.e., "Let's dally a while and enjoy each other's company before you choose and either fail or else, succeeding, win too much—win control not only over my person but also over my father's purse."

The undertone is louder in "beshrow your eyes, / They have o'erlook'd me and divided me" (III.ii.14–15). It is concentrated in the multiple pun on "o'erlook'd": (1) "given me the evil eye, bewitched me" (the sense under which the *OED* lists this line), and here she shifts blame to his eyes for her impulse to sin against her father's will; (2) "looked down on me from above," which suggests the danger of mastery encoded later in her prospective image of Bassanio Triumphant, "when true subjects bow / To a new-crowned monarch" (III.ii.49–50); (3) "looked over and beyond me"—toward the inheritance—"thus failing to see me, or disregarding me." Hence "you have divided me between the desire that induces me to surrender wholly to you, and the premonition that makes me afraid of letting myself be reduced to the golden fleece and locked in a marital casket."

"O these naughty times / Puts bars between the owners and their rights" (III.ii.18–19): desire tells Portia that her father bars Bassanio from rights conferred by the law of love, while apprehension tells her that her father and Bassanio bar her from her rightful ownership of her own person and, by extension, of her father's purse. The generalized form of her statement blames the naughty times for this predicament, and also, we may infer, for any prospective violation of the letter of her father's will. Self-division makes Portia address their relationship as a struggle for power and possession, a struggle which her words register as they shift back and forth between the two poles of the division—either "mine" or "yours," but not "ours":

> Mine own I would say; but if mine then yours,
> And so all yours! O these naughty times
> Puts bars between the owners and their rights!
> And so, though yours, not yours. . . .
>   (III.ii.17–20)

She wants him but does not want to betray herself to him, and perhaps she would like it if she could somehow unknowingly conspire with him to outwit her father while observing the letter of the law. It would be ideal if she could "let happen" what she wants to happen, if the issue could be decided by ordeal: "Prove it so, / Let fortune go to hell for it, not I" (cf. Macbeth's "If chance will have me King, why chance may crown me, / Without my stir" [I.iii.143]).

Since the knowledge that she could teach Bassanio "how to choose right," and the possibility of being forsworn, are never very far from her mind—for why else should Fortune go to *hell*—they cannot be absent from ours. In fact, I think they loom rather large in the odd dialogue leading up to her speech of encouragement. The dialogue is odd, even compelling, because some of the phrases we hear are muffled indicators that Bassanio and Portia would each like to draw from the other (without being found out) a signal of willingness to dupe the dead father. No clues are actually being given, but the words—if not the speakers—seem to be sounding out the feasibility of giving clues to the readiness to give or receive clues. In the following lines, the repeated term "confess," the question about treason, and the phrase "doth teach me answers for deliverance" are meta-clues trying to perform this task without seeming to do so. They tend to float away from their syntactical context toward a more complicit meaning, and they are barely held in place under the sweet nothings of love talk that veil them; they barely sustain the innocence of their speakers:

> *Bass.* Let me choose,
> For as I am, I live upon the rack.
> *Por.* Upon the rack, Bassanio? Then confess
> What treason there is mingled with your love.
> *Bass.* None but that ugly treason of mistrust
> Which makes me fear th'enjoying of my love.
> There may as well be amity and life
> 'Tween snow and fire, as treason and my love.
> *Por.* Ay, but I fear you speak upon the rack
> Where men enforced do speak anything.
> *Bass.* Promise me life, and I'll confess the truth.
> *Por.* Well then, confess and live.
> *Bass.* Confess and love
> Had been the very sum of my confession!
> O happy torment, when my torturer
> Doth teach me answers for deliverance.
> But let me to my fortune and the caskets.
> *Por.* Away then! I am locked in one of them.
> If you do love me, you will find me out.
> (III.ii.24–41)

Given Portia's apprehensions, she might well entertain varying responses to his impatience: fear of losing him if he fails; fear and desire of his importunate passion (and hers); fear of his haste to win her in order to secure his fortune. Yet her question about treason may also put out feelers that lightly probe his willingness to betray her father. Against Bassanio's hyperbole of the rack she will later pit the image of Hesione chained to a rock. The three lines beginning with "promise me life, and I'll confess the truth" are interchangeable: if Portia were asking for life and offering to teach him "how to choose right," Bassanio could be urging her to confess and live, and Portia would then seem to be recoiling from direct disclosure while keeping his hopes alive. That the assignment of lines is easily reversible indicates both the similarity and the conflict between them. Each says what she or he might like the other to say but would not dream of saying herself or himself. Portia plays the inquisitor, but this is a role which, if she were more crass, she could conceivably induce upon Bassanio, assigning him the function of torturing out of her the "answers for deliverance" (for her deliverance as well as his) which she would have too many scruples to offer voluntarily, not only the scruple about being forsworn but also the scruple about crowning Bassanio over her as her monarch. Bassanio's last two lines in the above passage come dangerously close to sounding as if she had in fact triggered in him a suspicion that she was ready to teach him how to choose. Portia quickly backs off, terminating the discussion. She would have reason to shrink from his possessive "let me to *my* fortune," and perhaps also from the aural trace of "lead" (the verb, not the metal) in "let." If we sense these submerged resonances, they vibrate in her final rejoinder: she might terminate the dialogue because she feels she has secured his complicity and because she fears he has already found her out. "That ugly treason of mistrust" (that ugly mistrust of treason) is at work beneath the surface of these lines.

It will not do to say, as I was on the verge of saying, that Bassanio and Portia *carefully* avoid the conspiratorial possibilities that play about these lines. I do not mean to attribute to either of them—not even to Portia—that much awareness of the desire to *actualize* the betrayal of the secret. The desire, however, hovers tantalizingly in the air of their language, and their airy words seem by themselves to submit to the pressure even as they assert the innocence of their speakers' love play. That Bassanio's subsequent demeanor gives absolutely nothing away does not mean that these subtextual implications are absent from the casket scene. Rather it means that they remain present throughout the remainder of the play, affecting our—and Portia's—response to ensuing events. And I think it is worth noting that we are not unprepared for the subtext of the casket scene, since it had been directly conveyed to us earlier by Jessica and Lorenzo in their elopement scene:

> *Jess.* Here, catch this casket; it is worth the pains.
> I am glad 'tis night—you do not look on me—
> For I am much asham'd of my exchange.
> But love is blind, and lovers cannot see
> The pretty follies that themselves commit;
> For if they could, Cupid himself would blush
> To see me thus transformed to a boy.
>   *Lor.* Descend, for you must be my torch-bearer.
> *Jess.* What, must I hold a candle to my shames?
> They in themselves, good sooth, are too too light.
> Why, 'tis an office of discovery, love—
> And I should be obscur'd.
>   (II.vi.33–44)

If these lines were engrossed in a plaque over the casket scene they would describe both the scenario Portia eschews when she says she will never be forsworn (III.ii.11–12) *and* the psychological conditions which would enable her to drop clues without being forsworn, letting blind Fortune go to hell for it. She will not descend to being Bassanio's torchbearer, holding a candle to her shames, and risking the obscurity of being his page and servant, his "boy," for life.[5] Whatever she and Bassanio do will be obscured in the blindness born when fancy—desire and self-deception—is engendered in the eye.

During the remainder of the play, Portia uses her wit to defend against the weakness for Bassanio which threatens to betray her into the power of the Royal Merchant Adventurers Club of Venice. Released from the bondage of her father's will into that of her own, she immediately goes to work to establish control over both herself and Bassanio. She does this by ostentatiously relinquishing control:

>   But now I was the lord
> Of this fair mansion, master of my servants,
> Queen o'er myself; and even now, but now,
> This house, these servants, and this same myself
> Are yours, my lord's.
>   (III.ii.167–71)

So free and generous a gift is nevertheless carefully itemized to remind him of her value and worth, and hence of his obligation. He comes, he says, like one contending for a prize, "to give *and to receive*"; she only gives, and gives him all, and with a flair for self-advertisement that lays him under a burden of gratitude beyond his means to discharge. She then uses the additional gift of the ring to convert this first gift to a loan, a bond, which can be forfeit, but even in imposing *that* qualification she brings it off as still another generous act. She is a Christian, and she knows the power of the charity that wounds.

When she regains the ring in the fifth act, the thematic resemblances to *Much Ado* become quite noticeable, and Portia's advantage is like that of the conquering Hero in Act V. She teases Bassanio about man's inconstancy, and threatens to be as unfaithful as he was. The fact that he gave the ring to a man rather than a woman may seem to clear him, but actually it points toward a more dangerous tendency. The act of giving the ring to a man may have the same value as that of giving it to another woman in return for favors, since both acts indicate man's assumption that men are superior to women, that it is men who save each other and the world and who perform great deeds and sacrifices; the pledge to a woman can be superseded by the debt of gratitude owed a man. Once again we see how a culture dominated by the masculine imagination devalues women and asserts male solidarity against feminine efforts to breach the barrier. In her own way, Portia is no less an outsider than Shylock, and her "I stand for sacrifice" is finally not much different from Shylock's "I stand for judgment."

If Shylock practices usury, Portia is the master mistress of negative usury. Usury, stripped of its subtleties, amounts to getting more than you give. Negative usury is giving more than you get. More efficient than Jewish or Christian fatherhood, it works like Jewish motherhood to sink hooks of gratitude and obligation deep into the beneficiary's bowels. Against Antonio's failure to get himself crucified, we can place Portia's divine power of mercifixion; she never rains but she pours. "Fair Ladies," says the admiring Lorenzo, "you drop manna in the way / Of starved people" (V.i.294–95). But the manna melts in Bassanio's mouth before he can swallow it. Confronted with his surrender of the ring, he flinches, pleads necessity, is forced to his knees (like Shylock), and is made to promise he will behave. This gives Antonio one last chance to compete with Portia by rescuing Bassanio from blame, but she foils that by making him the intermediary who formally returns the ring and bids Bassanio "keep it better than the other." Then in another divine shower, she mercifies Antonio by giving him back his life and living. The last vestige of his power over Bassanio is thus happily ended, and the age of good neighbors restored.

If Dogberry had been standing by, he would have been ready with an appropriate comment: "God save the foundation! . . . God keep your worship! . . . God restore you to health! I humbly give you leave to depart. And [turning now to Portia and Bassanio] if a merry ending may be wished, God prohibit it!" An amiable constabularial farewell: *Come, neighbors.*

Notes

1. "The Loss of Men and Getting of Children: 'All's Well that Ends Well' and 'Measure for Measure,'" *Modern Language Review*, 73 (1978), 18.

2. *The Merchant of Venice* and all other plays are quoted from the Penguin edition of *William Shakespeare: The Complete Works*, gen. ed. Alfred Harbage (London: The Penguin Press, 1969).

3. *Shakespeare Quarterly*, 21 (1970), 109.

4. For a recent argument against either or both of these views, and a return—unpersuasive, in my opinion—to a more traditional reading of the play, see Lawrence Danson, *The Harmonies of "The Merchant of Venice"* (New Haven: Yale Univ. Press, 1978).

5. Lorenzo's earlier comment, while making even clearer the difference between Jessica and Portia, still spells out both the outcome she desires and the page-like subservience she fears:

> she hath directed
> How I shall take her from her father's house,
> What gold and jewels she is furnished with,
> What page's suit she hath in readiness.
> (II.iv.29–32)

COPPÉLIA KAHN

The Cuckoo's Note: Male Friendship and Cuckoldry in The Merchant of Venice

Shakespeare's romantic comedies center on courtship, a holiday of jokes, disguisings, songs, word play, and merriment of many kinds, which culminates in marriage, the everyday institution which both inspires holiday and sets the boundaries of it. Shakespeare doesn't portray the quotidian realities of marriage in these comedies, of course. He simply lets marriage symbolize the ideal accommodation of eros with society, and the continuation of both lineage and personal identity into posterity. Yet at the same time he never fails to undercut this ideal. In *The Merchant of Venice* he goes farther than in the other comedies to imply that marriage is a state in which men and women "atone together," as Hymen says in *As You Like It*. Rather than concluding with a wedding dance as he does in *A Midsummer Night's Dream* or *Much Ado About Nothing*, a wedding masque like that in *As You Like It*, or a combination of family reunion, recognition scene, and troth plighting as in *Twelfth Night*, he ends *Merchant* with a combat of wits between men and women, a nervous flurry of accusations and denials, bawdy innuendos and threats of castration, which make up the final episode of a subplot rather than rounding off the main plot by celebrating marriage. Commonly referred to as "the ring plot," this intrigue may seem trivial, but is actually entwined with the main courtship plot from the middle of the play, and

From *Shakespeare's "Rough Magic": Renaissance Essays in Honor of C. L. Barber*, edited by Peter Erickson and Coppélia Kahn, pp. 104–12. Copyright © 1985 by Associated University Presses.

accomplishes more than one darker purpose on which the romantic moon-light of Belmont does not fall.[1]

To begin with, Shakespeare structures the ring plot so as to parallel and contrast Antonio and Portia as rivals for Bassanio's affection, bringing out a conflict between male friendship and marriage which runs throughout his works.[2] As Janet Adelman points out in her penetrating essay on the early comedies, same sex friendships in Shakespeare (as in the typical life cycle) are chronologically and psychologically prior to marriage. "The complications posed by male identity and male friendship," she argues, rather than heavy fathers or irrational laws, provide the most dramatically and emotionally significant obstacles to marriage in *The Comedy of Errors, The Two Gentlemen of Verona, The Taming of a Shrew*, and *Love's Labor's Lost*.[3] In these plays, Shakespeare tends toward what Adelman calls "magical solutions," facile twists of plot and changes of character in which the heroes are enabled to pursue friendships with other men while also contracting relationships with women, even though these relationships jeopardize or conflict with their earlier ties with men. *Merchant*, I think, is perhaps the first play in which Shakespeare avoids this kind of magical solution and gives probing attention to the conflict between the two kinds of bonds, and to the psychological needs they satisfy.

Second, the ring plot comes to rest on the idea of cuckoldry, a theme as persistent in the comedies as that of male friendship. Bonds with men precede marriage and interfere with it; cuckoldry, men fear, follows marriage and threatens it. I wish to demonstrate the interdependence of these two motifs. First, though, it may be helpful to summarize the ring plot.

Articulated in three scenes, it begins at the very moment of Portia's and Bassanio's betrothal, after he has correctly chosen the lead casket. As Portia formally surrenders lordship over her mansion, her servants, and herself to Bassanio, she gives him a ring, enjoining him not to part with it. If he does, she cautions, he will bring their love to ruin and give her cause to reproach him. The next turn of the plot occurs during Shylock's trial. When there appears to be no recourse from the payment of the pound of flesh, Bassanio declares that though his wife be dear to him "as life itself," he would sacrifice her (and his own life) to save his friend. Portia in her lawyer's robes drily remarks, "Your wife would give you little thanks for that / If she were by to hear you make the offer" (4.1.28–85).[4] Thus Shakespeare establishes a motive for the trick the wives play on their husbands: they want to teach them a lesson about the primacy of their marital obligations over obligations to their male friends. Next, the rings reappear at the end of the trial scene. When Bassanio offers the lawyer "some remembrance" for his services, the disguised Portia asks for the ring, and persists in asking for it even when Bassanio protests,

> Good sir, this ring was given me by my wife,
> And when she put it on, she made me vow
> That I should neither sell, nor give, nor lose it.
>   (4.1.437–39)

At this point, it would seem that Bassanio has passed the test his wife devised: he knows how to value her ring. A moment later, though, at Antonio's urging he gives the ring away. Finally, reunited with their husbands, Portia and Nerissa demand the rings (which, of course, they still have) as proof of fidelity. Pretending to believe that Bassanio and Gratiano gave the tokens to Venetian mistresses, while the men try to defend themselves the women threaten retaliation in the form of cuckoldry. All the while, we as audience are in on the joke, titillated, but reminded by numerous double-entendres that the doctor and his clerk, whom Portia and Nerissa pretend to regard as fictions concocted by their guilty husbands, are in fact the two wives, who know better than anyone that their husbands are blameless.

Two complementary anxieties run through this intrigue: that men, if they are to marry, must renounce their friendships with each other—must even, perhaps, betray them; and that once they are married, their wives will betray *them*. Each anxiety constitutes a threat to the men's sense of themselves as men. In Shakespeare's psychology, men first seek to mirror themselves in a homoerotic attachment (the Antipholi in *The Comedy of Errors* offer the best example of this state) and then to confirm themselves through difference, in a bond with the opposite sex—the marital bond, which gives them exclusive possession of a woman.[5] As I have argued elsewhere, the very exclusiveness of this possession puts Shakespeare's male characters at risk; their honor, on which their identities depend so deeply, is irrevocably lost if they suffer the peculiarly galling shame of being cuckolded.[6] The double standard by which their infidelities are tolerated and women's are inexcusable conceals the liability of betrayal by women. In fact, the ring plot as a whole can be viewed as a kind of cadenza inspired by a bawdy story in a Tudor jestbook, the point of which is that the only way a jealous husband can be wholly assured of not being cuckolded is to keep his finger in his wife's "ring." The joke stresses both the intense fear of cuckoldry of which men are capable, and the folly of such fear.[7]

Until the trial scene, it might seem that Shakespeare is preparing for a fairy-tale conclusion, in which both Antonio's and Portia's claims on Bassanio could be satisfied. Though they are paralleled and contrasted with each other (for example, both enter the play with a sigh expressing an inexplicable sadness, Antonio puzzling "In sooth I know not why I am so sad," and Portia declaring, "By my troth, Nerissa, my little body is aweary of this great world"), neither the friend nor the beloved behaves competitively at first.[8] When Bassanio needs money to court Portia, Antonio's purse is his; when he needs it (as it seems at one point) to rescue Antonio, Portia's wealth is at his disposal. But when Antonio's ships fail to return and his bond with Shylock falls due, he sends a heartrending letter to Bassanio which arrives, significantly, just when he and Portia are pledging their love, and prevents them from consummating their marriage. Bassanio's two bonds of love, one with a man, the other with a woman, are thus brought into conflict. Portia immediately offers Bassanio her fortune to redeem his friend, but remarks, "Since you are dear bought, I will love you dear" (3.2.312), calling attention to her generosity and his indebtedness. In contrast, Antonio's letter reads,

> Sweet Bassanio, . . . all debts are clear'd between you and I, if
> I might but see you at my death: notwithstanding, use your
> pleasure,—if your love do not persuade you to come, let not my
> letter.
>   (3.2.317–20)

As others have noted, the generosity of both rivals is actually an attempt "to sink hooks of gratitude and obligation deep into the beneficiary's bowels."[9]

At the trial, Bassanio's implicit conflict of obligations comes out in the open when, in language far more impassioned than that he used when he won Portia, he declares he would give her life for his friend's:

> Antonio, I am married to a wife
> Which is as dear to me as life itself,
> But life itself, my wife, and all the world,
> Are not with me esteem'd above thy life.
> I would lose all, ay sacrifice them all
> Here to this devil, to deliver you.
>   (4.1.278–83)

How neatly ironic that, in successfully urging Bassanio to give away Portia's ring, Antonio actually helps her to carry out her plot against her erring husband: again, the two claims are irreconcilable, and the friend's gives place to the wife's. "Let . . . my love withal / Be valued 'gainst your wife's commandement," pleads Antonio, making the contest perfectly explicit (4.1.455–46). In the final scene, Shakespeare maintains the tension between the friend's claim and the wife's until Antonio offers to pledge a pound of his flesh that his friend "Will never more break faith"; only then does Portia drop her ruse, when Antonio offers to sacrifice himself once again. Thus Shakespeare suggests that marriage will triumph over friendship between men.

Nevertheless, it takes a strong, shrewd woman like Portia to combat the continuing appeal of such ties between men. At first, her power derives from her father; the wealth he bequeathed and the challenge he devised make her a magnet, drawing nobles from all over Europe who hazard all to win her. Though in her opening scene Portia sees herself as caught in the constraints of her father's will, Shakespeare soon makes it clear that she has a will of her own. In her merrily stinging put-downs of the suitors, wit and verbal force substitute for sexual force and prerogative—as they also do when she prompts Bassanio to choose the right casket, when she manipulates the letter of the law, and when she uses the ring to get the upper hand over her husband.

Portia's masculine disguise, however, also produces the suggestion that she is not just a clever woman, but something of a man as well. For example, when Bassanio protests concerning the ring, "No woman had it, but a civil doctor" (5.1.210), or when Portia jokes, "For by this ring the doctor lay with me" (5.1.259), it is as though images of her as male and as female are superimposed. When Portia shares her plans for disguise with Nerissa, she says their husbands "shall think we are accomplished with that we lack" (3.4.61–62), slyly suggesting not a complete physical transformation from female to male, but the discrete addition of a phallus to the womanly body. The line carries two implications, at least. One is that the phallus symbolizes not just masculinity *per se* but the real power to act in the world which masculinity confers. The arguments she presents as Dr. Bellario would have little force if she delivered them as Portia, a lady of Belmont. Another implication is that Portia as androgyne is a fantasy figure who resolves the conflict between homoerotic and heterosexual ties, like the "woman … first created" of sonnet 20, who is also "pricked out." As the concluding episode of the ring plot proceeds, however, the double-entendres about Portia's double gender become mere embellishments to the action, in which she uses her specifically female power as wife to establish her priority over Antonio and her control over Bassanio.

The power is based on the threat of cuckoldry, the other strand of meaning woven into the ring plot. When Portia gives the ring to her future husband, she says,

> This house, these servants, and this same myself
> Are yours,—my lord's!—I give them with this ring,
> Which when you part from, lose, or give away,
> Let it presage the ruin of your love,
> And be my vantage to exclaim on you.
>   (3.2.170–74)

Portia's gift limits the generosity of her love by a stringent condition. She gives all to her bridegroom; he in turn must keep her ring, or their love will turn to "ruin." This ominous note recalls another Shakespearean love token, the handkerchief Othello gives Desdemona. He calls it a "recognizance and pledge of love," but as he describes its history, it seems not so much the symbol of an existing love as a charm on which the continuation of that love magically depends. The handkerchief was first used to "subdue" Othello's father to his mother's love, and Othello hints that it should have the same effect on him when he warns, in lines reminiscent of Portia's, "To lose, or give't away were such perdition / As nothing else could match" (3.4.53–66). However, Portia's ring has less to do with magic than with rights and obligations. Unlike Othello, she is concerned more with "vantage," which the OED defines as gain or profit, than with some vaguer "ruin." She sees marriage as a contract of sexual fidelity equally binding on both parties, for their mutual "vantage."

On one level, the ring obviously represents the marriage bond, as it does in the wedding ceremony. But on another, it bears a specifically sexual meaning alluded to in the play's final lines, spoken by Gratiano: "Well, while I live, I'll fear no other thing / So sore as keeping safe Nerissa's ring" (5.1.306–7). Rings, circles, and O's are frequently, in Shakespeare's works and elsewhere, metaphors for female sexual parts.[10] In the last scene, speaking to Bassanio, Portia refers to the ring as "your wife's first gift" (5.2.166), that is, her virginity. In giving Bassanio her "ring," Portia gives him her virginity, and a husband's traditionally exclusive sexual rights to her. In *All's Well That Ends Well*, Diana voices the same metaphorical equation when Bertram compares his masculine honor to the ring he wears: "Mine honor's such a ring," she replies; "My chastity's the jewel of our house" (4.2.45–46).[11] When Bassanio accepts the ring from his bride, he vows to keep it on his finger or die. Again, the two meanings, proper and bawdy, come into play. He promises to be faithful to his wife, and also to keep her sexuality under his control—by keeping her "ring" on his "finger."

When Bassanio's passionate outburst in the trial scene reveals the intensity of his friendship with Antonio, Portia feels threatened, and later retaliates with the only weapon at a wife's command: the threat of infidelity. In a turnabout of the conventional metaphor for female chastity, she declares that her supposed rival "hath got the jewel that I love"—the ring, representing her husband's sexual favors and his fidelity. She continues with an even more unorthodox assertion of sexual equality:

I will become as liberal as you,
I'll not deny him anything I have,

No, not my body, nor my husband's bed:
Know him I shall, I am well sure of it.
   (5.1.226–29)

Refusing to honor the double standard on which the whole idea of cuck-oldry depends, and refusing to overlook her husband's supposed sexual fault, she threatens to seize a comparable sexual freedom for herself. One facet of Shakespeare's genius is his perception that men don't see women as they are, but project onto them certain needs and fears instilled by our culture. He and a few other writers stand apart in being critically aware that these distorted but deeply felt conceptions of women can be distinguished from women themselves—their behavior, their feelings, their desires. From Portia's point of view, women aren't inherently fickle, as misogyny holds them to be; rather, they practice betrayal defensively, in retaliation for comparable injuries.

The ring plot culminates in fictions: though Bassanio did give Portia's ring away, in fact he wasn't unfaithful to her as she claims he was, and though she threatens revenge she clearly never intends to carry it out. This transparent fictitiousness makes the intrigue like a fantasy—a story we make up to play out urges on which we fear to act. In terms of fantasy, Bassanio does betray Portia, both by sleeping with another woman and by loving Antonio. Portia, in turn, does get back at him, by cuckolding him. At the level of fantasy, Shakespeare seems to imply that male friendship continues to compete with marriage even after the nuptial knot is tied, and that men's fears of cuckoldry may be rooted in an awareness that they deserve to be punished for failing to honor marriage vows in the spirit as well as in the letter.

René Girard has argued that the binary oppositions on which the play seems to be built—Christian versus Jew, realism versus romance, the spirit ver-sus the letter, and so on, collapse into symmetry and reciprocity. Girard holds that, though "The Venetians appear different from Shylock, up to a point,"

They do not live by the law of charity, but this law is enough of a presence in their language to drive the law of revenge underground, to make this revenge almost invisible. As a result, this revenge becomes more subtle, skillful, and feline than the revenge of Shylock.[12]

By trivializing serious issues into jokes which rest on playful fictions, the ring plot serves to disguise the extent to which the Venetians do resemble Shylock. But it also articulates serious issues; in it as in the main plot, ironic similarities between Jew and Christian abound. Portia's gift to

Bassanio seems innocent, like Shylock's "merry bond," but it too is used to catch a Venetian on the hip and feed a grudge. Her vow of revenge through cuckoldry parallels Shylock's in his "Hath not a Jew eyes?" speech: both justify revenge on the grounds that what their adversaries denounce they actually practice. Just as in the trial Portia pleads for the spirit of mercy but actually takes revenge against Shylock through the letter of the law, so her original professions of boundless love are undercut by her later desire to even the sexual score. As Shylock says, "These be the Christian husbands!" (4.1.291). He was once a husband, too, and pledged his love to Leah with a ring—a pledge dishonored (so far as we know) only by his daughter when she turned Christian.

Finally, though, the ring plot emphasizes sexual differences more than it undercuts social and moral ones. It portrays a tug of war in which women and men compete—for the affections of men. Bassanio's final lines recapitulate the progression from homoerotic bonds to the marital bond ironically affirmed through cuckoldry which the action of the ring plot implies:

> Sweet doctor, you shall be my bedfellow,—
> When I am absent then lie with my wife.
>   (5.1.284–85)

Similarly, the very last lines in the play, spoken by Gratiano, voice the homoerotic wish, succeeded by the heterosexual anxiety:

> But were the day come, I should wish it dark,
> Till I were couching with the doctor's clerk.
> Well, while I live, I'll fear no other thing,
> So sore, as keeping safe Nerissa's ring.
>   (5.1.304–7)

Notes

1. Norman Rabkin has written perceptively about the ring plot as one of many "signals" in *The Merchant of Venice* which "create discomfort, point to centrifugality." See his *Shakespeare and the Problem of Meaning* (Chicago: University of Chicago Press, 1981), p. 29. Interesting essays on the ring plot are: Marilyn L. Williamson, "The Ring Episode in *The Merchant of Venice*," *South Atlantic Quarterly* 71 (1972): 587–94; James E. Siemon, "*The Merchant of Venice*: Act V as Ritual Reiteration," *Studies in Philosophy* 67 (1970): 201–9. For an interpretation centering on Portia's power and how the ring plot resolves its threat to male dominance, see Anne Parten, "Re-establishing the Sexual Order: The Ring Episode in *The Merchant of Venice*," *Women Studies* 9, no. 1 (Spring 1982), Special Issue on Feminist Criticism of Shakespeare II, ed. Gayle Greene and Carolyn Swift: 145–56. While I share her view that cuckoldry is "a particularly disturbing specter which is bound up with the idea

of female ascendancy" (pp. 149–50), we disagree about how the ring plot represents this specter. She holds that, by making explicit the male anxieties which cuckoldry inspires and then exposing them as "*only* a game" (p. 150), it dispels those anxieties; I believe that by voicing them loudly in the final scene, in lieu of conventional conclusions which celebrate marriage, the ring plot seriously undermines any comic affirmation of marriage. For a reading of the final scene as Portia's way of getting back at Antonio, see Leslie Fiedler, "The Jew As Stranger," in *The Stranger in Shakespeare* (New York: Stein and Day, 1972), esp. pp. 134–36.

2. Others have commented on the triangulated rivalry which the ring plot brings out. In her introduction to *The Merchant of Venice* in *The Riverside Shakespeare*, ed. G. Blakemore Evans (Boston: Houghton-Mifflin, 1974), Anne Barton notes that the ring plot is "a test which forces Bassanio to weigh his obligations to his wife against those to his friend and to recognize the latent antagonism between them" (p. 253). Leonard Tennenhouse, in "The Counterfeit Order of *The Merchant of Venice*," in *Representing Shakespeare: New Psychoanalytic Essays*, ed. Murray Schwartz and Coppélia Kahn (Baltimore: Johns Hopkins University Press, 1980), observes that "This test of Bassanio's fidelity to Portia becomes, at Antonio's insistence, a test of Bassanio's love for Antonio" (p. 62). Lawrence W. Hyman, "The Rival Loves in *The Merchant of Venice*," *Shakespeare Quarterly* 21 no. 2 (Spring 1970): 109–16, sees the main action of the play as a struggle between Portia and Antonio for Bassanio, and interprets Antonio's bond with Shylock as a metaphor for the bond of love between him and Bassanio. See also Robert W. Hapgood, "Portia and *The Merchant of Venice*: The Gentle Bond," *MLQ* 28, no. 1 (March 1967): 19–32; on the ring plot, pp. 26–29.

3. Janet Adelman, "Male Bonding in Shakespeare's Comedies."

4. This and all subsequent quotations from *Merchant* are taken from the new Arden edition of *The Merchant of Venice*, ed. John Russell Brown (1955; reprint, London: Methuen; Cambridge: Harvard University Press, 1961, 1966).

5. Peter Erickson deals extensively with the psychology of homoerotic bonds in Shakespeare in his book *Patriarchal Structures in Shakespeare's Drama*, . . . from the University of California Press. See also Shirley Nelson Garner's interesting treatment of this theme in "A Midsummer Night's Dream: 'Jack shall have Jill; / Nought shall go ill,'" *Feminist Studies* 9, no. 1 (1981), Special Issue on Feminist Criticism of Shakespeare I, ed. Gayle Greene and Carolyn Lenz: 47–64.

6. See my book *Man's Estate: Masculine Identity in Shakespeare* (Berkeley and Los Angeles: University of California Press, 1981), passim, but esp. chap. 4.

7. The story can be found in *Tales and Quick Answers* (1530), reprinted in *Shakespeare's Jestbook* (Chiswick: C. Wittingham, 1814), p. 14.

8. There is a hint, however, that Antonio's sadness is caused by the prospect of Bassanio's marriage. When noting Antonio's mood, Gratiano comments that he is "marvelously chang'd" (1.1.76), and a few lines later we learn that Bassanio had earlier promised to tell him about a vow to make "a secret pilgrimage" to a certain lady (1.1.119–20).

9. The phrase is Harry Berger's in "Marriage and Mercifixion in *The Merchant of Venice*: The Casket Scene Revisited," *Shakespeare Quarterly* 32, no. 2 (Summer 1981): 161, and describes what he regards as Portia's attempt to control Bassanio by giving him the ring. Regarding the secret agenda behind Antonio's generosity, see Robert Hapgood, cited in n. 2: "Antonio is at once too generous and too possessive. . . . He wants Bassanio to see him die for his sake" (p. 261).

10. See David Willbern, "Shakespeare's Nothing," in *Representing Shakespeare: New Psychoanalytic Essays*, cited in n. 2, and the story cited in n. 7.

11. This quotation is taken from the new Arden edition of *All's Well That Ends Well*, ed. G. K. Hunter (1959; reprint, London: Methuen; Cambridge: Harvard University Press, 1962).

12. René Girard, "'To Entrap the Wisest': A Reading of *The Merchant of Venice*," in *Textual Strategies: Perspectives in Post-Structuralist Criticism*, ed. Josué Harari (Ithaca: Cornell University Press, 1979), pp. 100–119.

RICHARD A. LEVIN

Portia's Belmont

Shylock is a product of forces in Venice and as a mirror image of that city. One might concede some degree of likeness between Shylock and Christian Venice, however, and still hold that Christian Venice comes closer to an ideal fully expressed in Belmont. The nature of Belmont, then, is crucial to one's interpretation of *The Merchant of Venice*. Is Belmont best seen as an expression of a culture's highest values or as a suburban retreat for the privileged? The latter alternative has been gaining adherents, partly because contemporary interest in the outsider in Shakespeare creates unease about the plight of Shylock at Portia's hands in act 4 and the marginal status she imposes on Antonio in act 5.[1] Portia's assertion of authority is, I believe, at the heart of the play; it allows one to see that not until the end are the dual questions settled: who will be admitted into society, and on what terms? In answering these questions, the play reveals that life in Belmont, no less than life in Venice, is shaped by the struggle for position.

Through Launcelot Shakespeare indicates the continuity between Venice and Belmont. In Venice, when Bassanio took Launcelot into service, in an ebullient mood he bid Jessica, the Jewess, farewell. When Launcelot first appears in Belmont, however, his fortunes are in temporary eclipse: in the absence of Portia and his master, Lorenzo and Jessica have authority in the household.

From *Love and Society in Shakespearean Comedy: A Study of Dramatic Form and Content*, pp. 53–85, 178–79. Copyright © 1985 by Associated University Presses.

Resentfully, Launcelot jests at Jessica's expense. She is damned, he tells her, by virtue of her birth; she is either the Jew Shylock's daughter, or else she is a bastard (3.5.1–18). Moreover, Jews ought not to convert, because in doing so they "raise the price of hogs" (24). Launcelot implies that society has a limited number of privileges to offer, so that the success of one person implies another's failure. Marginally situated as Launcelot is, he tries to reaffirm his right to belong by declaring Jessica the outsider. The question, then, is whether those more advantageously placed in Belmont are as competitive as Launcelot.

The answer to this question is complex. A privileged life has room for generosity; thus, just as Christian Venice is sometimes gracious when Shylock is not, so Belmont can rise superior to Venice. However, even at the pinnacle of society Portia feels herself the outsider among herself, Bassanio, and Antonio. The privileged, and Portia preeminently, also have the power to protect their own interests. Portia, for example, is poised, charming, and well-connected; she proves able to set the terms that others must accept, if they are to end up with any portion of the pie.

It is not simply because competition takes subtle forms at Belmont that the action there often seems the best evidence that *The Merchant* is genuinely romantic comedy. The casket plot, in which a suitor must choose the right casket to win Portia, comes right out of romance and is at the furthest remove from actual social practices. I believe, however, that even this plot can be interpreted, symbolically at least, as an antiromantic comment on social reality. We will approach such an understanding of this plot and of Belmont in general by analyzing Portia's development. Even when she is introduced, in 1.2, she possesses shortcomings sometimes to be found in one of her privileged class and background: ennui, intolerance for outsiders, and moral complacency. Her present circumstances have already begun to make her aware that she has interests to protect; later, when the veil falls fully from her eyes, she discovers, and we with her, that the struggle for position continues unabated in Belmont.

* * *

The scene opens with Portia complaining, "By my troth, Nerissa, my little body is a-weary of this great world." One is inclined to be sympathetic, for although we have not yet heard how the will of Portia's father limits her freedom, her words recall Antonio's melancholy at the play's outset. Nerissa, however, puts Portia's predicament in a different light. To Nerissa, Portia "surfeits" with too much and her "good fortunes" far outweigh her miseries. Nerissa reveals Portia as an immensely privileged woman, whose "great world" is a palace and whose troubles are, at most, momentary. Nerissa advises Portia that those who possess mere "competency" are often happier than those with "superfluity"; Portia should learn to be content with what she has (8–9).

Portia laconically replies, "Good sentences, and well pronounc'd" (10); she elaborates after Nerissa insists that Portia should follow the advice she has been given. Portia pours forth a stream of sententious wisdom to the effect that there is all the difference in the world between giving good advice and following it. The implication seems to be that one ought to accept the way of the world and not have compunctions about falling short of ideals.

There is another implication, too, one directed at Nerissa; it is heard most strongly in the first of Portia's gnomic utterances:

> If to do were as easy as to know what were good to do, chapels
> had been churches, and poor men's cottages princes' palaces.
> (1.2.12–14)

Portia nudges her lady-in-waiting back into place, saying, in effect, that the poor would like to be rich, and if they were, they would behave precisely as the rich do. Portia is unapologetic about her privileges.

It is at this point that Portia first mentions her father's will. She finds it "hard" not to have choice, and complains that her own "will"—that is, her volition—is constrained by her father's "will" (24–26). Portia wittily sums up her predicament and inclines the viewer in her favor. If she is indeed committed to adhering to the will, then she has simply been letting off steam. And yet her real intentions are still hidden, for at this point only Nerissa endorses the scheme contrived by Portia's father. Before hearing Portia again on the will, attention shifts: Nerissa offers to name the suitors who have already arrived, while Portia's comments will reveal her "affection" for them.

Portia's tart remarks about her suitors perhaps reveal only an impressively spirited young lady, doing what she can to pass her time and Nerissa's under arduous circumstances: she is encroached upon by suitors not at all to her liking. A harsher judgment is also possible. Portia continues to reveal the limitations characteristic of her class and background. For example, Portia mocks all her suitors even though she knows "it is a sin to be a mocker" (57): she still shows no compunction about failing to bring her conduct into line with moral standards. Then, too, Portia caricatures her suitors by employing foreign stereotypes.[2] Thus she finds the Englishman ludicrously outfitted in an assortment of imported styles of dress, the German a drunkard, and the Scotsman a coward who depends on French backing. Such mocking may be standard Elizabethan fare or else the clever but brittle humor of a woman who does not delve very deeply into the intrinsic merits of her suitors.

Portia's stereotyping of the suitors helps to link her with the less attractive traits of her countrymen in Venice. As a way of affirming her own qualifications as an insider, she mocks the foreigners, much as Salerio and Solanio mock Antonio as a "strange fellow." Portia also resembles Venetians when she ridicules the Count Palatine because he is a "weeping philosopher" who does "nothing but frown" (49, 46). Her desire for amusement also recalls the Venetian worldlings of 1.1, and especially Gratiano, who rejects "wisdom" and "gravity" in favor of "mirth" and "laughter."

At the end of the scene, Portia expresses two contrasting opinions that help confirm her link with Venice. After Nerissa names all the suitors, she recalls an earlier guest, "a Venetian, a scholar and a soldier, that came hither [to Belmont] in company of the Marquis of Montferrat" (113–14). Portia also remembers this guest, Bassanio, and agrees that he was attractive. Bassanio, likewise, was impressed by Portia's appearance. Moreover, just as Bassanio spoke of a marriage to Portia as "fortunate," so Portia seems to regard Bassanio as a good catch; he is a well-born Venetian who traveled to Belmont in the company of an Italian nobleman. (Bassanio's credentials need not include wealth, of course; Portia has wealth in abundance.)

No sooner has Portia rendered one favorable verdict for dubious reasons than she renders an unfavorable one for equally dubious reasons. A servant announcing the imminent departure of the suitors mentions the unexpected arrival of another, the Prince of Morocco. Though Portia has never met him, she already knows he is unwelcome: "If he have the condition of a saint, and the complexion of a devil, I had rather he should shrive me than wive me" (129–31). Though an Elizabethan audience might be expected to share Portia's prejudice, her comment jars; she wants nothing to do with a black man, whatever his merits. She unapologetically falls short of the ideals of Christian culture.

Were Portia seen as wholeheartedly committed to respecting her father's will, her faults and blemishes might be extenuated. However, her intentions remain obscured throughout the scene, though at one point she seems to declare them unambiguously: "If I live to be as old as Sibylla, I will die as chaste as Diana, unless I be obtained by the manner of my father's will" (106–8). The context of this remark is pertinent, however. Nerissa has just told Portia that the detested suitors have resolved to leave unless Portia breaks the will. It seems, then, that she is communicating a message designed to insure her guests' departure.

Slightly earlier in the scene, Portia has something rather different to say about the will. She remarks of the German suitor: If "the worst fall that ever fell, I hope I shall make shift to go without him" (90–91). When Nerissa points out that Portia would be breaking the will if she rejected the German after he chose correctly, Portia suggests that Nerissa tempt him by placing "a deep glass of Rhenish wine on the contrary casket." "I will do any thing," Portia adds, "ere I will be married to a spunge."

Portia seems to be hinting that if necessary she might be relieved of responsibility by Nerissa, who could take it upon herself to protect Portia's interests. In this connection, note that Nerissa is kept informed by Portia of her opinion of all the suitors—and potential suitors, for Bassanio's name is introduced as if both Nerissa and Portia understood that he might possibly become a suitor.

The conflicting evidence about Portia's intentions suggests that she experiences opposing impulses: she feels both loyal and rebellious to her father. The circumstances of Portia's life, as they are sketched in during this scene, suggest the nature of the conflict. Thus far, Portia has lived in total comfort, protected by her father from the world. She is a devoted daughter who half-believes that when her father dies, the right man will magically appear to win her. Nevertheless, Portia senses that her father's death fundamentally alters her circumstances. But for his will, she would be as free to shape her destiny as, for example, Olivia is in *Twelfth Night*. More important still, the father's will puts her into danger, potentially delivering her to a man she will find abhorrent. It is not surprising, therefore, if some harsher elements in Portia's character have begun to emerge.

The scene makes one curious about the direction Portia's development will take. It is not clear, for example, that respect and devotion for her father provide the only explanation for her reluctance to break the will; she may have less admirable motives. Consider Portia's witty pronouncements concerning this will:

The brain may devise laws for the blood, but a hot temper leaps
o'er a cold decree—such a hare is madness the youth, to skip o'er
the meshes of good counsel the cripple. (1.2.18–21)

Portia contrasts law and license, reason and passion, and age and youth; though she sides with license, passion, and youth, the imagery she employs suggests that she understands the need for agile movement around a barrier—one avoids breaking the law outright. Portia is the quintessential insider, loath to break the law because she understands that aristocracy exists by virtue of law and precedent. Portia uses other legal imagery in the scene,[3] anticipating her impersonation of a judge in a Venetian court of law. She already appears to recognize the value of stealth and takes a totally unsentimental view of outsiders who encroach on her life.

Nevertheless, 1.2 conspicuously consists of conversation, not action. Portia has yet to take her place on the world's stage, and the relationship between her words and her deeds has yet to be established. While it is possible that Portia privately discloses her settled convictions, it is likelier that Portia herself does not understand whether her rebelliousness and cynicism are anything more than a pose.

Consider first matters related to her father's will. Must this will express an ideal value and nothing else, or can it alternately symbolize certain realistic social facts? Similarly, will the casket test locate the perfect suitor, or will it work imperfectly, as any test would in the actual world? These questions have obvious importance; Portia is not likely to reflect the values of a specific class unless she exists in a plausible social milieu.

Nerissa's description of the will makes it appear as a donnée from the world of romance:

> Your father was ever virtuous, and holy men at their death have
> good inspirations; therefore the lott'ry that he hath devis'd in
> these three chests of gold, silver, and lead, whereof who chooses
> his meaning chooses you, will no doubt never be chosen by any
> rightly but one who you shall rightly love. (1.2.27–33)

In Nerissa's view, Portia's father has contrived a means for bringing together two people perfectly in love. As the test unfolds, it indeed may be interpreted as a conventional romance motif testing the purity of love. Each casket has its own inscription. The gold one reads: "Who chooseth me shall gain what many men desire." The silver: "Who chooseth me shall get as much as he deserves." And the lead: "Who chooseth me must give and hazard all he hath." We eventually discover that the gold and silver caskets represent different faces of fortune. The gold one symbolizes the outright desire for worldly wealth or position; the silver casket represents false self-esteem based on one's own fortune. Only the lead one, then, identifies a love not "mingled with regards that stands / Aloof from th' entire point" (*Lr.* 1.1.239–40). Nevertheless, while granting that her father intends to identify true love, the morality of his scheme is still questionable.

Portia's silence in the face of Nerissa's affirmation suggests that he has imposed on his daughter. Though he seems to Nerissa to have affirmed high values, he has done so at no expense to himself: the cost of his idealism is to be borne by his daughter. Indeed, the virtue that Nerissa finds not only in the father's will but in his whole life is subject to the same criticism. Possessed of almost limitless wealth, he could avoid many common moral compromises and safely indulge in virtuous deeds.

Doubts about the motives behind the will are strengthened if it ultimately fails to function as one would expect it to in a romance. For the play to work as a romance, the intrinsic worth of each suitor must be perfectly reflected in his choice of a casket; the suitors therefore must have the simplicity of allegorical figures. I shall try to show, however, that the characters are sufficiently "rounded" (to use Maurice Morgann's term) and the motives behind their choices sufficiently complex so that the connection between their merit and their fate is imperfect at best. One is free to feel that the worthiest suitor does not win and that various elements that should be extraneous influence the outcome of the test.

The Prince of Morocco has won the sympathy of many viewers, and he may be the worthiest. Although Morocco chooses the gold casket, he cannot easily be regarded as a fortune-hunter, for his wealth and status are comparable with Portia's (2.7.31–33) and in the hopes of winning her he willingly agrees never to woo any woman again if he fails. Moreover, a laudable motive seems to lie behind his choice of the gold casket. Morocco heretofore had fought valorously; not satisfied with past tests of his character, however, he set out for Belmont. The reason behind his quest seems to be revealed by the motive he imputes to others: "All the world desires [Portia]. / From the four corners of the earth they come / To kiss this shrine, this mortal breathing saint" (38–40). To say the least, Morocco very generously explains why so many men have arrived on the shores of a wealthy heiress. But the tawny Moor neither sees base motives in others nor possesses them himself; his choice of the gold casket represents not desire for wealth but homage to Portia: "Never so rich a gem / Was set in worse than gold" (2.7.54–55). Morocco is the play's one true romantic. Moreover, discovering his wrong choice, Morocco remains dignified and leaves with a "griev'd heart," promising to abide by his vow not to court again (75–76). His few blemishes, considered below, are far from serious and perhaps largely the product of his reception in Belmont.

The Prince of Arragon is less admirable than Morocco. He is an "arrogant" Spaniard who haughtily rejects the gold casket as the choice of the "fool multitude," and then, convinced of his own worth, chooses the silver. But although smug, he is not a completely negligible figure.[4] Like Morocco, he willingly vows not to woo another if he fails to win Portia. Moreover, the inscription on the silver casket, "Who chooseth me shall get as much as he deserves," strikes in him a powerful and responsive chord, and he elaborates upon it with conviction: no one, he says, should "presume / To wear an undeserved dignity" (2.9.39–40). Arragon endorses the enlightened Tudor doctrine that the social hierarchy should be sensitive to merit, and his choice suggests that he has tried to be worthy of his rank. He opens the silver casket and is humiliatingly confronted with "the portrait of a blinking idiot" (54) as a measure of his true worth. No doubt Arragon does fail to meet the standard he sets for himself—but at least he makes an effort.

On the other hand, the successful suitor, Bassanio, deliberately tries to assume an undeserved dignity by "cozening fortune."[5] Bassanio outfits a lavish retinue and sends ahead to Belmont "gifts of rich value" (91) as a token of the wealth that is actually only borrowed. Moreover, although Bassanio chooses the lead casket, his present poverty and past prodigality give reason for thinking that fortune is his principal motive in undertaking the courtship, and his interview with Portia at the opening of 3.2 does not suggest he has fundamentally altered. He is very much the man with a rented limousine, anxious to conduct his business and, if unsuccessful, depart. Moreover, he has nothing to lose, since Portia has apparently not repeated the key stipulation that a losing suitor must vow never to marry.

Before Bassanio picks the lead casket, the merit of his choice is further eroded. The song Portia orders to accompany his deliberations provides him with a number of hints. The song warns against "fancy," which is "engend'red in the eyes" and then quickly "dies" (3.2.67–68). Bassanio seems to infer that the song counsels against trusting appearances, for the speech in which he announces his choice begins, "So may the outward shows be least themselves. . . ." The song has also pointed towards the lead casket by introducing five "-ed" rhymes and by introducing a tolling bell, which, along with the references to fancy's death, invokes "the lead in which the dead [of the period] were folded."[6] "In that age of anagrams and acrostics," one critic observes, the song might be expected to provide Bassanio hints; another critic identifies Renaissance plays in which a song discloses what a character is sworn to conceal.[7]

Several of Bassanio's earlier aphorisms on the theme of deceptive appearance strike a suitably grave note, as for example, the first: "In law, what plea so tainted and corrupt / But, being season'd with a gracious voice, / Obscures the show of evil?" (75–77). (That a "gracious voice" in the courtroom can "obscure" evil is evident in act 4.) Soon, however, Bassanio's examples derive from the woman's toilette; she may deceive by wearing wigs, and through other arts as well she may manage to "veil an Indian beauty" (99). Without a trace of self-consciousness, Bassanio has descended from a high spiritual plane to invoke society's prejudice against dark-skinned people.

Bassanio's indifference to spiritual values seems confirmed when, upon opening the casket and finding Portia's picture, he becomes absorbed in praising her painted likeness (115–26); when he does turn to the woman herself, it is her physical beauty that he notices. Finally, he reads the enclosed scroll, which incongruously praises him as one who "choose[s] not by the view" (131). Instructed by the scroll to "claim [Portia] with a loving kiss," he does so, but with words that make his affection doubtful. He describes himself as like one who has "contend[ed] in a prize"; now, "giddy" as if he were hearing applause, he wishes to have his victory "confirmed, sign'd, [and] ratified" by Portia's kiss (148). Though we need not doubt that Bassanio is by this time infatuated with his "thrice-fair lady," his imagery is telltale: beyond his wildest dreams he has achieved a preeminently "fortunate" (1.1.176) match. His love is emphatically not that pure love which the lead casket was supposed to identify.

If the casket test does not work ideally, alternate explanations of how it does work are available. The test is twice referred to as a "lottery" (1.2.29, 2.1.15) and Morocco compares the test to the game of dice, where "blind fortune" can deprive "the better man" of victory (2.1.32–38). Nor is he alone in identifying the role of fortune (see 3.2.21). One may also notice that the winner, aside from whatever hints he may get, is aided by his insider's knowledge of the culture; whereas Morocco rejects the lead casket, saying that "men that hazard all / Do it in hope of fair advantages" (2.7.18–19), Bassanio has a better sense of what the occasion calls for.

Portia's response to her three suitors can also be discussed outside the context of romance. She has no interest in Arragon and Morocco; Bassanio is her clear choice. There is good reason for thinking that her feelings are in large measure dictated by her class and background. It is noticeable, for example, that she never takes any interest in Morocco's personal qualities; she has the same objection to him before she meets him and after he fails the test: "Let all of his complexion choose me so."[8] By way of contrast, Portia shows immediate interest upon hearing that a wealthy Venetian approaches, and when 3.2 opens shortly after Bassanio's arrival, Portia showers him with the affection she has reserved for the first eminently suitable bachelor to make his way to the shores of Belmont.

Yet it is necessary to define Portia's development more precisely. Earlier, encroached upon by two unwelcome suitors, her less attractive features predominate. With Bassanio, on the other hand, far more appealing characteristics surface. Only when she again feels threatened does she relentlessly pursue her interests.

To Portia's credit it can be said that she honors her father's will and allows both Arragon and Morocco to make their choices. Nevertheless, a rebellious spirit sometimes threatens to overcome her inhibitions. Without breaking the will, she does what she can to discourage Morocco and Arragon. For example, she communicates to the former her dislike of him and postpones his choice in the hope he will be discouraged; more important, she seems to invent the stipulation that a failed wooer cannot court again, for when Arragon later opens the wrong casket, he discovers a scroll inviting him subsequently to "take what wife [he] will to bed" (2.9.70). Lest Bassanio be discouraged, he is never confronted with the inhibition, as noted earlier.

Portia's rudeness also helps to develop the darker notes in her character. Act 2, scene 1 opens with Morocco pleading, "Mislike me not for my complexion." In view of a knowledge of Portia's prejudices, one infers that she has communicated her feelings to him. Confirmation soon arrives. Portia observes equivocally that she is not sol[el]y led / By nice direction of a maiden's eyes," and then says of Morocco that he is "as fair / As any comer [she has] look'd on yet" (20–21)—a dubious compliment, even if we overlook Morocco's having just used "fair" to mean "light-complexioned" (4). Morocco, trying to keep his chin up, responds, "Even for that I thank you," and boasts of his achievements, awkwardly proclaiming that women of his own color have found him attractive. He either is a braggart or is trying to steady himself, meanwhile remaining studiously polite to his hostess. His manners show to advantage against hers. And even if in a strange way her behavior can be extenuated on the grounds that she needs to discourage Morocco, the hint of gratuitous cruelty is confirmed when she taunts her next suitor, Arragon, *after* he has made his wrong choice (2.9.53 and 61–62).

Just as Portia's attitude towards Morocco and Arragon highlights her intolerance for outsiders encroaching on her life, so her very different reception for Bassanio shows her insularity. Nevertheless, Portia does reveal genuinely attractive aspects of her character. While Bassanio is precipitating the moment of choice, Portia pours forth her heart. It is all the more important to notice, therefore, that even as she rides the high tide of romantic passion, she experiences an undertow that strengthens her self-protective urges. That she has pleaded unavailingly for Bassanio to postpone his choice suggests to her that her feelings are not reciprocated; she asks him to "confess / What treason there is mingled with [his] love" (3.2.26–27). Portia shows that her infatuation and caution exist side-by-side and that highly emotional circumstances are likely to shift her in one direction or the other.

On all sides at this time is evidence of the two Portias. They are seen in her apparent decision to adhere to her father's will. She is, on the one hand, the trusting and dutiful daughter, but she is also a sceptical woman who apparently resolves to let Bassanio be tested: "If you do love me, you will find me out" (41).[9] Similarly, Portia describes Bassanio's moment of choice romantically, but she adds sophisticated touches. From farfetched conceits one infers that she does not really confuse reality and fantasy; for example, before calling for music, she describes Bassanio's possible defeat as follows:

> if he loses he makes a swan-like end,
> Fading in music. That the comparison
> May stand more proper, my eye shall be the stream
> And wat'ry death-bed for him.
>   (3.2.44–47)

Portia's description of Bassanio's approach to the caskets more sharply reveals her dual self:

> Now he goes,
> With no less presence, but with much more love,
> Than young Alcides [Hercules], when he did redeem
> The virgin tribute paid by howling Troy
> To the sea-monster.
>   (3.2.53–57)

It is unlikely that Portia actually confuses the heroism of Hercules with Bassanio's challenge; moreover, by carefully distinguishing Bassanio's motives from Hercules's pecuniary interest, she reveals that she has considered their possible likeness.

If Portia, given her limited knowledge of Bassanio's background, nevertheless hovers between faith and doubt, the viewer who knows so much more, must wonder what lies in store for her. The song announces how quickly fancy dies, echoing as it does so Salerio and Gratiano's conclusion that romance soon gives way to disillusionment (2.6.5–19).

As Portia watches Bassanio choose the right casket, she expresses relief, meanwhile admitting to the doubts she has had:

> How all the other passions fleet to air,
> As doubtful thoughts, and rash-embrac'd despair,
> And shudd'ring fear, and green-eyed jealousy!
> O love, be moderate, allay thy ecstasy,
> In measure rain thy joy, scant this excess!
> I feel too much thy blessing; make it less,
> For fear I surfeit.
>   (3.2.108–14)

The passage not only clarifies what Portia felt earlier; it also ominously suggests the future. Though Portia wishes to take Bassanio's correct choice as magical confirmation of his love, she "fears" that she "surfeits." In effect, she has experienced one swing of the pendulum; the rest of the scene traces the return swing. The motion, imperceptible at first, gathers momentum.

Bassanio, having read the enclosed scroll, approaches Portia and requests a kiss. In granting the kiss, Portia generously bestows herself. All she possesses is Bassanio's; she only wishes that she were "a thousand times more fair, ten thousand times more rich," so that she might "stand high in [Bassanio's] account" (154–55). Implicit in her words is the knowledge that Bassanio does have an interest in her property and wealth. But this awareness does not fully measure Portia's sophistication. She calls herself "an unlesson'd girl, unschool'd, unpractic'd" (159), and says that she commits herself, her "fair mansion," and all her servants, to Bassanio to be directed, "as from her lord, her governor, her king" (164–71). However, is Portia teacher and not pupil, and is her gift not intended to be exemplary?[10] She slips a ring from her finger to Bassanio's, saying that should he lose or relinquish the ring, "let it presage the ruin of your love, / And be my vantage to exclaim on you" (173–74). Portia hints at the reciprocity that has been lacking, and by asking for a pledge of faith, she suggests her uncertainty about the faith she has so far been offered. Moreover, although Portia surely does not calculatedly deceive Bassanio, the totality with which she gives shows that she offers words and not deeds: her gift is sealed with a kiss only.

No sooner does Bassanio accept Portia's ring than Nerissa and Gratiano disclose that they have been eagerly waiting to see whether Bassanio would chose rightly. "My eyes can look as swift as yours," Gratiano tells Bassanio, adding, "Your fortune stood upon the casket there, / And so did mine too" (201–2). Gratiano reveals that he wooed Nerissa and obtained her agreement to marry him if Bassanio's "fortune" (207) was to achieve Portia. It takes no great stretch of the imagination to see that regardless of the affection Gratiano and Nerissa presumably feel for one another, both want marriage only if they can hang onto the coattails of a wealthy couple. Later, Gratiano exults to Salerio, "We are the Jasons, we have won the fleece" (241); even in Portia's presence, he comes very close to saying that both he and Bassanio were "swift" to fall in love partly because it was advantageous for them to do so.

Gratiano and Nerissa's disclosure should be disturbing to Portia for reasons other than what it implies about Bassanio's fortune-hunting. The prospect of a double wedding must make her wedding seem less precious, the ordinary course of the world, and not a unique event. Also, by asking in effect for a share of Bassanio's winnings, Gratiano makes Belmont appear as a pie to be divided up. We should not be surprised if Portia becomes newly alert to the question of how Bassanio's Venetian attachments will affect her marriage and her position at Belmont. The most serious danger from Venice is yet to emerge: Bassanio's emotional commitment to Antonio.

The key incident begins as simply a further Venetian encroachment. Lorenzo, Jessica, and Salerio arrive, the last bearing Antonio's letter for Bassanio.[11] Bassanio instinctively begins to welcome his friends to the home, then (perhaps with a glance from Portia) hesitates, wondering whether his "new int'rest" in Belmont permits him this privilege (221).[12] Portia informs Bassanio that his guests are "entirely welcome"; though cordial, she never greets the friends directly, and her adverb, "entirely," suggests that there are

degrees of welcome that have yet to be defined. Ralph Berry nicely para-
phrases Portia in order to catch her implication: "You haven't taken over my
household *yet*. Please make your friends welcome; and do not forget that I
am chatelaine here" (p. 13). When it comes to deeds and not words, Portia
has not yet transferred title to her property; in light of the latest intrusion,
it seems that she may become less and less inclined to relinquish any of the
constituents of her power.

When Bassanio receives from Salerio Antonio's letter and upon reading it turns pale, Portia becomes anxious. What can explain such a profound
change in Bassanio? "I am half yourself" (248), she says hopefully, and asks
him to share with her the contents of the letter.

The shamefaced young lord begins by admitting that he lied when he
said that his only wealth "ran in [his] veins" (255). He is not merely penniless;
he is in debt to a friend who placed himself in mortal jeopardy to make the
loan. Now this friend faces imminent death. Portia falls silent upon hearing
these disclosures. She must realize that Bassanio tells something short of the
whole truth; after all, only moments before she had put aside "green-eyed
jealousy" and her suspicions of "treason." Perhaps Bassanio, desperately short
of money, got Antonio to finance the lavish expedition to Belmont. Might it
be that Antonio did so, secure in the knowledge that Portia was only to be
a source of income for Bassanio, whose affections were otherwise engaged?
This is the worst possibility Portia can ponder; less threatening alternatives
soon become apparent.

When Portia does speak up, she asks Bassanio a curious question: "Is it
your dear friend that is thus in trouble?" (291). As Antonio has already been
identified as Bassanio's "dear friend" (261), Portia apparently probes for more
information about the relationship. Bassanio answers by describing Antonio
as "the dearest friend to me, the kindest man, / The best-condition'd and
unwearied spirit / In doing courtesies" (292–94). From these words, conflicting conclusions can be drawn. Antonio may be just as good a person as Bassanio describes, or he may appear better than he is through Bassanio's guilty
eyes. Possibly Antonio's generosity is calculated to have just the effect it seems
to be having on Bassanio. Portia has earlier heard Bassanio say of Antonio's
letter that "every word in it [is] a gaping wound / Issuing life-blood" (265–
66). Why has Antonio written such a letter, if not to influence Bassanio's feelings? Portia may be beginning to wonder whether her real worry ought not
to be Bassanio's present feelings for her, but how these feelings might alter as
Antonio's death approaches.

Portia responds to Bassanio with an offer that makes her appear a model
of kindness. She suggests that she and Bassanio should promptly marry and
that he should then leave for Venice with any sum of money he thinks he

needs to rescue Antonio. When Antonio is freed, she will welcome the two of them to her house. Portia is altogether too obliging to be sincere. How many wives, for example, would assure their husbands, without a trace of irony, that they should "hence upon [their] wedding-day"? (311). How many wives would cheerfully make Portia's offer: "My maid Nerissa and myself mean time / Will live as maids and widows" (309–10)? And how can Portia believe that her money will save Antonio, when she offers the precise sum Jessica has said Shylock would refuse—"twenty times" the principal? (307; cf. 287). I suggest that Portia's speech should arouse curiosity about her real attitude and her real intentions.

Portia seems conscious of the danger that Antonio may overwhelm Bassanio with feelings of guilt. She says, for example, that she will not let a friend like the one Bassanio describes "lose a hair through Bassanio's fault" (302). She adds that she sends Bassanio to Venice because she does not want him to lie by her side "with an unquiet soul" (306). Hence Portia's generosity may include a selfish motive; having seen how Antonio's generosity manipulates Bassanio, she resolves to outdo Antonio.

Portia's real feelings and underlying strategy are perhaps most strongly hinted at in three lines, the first two of which form a couplet that initially seems to close the scene:

> Bid your friends welcome, show a merry cheer—
> Since you are dear bought, I will love you dear.
> But let me hear the letter of your friend.
>   (3.2.312–14)

The couplet, as John Russell Brown notes, was relegated to the bottom of the page by Alexander Pope, who considered its commercial attitude unworthy of Shakespeare.[13] Brown answers that Portia makes "a joyful acknowledgement of the pleasures of giving for love." Yet it is not so easy to dismiss the couplet's discordant note. Traditionally, men court women with gifts, as Bassanio well knows—he came with gifts. Now Portia has heard evidence strongly suggesting that her wealth drew Bassanio hither; and her wealth is soon to be used in an attempt to rescue his friend. The couplet surely reveals a wry Portia, not unwilling to give, but not unaware of the imposition, either. Furthermore, her sudden request to hear Antonio's letter belies the "all's well" attitude conveyed by the couplet. Questions about the relationship of Bassanio and Antonio have caught her attention, and she is determined to learn more.

If Portia has feared that Antonio wishes to impose on both herself and Bassanio, the letter confirms her suspicions. Antonio, after describing his wretched plight to "sweet Bassanio" (315), asks that he return to be with him at his death, while implying that Bassanio may wish instead to indulge his "pleasure." "If your love do not persuade you to come," Antonio concludes, "let not my letter" (321–22). Antonio is of course disingenuous; his letter is calculated to bring Bassanio scurrying home. Portia would have every reason to wonder why Antonio attaches such significance to Bassanio's return. Could it be that Antonio wishes to impress his sacrifice on Bassanio?

Having heard the letter, Portia immediately instructs Bassanio: "O love! dispatch all business and be gone" (323). The "business" she refers to is their nuptials! A rebuke is implicit in her offer, and Bassanio, as if already responding to Portia's moral pressure, agrees to leave with the promise that until he returns "no bed shall e'er be guilty of [his] stay" (326). Bassanio promises a fidelity Portia will later enforce.

Portia's intentions begin to come clear a short while after Bassanio departs. Scene 4 opens with Lorenzo praising her patience. He compliments Portia's appreciation of "godlike amity"—the friendship that exists between her husband and Antonio—adding that if Portia "knew how dear a lover of" Bassanio was Antonio, she would be even prouder than she is of her good deed (1–9). This passage is commonly read as deserved praise. Yet the viewer may wonder whether any wife is as patient and selfless as the one Lorenzo thinks he sees in Portia. Is it not more likely that Lorenzo, perhaps to help make himself comfortable in Belmont, has taken to reading courtesy books? Having opened to a page praising the resolution of the conflict between Love and Friendship, he sincerely or flatteringly compliments Portia for her conformity to a Renaissance ideal of conduct.

Portia covertly mocks Lorenzo, I think. She is making no sacrifice at all, she says. Antonio, "being the bosom lover of [her] lord, / Must needs be like [her] lord" (17–18). And just as Antonio and Bassanio are alike, so she and her husband are alike. Thus, in sending her husband with money to rescue Antonio, she is merely "purchasing the semblance of [her own] soul, / From out the state of hellish cruelty" (20–21). As a proposition in geometry, it may be true that things equal to the same thing are equal to each other; but the logic of the human heart is different, as Shakespeare knew in Sonnet 42, where the speaker describes as "sweet flattery" the thought that because his friend and he are "one," his mistress, in loving his friend, loves him.

Lorenzo is certainly proven wrong; Portia, no patient Griselda, has already instructed her servants that Lorenzo and Jessica are to be put in charge of the household in her absence. Portia so informs her guests and after they exit, she sends a servant to Padua to her "cousin," Lord Bellario, from whom the servant is to get "garments" and "notes" (legal notes or memoranda), which he is then to deliver to Portia at the ferry to Venice. Although we do not yet know the details of her plan, we now anticipate her intervention in the courtroom.

Alone with Nerissa, Portia reveals something of her state of mind. Heretofore, she had been an unmarried woman, confined to Belmont while the men cavorted in Venice. Much as Bassanio did earlier, she plans to mix pleasure with business. She anticipates with glee the disguise she and Nerissa will don. With a new risqué touch, she remarks that the men will think the two of them "accomplished / With what [they] lack" (61–62). And when Nerissa asks, regarding their disguise, "Why, shall we turn to men?" (78)—meaning, "turn into men"—Portia remarks that a "lewd" interpreter might understand Nerissa very differently. These intimations of sexual liberation are slightly menacing because Portia also hints that she has a score to settle with the men. In her disguise, Portia will act "like a fine bragging youth" and tell of "honorable ladies [who] sought [his] love" and whom he betrayed. (Recall that earlier Bassanio had confessed to Portia that he had been a "braggart" on his arrival in Belmont [3.2.258].)

The new Portia is unfamiliar, of course; her transformation has been too sudden and she has yet to find a stage on which to display herself. Nevertheless, one can draw certain inferences about the change she has undergone and its likely influence on her subsequent actions. The last chapter showed that from the play's outset the Venetians give "business" priority. Portia, on the other hand, does not do so, even though she finds herself in newly exposed circumstances. Now, however, the veil of sentiment seems to have slipped from her eyes. Portia must realize that Bassanio, in coming to Belmont, betrayed a "twofold truth" (Sonnet 41), to Antonio and to herself. Bassanio betrayed Antonio by revealing a willingness to put marriage before friendship, as well as by allowing Antonio to place himself in danger. Bassanio betrayed Portia by seeming to be what he was not, an unencumbered lover. Portia might plausibly conclude that marriage, rather than being the journey's end where love conquers all, instead only involves her in a continuing struggle in which one person will betray another for advantage.

Although "fancy" may lie dying in Portia, she still wants marriage to Bassanio, presumably for reasons of the heart as well as for more pragmatic ones. Nevertheless, this marriage hurtles her into particularly vulnerable circumstances both within the marriage and within society. She cannot be sure either that she has secured Bassanio's affection or loyalty or that the distribution of power between herself and Bassanio will leave her any meaningful freedom or influence in society at large.

Indeed, considering for a moment matters from her point of view only—ignoring, that is, a sense of her still-overwhelming privileges—one can see that she feels herself as much an "odd one out" as Antonio and Shylock consider themselves. Between the time of her father's death and her own marriage, Belmont was Portia's. And far from struggling for the respectful attention of men, she was the cynosure of their eyes. Her marriage now risks making her a stranger in her own home, while Bassanio and perhaps a host of his friends and hangers-on flood her shores. Moreover, she cannot even be certain that her claim to Bassanio will prevail over Antonio's older and prior one. Thus, it would be logical for Portia to move vigorously to protect her interests, and, in light of the treatment she has received, to feel thoroughly justified in doing so.

However, many in the audience will be unwilling to share Portia's sense of injured merit, and *The Merchant* does, I think, portray her as overwhelmingly privileged. To the tasks that lie ahead, Portia brings advantages associated with her upbringing. She has an impeccably gracious and charming surface. Her poise allows her to convert to an asset what might elsewise be a liability: she is a woman in a world where men generally have the power. Portia can deceptively maneuver behind a mask of conformity. And, as one further advantage associated with her class, Portia has long been inclined to embrace the "way of the world." When to these assets bestowed by nurture are added others acquired by nature—Portia possesses high intelligence and attractive, not to say beguiling, looks—it appears that she may be ready to dominate others and to adjudicate the pending claims, legal and emotional, respectively, of Shylock and Antonio.

* * *

The courtroom scene, 4.1, constitutes the most decisive test of any society in all the comedies. Shylock justifies his demand for a pound of Antonio's flesh by likening the proposed forfeiture to other brutal actions carried out by society. For the audience, Shylock's accusation has a very direct meaning. He had promised, "the villainy you teach me, I will execute" (3.1.71–72); the course he now takes is shaped by the treatment he has received, or so he alleges. Some have argued that Shylock is proven wrong and that during the scene Venice ultimately extends to him the very mercy he has failed to grant Antonio. Other critics find that Venice acts reprehensibly—just how reprehensibly we have now to consider.

To think of Shylock as a monster is to misread fatally the scene. True, he contemplates a horrible crime with disconcerting eagerness—in all likelihood, for example, he sharpens a knife on the sole of his shoe (see 123–24). Yet Gratiano is significantly wrong when he describes Shylock as "wolvish, bloody, starv'd, and ravenous" (138); Shylock's humanity has diminished, not vanished. A comparison of Shylock in 1.3 and in the courtroom scene indicates at once that though he felt before the desire to "feed fat" the hatred he bore Antonio, he is now far closer to taking Antonio's life—without being fully resolved. He is still influenced by the action of others. One illustration will serve here. When Bassanio pleads for Antonio's life, Shylock, though he has been reluctant to admit his motives, remarks: "What, wouldst thou have a serpent sting thee twice?" (69). Shylock seems to be giving Antonio another opportunity to offer a reconciliation. Instead, Antonio responds, much as he did in the earlier scene, by antagonizing Shylock further. Antonio asks the court to proceed with judgment, explaining that it is useless to attempt "to soften that—than which what's harder?—/ His Jewish heart!" (79–80). Antonio's motive remains the same—to be seen making a sacrifice for Bassanio—and Shylock must not be allowed to stand in the way of Antonio's death.

This incident illustrates another important fact about the courtroom scene: the personal drama continues, although it is not always obvious. Three characters, all responding to the betrayals they have endured and their fears of isolation, maneuver for advantage. How does this personal conflict shed light on a situation in which, it is sometimes thought, the essential clash is between principles and not individuals?

If Shylock remains human for the viewer, then his charge against Venice is a serious matter. Shylock comes into the courtroom wishing to show society that its image of him is a mirror image of itself. This strategy also serves another purpose; it allows Shylock to avoid admitting the humiliation and suffering that has actually brought him to press his claim. Shylock therefore pretends he is not an abused Jew but a Venetian aristocrat whose "humor" (43) it is to claim Antonio's flesh. Just as a wealthy Venetian is free to spend "ten thousand ducats" to exterminate a rat (44–46), so Shylock will sacrifice three thousand ducats—or any sum he is offered, no matter how great—to have Antonio's life.

Bassanio finds outrageous Shylock's comparing the taking of a man's life with a rat's (63–64). Yet Shylock's example is intended to parody the abuses of human life tolerated in Venice. Shylock may well have in mind his own treatment as a "dog," but he will not say so now. Instead, he waits for a chance to illustrate how others besides himself have been abused. When the duke asks how he can "hope for mercy, rend'ring none" (88), Shylock replies that he fears no judgment because he acts no differently from privileged Venetians:

> You have among you many a purchas'd slave,
> Which like your asses, and your dogs and mules,
> You use in abject and in slavish parts,
> Because you bought them.
>   (4.1.90–93)

Dr. Johnson found Shylock's argument "conclusive": "I see not how Venetians or Englishmen, while they practice the purchase and sale of slaves, can
much enforce or demand the law of 'doing to others as we would that they
should do to us.'"[14] Johnson rightly draws out the implications of Shylock's
analogy: there is a contradiction between Venetian ideals and Venetian practice. Yet inasmuch as the audience has heard nothing so far about Venetian
slavery, it might be better to say that the audience, rather than granting
assent immediately, instead resolves to scrutinize the society more closely. In
fact, at this very moment new doubts arise about the fairness of the court.

From the opening of the scene, questions have occurred. The presiding
judicial officer is the duke—it is possible, then, that Venice does not always
maintain a firm line of demarcation between judicial and political considerations. Of interest is the fact that the scene begins not with Shylock and Antonio—plaintiff and defendant—facing the duke in open court; instead, before
Shylock is invited to enter, the duke offers Antonio sympathy, while describing
Shylock in stereotypical terms as "a stony adversary, an inhuman wretch, /
Uncapable of pity, void and empty / From any dram of mercy" (4–6).

When Shylock is called in, the duke arrogantly appoints him his role.
Shylock should not merely let Antonio live; he should also "forgive a moi'ty
of the principal" owed him, in consideration of the losses "that have of late
so huddled on [Antonio's] back" (28). Though the duke knows of Shylock's
own recent afflictions (having been called to investigate on the night Jessica
fled), they have made no impression on him. The explanation is that the duke
groups together Jews, Tartars, and Turks, all of whom must learn to imitate
the "gentile" virtue of mercy: "We all expect a gentle answer, Jew!" A ruler so
sure of the superiority of his own people is a danger, for he may feel justified
abusing outsiders. The duke therefore warrants close attention.

When Shylock confronts the court with the issue of Venetian slavery,
the duke attempts no rebuttal. Instead, he makes a startling announcement:

> Upon my power I may dismiss this court,
> Unless Bellario, a learned doctor,
> Whom I have sent for to determine this,
> Come here to-day.
> (4.1.104–7)

The court had seemed about to render a verdict supporting Shylock's position. Now the duke retains residual "power" and will use it rather than grant
Shylock's plea or answer his challenge to the society. Whether "dismiss" has
its usual meaning and the duke proposes to reject Shylock's plea entirely
or whether the duke only proposes to "adjourn" the hearing, it is clear that

he has every hope of circumventing what he takes to be the law.[15] Bellario is being called in not because the duke is in doubt about the law, but only because the law does not support the verdict the duke desires.

Yet this passage raises even more serious questions. The duke must be lying—unless an extraordinary coincidence has occurred or the dramatist is fumbling as he tries to synchronize details of his plot—because Bellario's interest in the case must derive not from the duke's inquiry but from Portia's. On the basis of what is known about the duke's predisposition, it seems possible that he may be scheming.

A few details help to strengthen the impression of a secret plot. The duke, told that Bellario's messenger has arrived with "letters," asks for him to be admitted. Nerissa, disguised as a lawyer's clerk, enters and delivers correspondence, which the duke reads silently while Gratiano and Shylock exchange insults. The duke then interrupts to say that Bellario has recommended a lawyer; upon learning that this lawyer waits outside, the duke agrees "with all [his] heart" to admit him, and asks that he be given "courteous conduct" into the courtroom.

Meanwhile, at the duke's request, a clerk reads Bellario's letter. Bellario writes that the duke's request for help found him ill. However, he had with him "a young doctor of Rome," Balthazar, with whom he consulted on the "cause in controversy between the Jew and Antonio the merchant." Bellario strongly recommends Balthazar to the court and asks for his "gracious acceptance," while testifying that Balthazar is wise in spite of his youth. The viewer of course knows that this "young doctor" is Portia, that she has not been to Padua, and that she lacks all legal training—but that she does have a personal interest in the case before the court.

When Portia enters, the duke warmly takes her hand (169) and at once puts her in full control of the hearing. It seems as if members of the ruling class are doing favors for one another. For his cousin, Bellario intervenes with the duke, while the duke helps a famous jurist from a neighboring city.

Consider for a moment the Venetian attitude towards justice, which Shakespeare began to establish prior to the court scene. In 3.2, one hears that rejection of Shylock's claim would "impeach the freedom of the state" (278). A few lines later, in the next scene, the phrase is virtually repeated (3.3.29), with a fuller explanation of the situation. "The trade and profit of the city" (30) depends on foreign commerce, and this commerce in turn depends on the confidence foreigners have in Venetian law. Thus it is not love of justice for her own sake, but mere self-interest, that keeps Venice within the law. By the beginning of act 4, Antonio testifies that the duke has exhausted all "lawful means" for trying to free him (9). Yet one possibility remains: that Venice, while seeming to adhere to law, will work stealthily.

Because of the circumstances under which Portia is admitted to the courtroom; she is considered as an Establishment figure who knows "the rules of the game" and will play by them. In due course, she proves her commitment. When Bassanio beseeches her to show compassion and save Antonio's life by "wrest[ing] once the law to [her] authority," Portia adamantly refuses:

> It must not be, there is no power in Venice
> Can alter a decree established.
> 'Twill be recorded for a precedent,
> And many an error by the same example
> Will rush into the state. It cannot be.
>   (4.1.218–22)

Portia knows that her own privileges depend on the preservation of the status quo; she will protect the reputation of the court.

Portia's initial effort is directed at persuading Shylock to show mercy—or so it seems. A question arises because in the first words she speaks to him she guarantees that "the Venetian law / Cannot impugn you as you do proceed" (178–79). This assurance becomes almost a refrain, repeated at the same time she is asking him to be merciful. It is possible, therefore, that she tempts him to expose his cruelty.

The most important evidence that Portia is devious involves her speech beginning "The quality of mercy is not strain'd" (184). As all readers of *The Merchant* know, these lines are as moving a paean to mercy as can be imagined. And the speech is never more forceful than when Portia describes mercy as the virtue best becoming the "throned monarch" (189); mercy, she says, "is an attribute to God himself; / And earthly power doth then show likest God's / When mercy seasons justice" (195–97). It would be very interesting to know whether Shakespeare intended any response from Shylock at this point; Portia's words might be expected to have an especially powerful effect on him, for he has come into court arguing that it is for those in authority to establish standards of conduct. Now Portia points out that in the present situation, "earthly power" is Shylock's—it is for him to establish a precedent, if he wishes.

Though we do not know Shylock's response, it is clear that Portia veers at midline and with an illogical "therefore" (she does not go on to draw a conclusion), suddenly introduces a far less compelling argument: because our salvation depends on divine mercy, in the hope of that mercy we ourselves should be merciful. This is an appeal that would make its greatest impact on one who believes in Christian doctrine, as Shakespeare's audience perhaps realized; in any event, the argument is less attractive than the first one because it asks Shylock to admit wrongdoing of his own. Yet even at this point, Portia does not pause for Shylock's response, but instead finishes her speech by once again assuring him that if he insists, "this strict court of Venice" remains prepared to render a verdict in his favor. As if seizing bait, Shylock does demand a verdict.

Whether or not Portia plots against Shylock from the outset, she does so eventually. She contrives to introduce a distinction between extracting a pound of flesh and taking Antonio's life in a way that does not allow Shylock to catch the potential legal significance of her point. Portia asks whether Shylock has provided a surgeon to staunch the flow of blood and prevent Antonio's bleeding to death. "It is predictable," A. D. Moody remarks, "that [Shylock] should declare himself under no obligation to spend money on his enemy—why should not his friends provide the surgeon?" (p. 43). Portia again distracts Shylock from the possible legal implications of his decision when she suggests "charity" as a motive for saving Antonio (261). Portia's trap is now set.

Before this moment arrives, another, more remote, possibility has developed: Portia might actually allow Antonio to die. When Antonio asks Portia (as he earlier asked the duke) not to plead further with Shylock and instead to render a verdict, Portia replies: "Why then thus it is: / You must prepare your bosom for his knife" (244–45). It is not difficult to imagine these lines spoken with irritation. Yet Portia proceeds cautiously. After setting the trap against Shylock, she draws Antonio out: "You, merchant, have you any thing to say?" (263). Antonio's life may depend on his answer.

He takes the opportunity to try to ensure that his death will have the desired effect:

> Commend me to your honorable wife,
> Tell her the process of Antonio's end,
> Say how I lov'd you, speak me fair in death;
> And when the tale is told, bid her be judge
> Whether Bassanio had not once a love.
> Repent but you that you shall lose your friend,
> And he repents not that he pays your debt.
>   (4.1.273–79)

Antonio puts himself forward as Portia's competitor: his death will prove that Bassanio "had once a love"—that is, Antonio's "love" surpasses Portia's, which has not proven itself with a comparable sacrifice. In the last two lines quoted, Antonio tries to make Bassanio feel guilt. By asking Bassanio to "repent," Antonio implies that Bassanio, if left to himself,

might not lament the loss of his friend. The word "repent" of course rein-
forces Antonio's message, for while it ostensibly means only "regret," it also
hints at the need for contrition.

Bassanio promptly gives the desired response; he would willingly sacrifice "life itself, [his] wife, and all the world" to save Antonio (284). Of course,
Bassanio offers mere words—he does not contemplate being asked to prove
his love. Yet Portia has every reason to think that the memory of Antonio's
death may in time work its effect on Bassanio; she cannot afford to let Antonio die. She must deal with his threat to her marriage differently.

She prepares to close in on Shylock. Twice she declares the bond forfeit;
then, halting Shylock, she declares: "The words [of the bond] expressly are a
'pound of flesh'" (307). If Shylock sheds "one drop of Christian blood," Venetian law provides that the state is to confiscate all his wealth and property.

The scene has reached a turning point. So far, Shylock has held the
power and the viewer feared the use he would make of it. Portia's stealthy
entrance and the duke's complicity have only created the potential for a reversal. But Portia is now about to gain the upper hand. Her own use of "earthly
power" will be tested.

As if wary from long experience, the moment Portia reveals the law, Shylock senses danger and becomes cautious. First he tries to leave with "thrice"
the value of the bond, the latest offer Bassanio has made him (318). Bassanio
is willing, but Portia will not let him; she leaves Shylock free only to exact the
forfeiture, at his peril. Shylock quickly asks for only the principal. Bassanio
is again willing; Portia is not. Finally, Shylock makes to leave with nothing.
"Tarry, Jew," Portia commands, and informs him of another law. If any alien is
discovered plotting against the life of a Venetian citizen, the intended victim
is to seize half the alien's wealth, and the state the other half, while the alien's
life lies at the mercy of the duke. Thus Shylock, without so much as touching
Antonio, stands in mortal danger, as Portia triumphantly declares: "Down
therefore, and beg mercy of the Duke."

How is Portia's rigorous pursuit of Shylock to be understood? Apolo-
gists for the Venetians generally offer an explanation along the lines suggested
by Nevill Coghill: behind the human drama lies an allegorical one; Shylock
stands for Justice, Portia for Mercy.[16] Before extending mercy, Portia must
demonstrate the exhaustion of the law: everyone—Shylock included—stands
guilty before it.

One would expect, however, that to demonstrate universal human fal-
libility, Portia would condemn Shylock under a law applicable to all people;
instead she invokes a law prejudicial to foreigners. She is therefore a person
with Venetian prejudices and an interest in protecting the city. A foreigner
has stepped out of line and she pushes him back, as a warning to him and to

others. Her ingenious manipulation of the law perhaps serves as a reminder of her privileged place in society, for she acts like a high-powered lawyer, such as the rich are able to hire. Until Portia's appearance, everyone had assumed that the extraction of a pound of flesh "nearest the heart" meant certain death for Antonio. Only Portia thinks to interpret the bond literally ("the words expressly are 'a pound of flesh'" [307]), so that it no longer permits the taking of Antonio's life. At one point, Portia even conforms to a proverb and "splits hairs"; she says that if Shylock takes even so small an amount above a pound that "the scale do turn / But in the estimation of a hair," his life is forfeit (330–31). The poor and the disadvantaged do not get such clever lawyers.

Portia's performance appeals to Gratiano, who cheers her on and taunts Shylock. One wonders whether Portia is able to please Gratiano because her emotions and his have more than a little in common. She observes correct courtroom decorum and her surface is far more polished than Gratiano's. Yet Portia, and perhaps the other refined members of society, share Gratiano's intolerance for the Jew.

As disturbing as Portia's "justice" may be, once she mentions "mercy" one waits to see whether Venice will finally prove itself superior to Shylock. The duke promptly says to Shylock: "That thou shalt see the difference of our spirit, / I pardon thee thy life before thou ask it" (368–69). The wording suggests that the duke's underlying motive is to exhibit the superiority of the Venetians. Similarly, though the duke offers to reduce the fine Shylock owes the state, he sets a telling condition—Shylock must show his "humbleness" (372). The duke's underlying hostility towards the Jew is confirmed after Antonio speaks.

Antonio, having been awarded half Shylock's estate, must take his turn offering mercy. His speech contains so many ambiguities that his precise motives remain obscure, as Shakespeare perhaps intended they should. Antonio is apparently willing to let the state reduce its share to a fine, and even to relinquish the half due him, so long as Shylock agrees to certain conditions. First, Antonio must be permitted to have "in use" the share that he could seize outright (383). Antonio's phrase "in use" is most curious, because it may refer to the interest on a loan.[17] Possibly, then, Antonio, for his own advantage, is again willing to violate what he earlier described as his practice, "neither [to] lend nor borrow" upon interest (1.3.61). Some editors, wishing to save Antonio from thus incriminating himself, have glossed the phrase differently; perhaps Antonio demands to hold the estate "in trust," either for Shylock, who would receive income on it, or for Jessica and Lorenzo. Yet however the phrase is glossed, it seems as if Antonio subtly combines self-interest—the provision of seed money for himself—with the appearance of generosity in the form of an inheritance for Jessica and Lorenzo. The one person towards whom Antonio shows no charitable feeling is Shylock.

As if to confirm his lack of charity, Antonio adds two further stipulations: Shylock must agree that at his death all his wealth will pass to Lorenzo and Jessica; and Shylock must now convert to Christianity. This last demand has been debated by the critics. Some have held that Shakespeare's audience would have felt that Antonio was doing Shylock a favor since his only chance for salvation would be thought to come through conversion. Yet nothing in Antonio's language suggests he has in mind a kindness for Shylock; the contrary is the case. And in the present scene, which tests whether Christians are in actual practice superior to Jews or to any other group, Antonio is doing little more than assuming what remains to be proven. Antonio's own behavior falls short of Christian ideals.

Perhaps the nature of the court's "mercy" is best revealed by Shylock's reaction. When Portia demands that Shylock "beg mercy," he apparently does not do so (369); he may well be stunned, for when the duke goes on to offer ameliorating conditions, Shylock seems not to notice that some of his wealth may be returned to him: "Nay, take my life and all, pardon not that . . . You take my life / When you do take the means whereby I live" (374, 376–77). Shakespeare has been careful to suggest that Shylock's dependence on his wealth is not mercenary. Just a few lines above (267–72), Antonio had painted a bleak picture of a penurious old age, from which, he said, he was glad to escape through death. Furthermore, Shylock's lament echoes the Bible: "He that taketh away his neighbor's living, slayeth him" (Eccles. 34:12). The seizing of Shylock's property is certainly a grievous offense.

After Antonio's carefully qualified offer, Shylock is again silent, and only when the duke suddenly threatens to "recant [his] pardon," does Shylock acquiesce: "I am content" (394). Then he adds, "I am not well," and begs permission to leave the courtroom, a request granted with the words "Get thee gone," and a demand that he agree to sign a deed of gift. There is every indication that Shylock is in anguish, broken, or very nearly so, by the court's "mercy."

Once Shylock is gone, the Venetians are "smugly amiable among themselves, assuring themselves of their gentle community with mutual compliments and courtesies."[18] Every detail is telling. The duke asks Portia home for dinner (she declines); then he suggests that Antonio "gratify" her with a gift (406)—as if Portia had been a lawyer donating her services to Antonio and not a judge charged with impartial determination of the law. For Shylock, they have not a word; their mercy was for display, his anguish has left them untouched.

One might argue that the outcome of the courtroom scene is satisfactory; Antonio is saved, while Shylock is called to account and treated with a minimum of kindness—all he deserves. Yet right things sometimes happen for the wrong reasons. The real drama in the courtroom scene takes place in the hearts of the three principal protagonists, Shylock, Antonio, and Portia.

Even while Shylock is pretending to be a "humorous" aristocrat, he introduces one image that tells another story. He compares himself to men who at the sound of a bagpipe "cannot contain their urine" (50). He must, he says, "yield to such inevitable shame, / As to offend himself being offended" (57–58).[19] He realizes that the action he feels compelled to take will shame him. A few lines later, he refers to his as a "losing suit." Though the phrase has sometimes been glossed as a reference to the three thousand ducats he is prepared to forego, Shylock surely expresses a profounder sense of loss. He had once hoped to show Antonio the path to human compassion and had hoped to gain social acceptance in the process. Now he is forfeiting both esteem and any hope of belonging. Shylock's reference to a "losing suit" suggests that he might wish to be saved from himself. Instead, Portia and Antonio, for their own reasons, let him demand more adamantly the pound of flesh due him.

Antonio, like Shylock, is a pitiable figure. Though he attempts to use his death strategically, his desire for death is an expression of both melancholy and desperation. Like Shylock he chances to use images that reveal his underlying condition: "I am a tainted wether of the flock, / Meetest for death; the weakest kind of fruit / Drops earliest to the ground, and so let me" (114–16). Antonio reveals his innermost feeling and does not present his death as a noble sacrifice for a friend.

Like Antonio and Shylock, Portia feels that she has been betrayed and is in danger. Yet in actual fact she is greatly privileged. Her advantages are much in evidence. The duke lets her sneak into the courtroom. The confidence her status gives her allows her to remain in control of herself as Shylock cannot. In her hands Shylock becomes a maddened bull, dangerous only if met head-on. She builds his trust and he comes to think of her as "a well-deserving pillar" of the law (239). She prevails with ease.

If my interpretation of the courtroom scene is correct, then several years before *King Lear* Shakespeare illustrated some of that play's most important lessons. Lear knows how easily the privileged can conceal their guilt: "Thorough tatter'd clothes small vices do appear; / Robes and furr'd gowns hide all." And he knows that if appearances could be penetrated, the moral position of social insider and outsider would be found equivalent. In adversity, Lear and Gloucester learn "to feel what wretches feel." The "superfluity" of the Venetians closes their hearts to the most important event in the entire scene, the crushing of Shylock's spirit.

* * *

After the tense confrontations and the near-violence of act 4, *The Merchant*'s final act effects a remarkable change in tone: the single scene of the act begins with one of the newlywed couples on a tranquil moonlit evening and ends with the reuniting of the two other newlywed couples. And while act 4 confirms Shylock as an outsider, act 5 safely ensconces in Belmont two potential outsiders: the Jewess Jessica and Antonio, the man who, along with Shylock, placed an impediment in the path of Portia and Bassanio's marriage. What has happened, then, to the desire for inclusion and the fear of betrayal and exclusion? I believe that the past subtly impinges on the present.

The journey that *The Merchant* has been tracing from single to married life and social position is still incomplete. Two of the marriages were actually left unconsummated when the husbands left for Venice. From the hurried arrival and departure of the men, the women infer that they need to ensure their husband's future loyalty. And so, as soon as Portia can, she turns all her attention back to her marriage: after defeating Shylock and while still disguised as Balthazar, she begs as a reward the ring she once gave Bassanio to wear as a pledge of faith. Then in a short second scene closing the act, Portia explains to Nerissa that the two women must leave Venice hastily in order to arrive home before their husbands. Portia clearly plans a reckoning with Bassanio.

The alacrity with which Nerissa falls in line behind Portia and maneuvers for Gratiano's ring suggests that her husband will also be taught a lesson in fidelity. How a question about fidelity also affects the third marriage, between Lorenzo and Jessica, can best be discussed after considering the broader dimensions of the journey undertaken in *The Merchant*, the journey to social position. By the time the last act begins, it is clear that acceptance at Belmont will symbolize social inclusion; moreover, although the three couples and Antonio are likely to be admitted, the terms by which admission will be granted are unknown.

That the gates of Belmont will not simply open wide to receive the guests and that, instead, terms of some kind will be imposed is quite evident. For one thing, Belmont is sure to express a variety of Venice's preferences and prejudices. More important, perhaps, Belmont cannot afford to ignore the deity of Venice, fortune. To welcome Venetians unqualifiedly is to invite dangerous illusions about how the pie might be further divided. Already some Venetians have tentatively encroached on Belmont: Gratiano and Nerissa bid to share the spotlight with Bassanio and Portia, Lorenzo happened by Belmont and remained, Bassanio unexpectedly disclosed a prior obligation to Antonio. Events such as these indicate that the pulling and tugging for social position will continue, unless, as a condition of admission to Belmont, a pledge of loyalty is exacted.

Portia has already shown herself to be realistic about human motives, and she has carefully looked after herself, employing, when need be, a veil of courtesy and even generosity. In act 5 she will attempt to reassume and make secure her position at the pinnacle of her household. Her guests must be made to see the wisdom of accepting both the privileges and the limitations that she defines for them.

An effective and perhaps indispensable sanction that authority must hold in reserve is the possibility of exclusion. Without such a threat, how is society to establish the limits of the permissible? Thus, among those who are included, some must be placed at the margin in order to demonstrate to one and all the provisional nature of social status. Of course, those placed at the margin continue to experience to an inordinate degree the fears and tensions they knew earlier, before they found acceptance. And just as one outsider turns on a still more vulnerable one—Antonio on Shylock, for example—so one insider can turn on another. In Belmont, Lorenzo and Jessica, as hangers-on, are least secure, and Jessica is the more vulnerable of the two. Their relationship is affected—their enjoyment of one another and their confidence in one another's fidelity.

After the impoverished Lorenzo eloped with the Jewess and her father's ducats, the chance to travel to Belmont fell his way. A well-born Christian Venetian, Lorenzo tries with some success to make himself at ease in opulent surroundings. Jessica has more difficulty, for good reason. Upon their arrival, Lorenzo is greeted warmly, but she is not greeted at all. Instead, she is noticed as a "stranger" in need of "cheer[ing]" (3.2.237). After Antonio's letter reveals his plight at Shylock's hands, Jessica makes an awkward bid for acceptance by offering damaging testimony against her father (284–90); everyone ignores her. Later, after Bassanio and Gratiano have left for Venice, Jessica stands by silently while her husband compliments Portia on her capacity for friendship. Then Portia, addressing only Lorenzo, delegates authority in her absence to both him and his wife. At last, Jessica gamely speaks up, offering Portia "all heart's content" as a farewell (3.4.42). Portia ironically returns the wish, as if Jessica's well-rehearsed speech were better directed at herself, a sad-eyed Jewess. This moment characterizes Portia's dealings with Jessica throughout; she always shows "an icy courtesy that projects a very strong sense of distance and distaste."[20] The Jewess has not been excluded from Belmont, but she has not been warmly welcomed either.

The next scene (3.5) opens with Launcelot making Jessica feel uncomfortable about converting to Christianity and thereby raising the price of hogs. By the end of the scene, even her husband is regarding her as alien. Though noticing her wan expression ("How cheer'st thou, Jessica?"), he again brings up Portia as a subject for praise (71–72). Jessica, standing in the great lady's shadow, dutifully rehearses her virtues. The viewer is pained by this but Lorenzo, rather than putting Jessica at ease by naming attractions of her own, remarks:

"Even such a husband / Hast thou of me as [Portia] is for a wife" (3.3.83–84). The implication is that Portia and Lorenzo are alike, while Jessica is "different." Of course, Lorenzo's remark could merely contribute to the teasing repartee between him and his bride. Nevertheless, Gratiano and Salerio have prophesied that disillusionment would follow marriage. Lorenzo, unexpectedly achieving a temporary place at Belmont, finds Jessica a clog to his future success. He blames her and makes her feel his own sense of precariousness.

Act 5 opens with a verbal duet performed by Lorenzo and Jessica, each trying to "out-night" the other in a series of allusions to mythical loves. A perfect opening for a romantic scene, one might say, but the duet is problematic, as many critics have realized, because a dark theme emerges from the Ovidian lore. The allusions are to lovers who have betrayed others or else been betrayed: Troilus and Cressida, Dido and Aeneas, Medea and Jason. The only exception—the allusion to Pyramus and Thisbe—seems interjected by Jessica to deflect Lorenzo from the theme of betrayal. And when he persists, Jessica, as if covertly defending herself, introduces Medea, who, though disloyal to her father, restored Jason's father to health and was loyal to Jason—it was he who was disloyal to her. Lorenzo parries by dropping myth altogether and alluding, instead, to the recent past he shares with Jessica: "In such a night" as the present one, Jessica did "steal from the wealthy Jew" and eloped with Lorenzo. Jessica promptly rejoins that she fled because Lorenzo stole her "soul with many vows of faith, / And ne'er a true one" (19–20). The journey to Belmont apparently remains alive for Jessica and Lorenzo. The magical aura they try to give their evening as they play lord and lady of the manor fails them; a wistful melancholy note reveals they are not secure enough to be at ease, loving and trusting one another.

It would of course be wrong to give too much prominence to the darker suggestions of the duet, for the recriminations never completely destroy its delicate surface and Lorenzo himself soon "forgives" Jessica her "slander." The troubling note serves primarily to create uncertainty about the turbulence that may lie beneath the tranquillity of Belmont. A series of intrusions now confirms these suspicions.

The family servant, Stephano, enters and identifies himself as a "friend" (26), that is, a friend of the house and therefore a man to be trusted.[21] His assurances are false, however; he has hidden motives. After announcing that Portia will arrive before dawn, he confirms the story she previously gave out, that together with Nerissa she has spent her time "kneel[ing] and pray[ing] / For happy wedlock hours" (31–32). Then Stephano quickly asks whether Bassanio has returned. Portia needs to know whether she can be sure of arriving before her husband. Act 5, like act 4, shows Portia gaining an advantage through secret planning.

Missing the drama pressing in upon him, Lorenzo simply tries to enjoy his last moments of authority. Instead of going into the house to prepare for Portia's return, he remains outside and asks that musicians be called. Then, looking up at the stars, he lectures Jessica on the music of the spheres: "There's not the smallest orb which thou behold'st / But in his motion like an angel sings" (60–61). Although Lorenzo speaks as if he could almost hear the music, he admits that while the soul is enclosed in "this muddy vesture of decay," he cannot. The lines are reminders that in spite of Lorenzo's neoplatonic yearnings, man and society may be filled with imperfections.[22]

His marriage is itself imperfect. No sooner have the musicians begun to play than Jessica laments: "I am never merry when I hear sweet music." The National Theatre Company's 1970 production of *The Merchant* rightly takes her remark as evidence of Jessica's alienation from Belmont and from her husband. She has again been a silent listener while her husband displays his refinement by rehearsing his culture's ideals. To make matters worse, he has just reintroduced admiration of Portia (67–68). Then, as if to confirm Jessica's isolation, Lorenzo misunderstands her remark and her mood. He takes her word "merry" to mean joyous or mirthful—it must really mean something more like "cheerful" (see OED adj. and adv. A2&3)—identifies her reaction as the proper one ("your spirits are attentive"), and goes on to lecture her further on the civilizing power of music. Even the "savage eyes" of a "wild and wanton herd" will turn to a "modest gaze" upon hearing music. The music of Orpheus similarly affected "trees, stones, and floods" (80). Finally, Lorenzo says that "the man that hath no music in himself . . . Is fit for treasons, stratagems, and spoils" and should not be "trusted." Lorenzo reveals here not only insensitivity to his wife's mood but ignorance of Portia's. She is about to enter, silence the music, and put into effect her own "stratagem."[23]

With her every word Portia deliberately breaks the romantic atmosphere. In the darkness Lorenzo recognizes Portia's voice as she silences the music; she replies to his greeting, "He knows me as the blind man knows the cuckoo, / By the bad voice!" (112–13). Not only does Portia allude to cuckoldry; she identifies herself as the cuckoo who will now obtrusively remind Bassanio of a husband's vulnerability. He enters unsuspecting and with a compliment for her: "In absence of the sun," he says, she would make night into day. Portia answers: "Let me give light, but let me not be light, / For a light wife doth make a heavy husband" (129–30). Portia intimates that she has in mind a lesson in sexual politics.

She has prepared carefully and gains an advantage through the element of surprise. Their ordeal over, the men have traveled to Belmont expecting a warm welcome. They do not know that their every move has been watched over by the women, who now lie in wait. Portia inaugurates her scheme by failing to greet Antonio. A small omission, one might say, but a significant one, and Bassanio tries casually to correct it by asking his wife to greet his friend. However, she begs off, saying that her welcome "must appear in other ways than words" and she therefore "scant[s] this breathing courtesy" (141). Its preamble complete, Portia's lesson follows.

Portia is first interrupted by Gratiano, for Nerissa has already confronted him with his loss of her ring and he must defend himself, arguing that he gave it not to a woman but to the judge's clerk. Nerissa pretends not to believe him, however, and Portia promptly sides with Nerissa, adding, as if for emphasis, that were Bassanio found to be without his ring, she would be no more forgiving with him than Nerissa has been with Gratiano. Of course, Portia has long since learned to manipulate Bassanio by making him feel shame; at this moment, he must surely appear ready to shrink into a corner. Gratiano quickly betrays Bassanio by disclosing that he too has lost his ring. Portia has him squirming, and no pleading on his part makes her relent. Instead, both women promise to be unfaithful at every opportunity—until their husbands produce the rings.

Portia and Nerissa have drawn the rope tighter and tighter. Finally it is Antonio's turn to be driven out into the open: "I am th' unhappy subject of these quarrels," he confesses (238). "You are welcome notwithstanding," Portia replies, but she continues to give her husband no quarter. Antonio finally capitulates:

> I once did lend my body for his wealth,
> Which but for him that had your husband's ring
> Had quite miscarried. I dare be bound again,
> My soul upon the forfeit, that your lord
> Will never more break faith advisedly.
>   (5.1.249–53)

As Antonio remarks, this is his second offer to stand surety for his friend. This time, however, the implications are far starker than they were before. His first offer was voluntarily made in the hope of keeping Bassanio. Now Portia demands the renunciation of Bassanio. Also, as Leslie Fiedler notices, Antonio this time pledges his soul, not his body, as surety, "as if to make quite clear that Portia, like some super-Shylock, will not be contented with a pledge of flesh."[24] Portia has won the day; she instructs Antonio to take a ring she has until now concealed and place it on Bassanio's finger, meanwhile obtaining from him a promise of future loyalty to his wife.

Since this ring is the same one she once gave Bassanio, it causes amazement; and there is more amazement when Nerissa reveals the ring she once gave Gratiano. The women tease the men, saying they got the rings by sleeping with the judge and the clerk respectively—and only then do the wives reveal their ruse. Finally, and still without pause, Portia distributes largesse. For Antonio she has news that three of his ships have mysteriously reappeared; for Lorenzo and Jessica, Portia brings Shylock's "deed of gift" bestowing his wealth on them after his death. Of course, to be thus generous with Lorenzo and Jessica, Portia has been correspondingly ungenerous with Shylock. Moreover, Portia's munificence, following so closely upon the ring trick and in such contrast to it, suggests that only upon the satisfactory completion of "business" is Portia willing to commence celebrating. Finally, given Renaissance suspicions about the practice of magic, Portia's ability to, as it were, new-create Antonio's lost ships, suggests that the power she employs to dominate act 5 has about it something disturbing and "more than natural."

Of course, the critical question is whether one can sympathize with Portia's achievement. She has obtained Bassanio's pledge of future loyalty and Antonio's promise to let marriage take precedence over friendship. We know that Portia has good reason for making the demands she does. The iterative language of this brief episode focuses on fidelity and on the swearing and the keeping of oaths; the betrayals that allowed the men to travel to Belmont must now be brought to a halt. Nevertheless, there is some question as to whether Portia's credentials are any better than any one else's. Whether she broke her father's will or not, she certainly seemed willing to. She built up Shylock's trust in her, then betrayed him. She betrayed Bassanio, secretly observing him and virtually coercing him into relinquishing the ring (he parted with it, he says, "unwillingly," when "naught would be accepted but the ring" [196–97]). In short, the greatest winner at Belmont, Portia, succeeds not because of her preeminent moral position, but rather because she successfully exploits opportunities that her privileges open up for her. And if she has managed to halt a chain of betrayals, it is not because she or others have experienced a change of heart. Rather, she has delineated a social order and demonstrated to others the advisability of respecting it.

Except for Portia's revelation of Shylock's "deed of gift" and Lorenzo's allusion to Jessica's theft of her father's wealth, act 5 contains no mention of Shylock. The characters might well have more to say, since their success is made possible by his defeat. Belmont's silence implies that Shylock has been expunged as an alien presence; is this true or is Shylock too close for comfort because his bitterness reflects feelings that are present at Belmont? Surely this question is in the audience's mind throughout act 5, since the emotional pitch of the courtroom scene is so great that appearances on a moonlit evening are constantly tested against deeper emotional realities. We continue to detect a struggle for power and the emotional lack it brings: Belmont is still unable to bridge through love the gap between individuals. The play ends with a forceful reminder of this failure. Lorenzo, hearing of Shylock's "gift," expresses his gratitude to Portia by saying: "You drop manna in the way / Of starved people" (294). This allusion to a biblical journey that was watched over by God and was as much a spiritual journey as a physical one sorts oddly with Lorenzo's materialism. Furthermore, by describing himself as "starved," he suggests the peculiar intensity of the quest—a quest not for mere subsistence (which he already had) but for abundance. He and the others at Belmont have abundant fortune—and little love.

Act 5 exhibits in its most delicate form an ambiguity present in *The Merchant* as a whole and in the two other comedies I will be considering. Though I have not said enough about them, the scene has a number of conventional comic guideposts that, if followed, make the action good-humored and joyous. For example, the ring trick can be seen as a clever and flirtatious offering and not at all as a piece of "business." One's response depends on the response to any number of earlier events; a reading of the act develops from a reading of the entire play. But two centuries of inconclusive debate suggest that even the entire play, with its massive structure and finely wrought detail, yields no final answer. Perhaps Shakespeare left out some necessary ingredient, or history has made the play inaccessible, or else *The Merchant* is still vitally alive, giving conflicting signals that are interpreted in the light of one's own deepest feelings and perceptions.

Notes

1. Norman Rabkin sketches the contemporary division of critical opinion over *The Merchant of Venice* in *Shakespeare and the Problem of Meaning*, 1–32.

2. Leslie A. Fiedler notices the national stereotyping in *The Stranger in Shakespeare* (London: Croon Helm, 1973), 103.

3. For Portia's use of legal imagery, see the New Arden *Merchant of Venice*, 1.2.10n.

4. For a different defense of Arragon, see Grudin, 57.

5. Moody, *Shakespeare: "The Merchant of Venice,"* 35.

6. Ibid., 36.

7. The first critic, quoted in the New Shakespeare *Merchant*, 149, is A. H. Fox-Strangways, *Times Literary Supplement*, 12 July 1923; the second critic is M. C. Bradbrook, *Themes and Conventions of Elizabethan Tragedy*, 2d ed. (Cambridge: At the University Press, 1980), 102–3.

8. Consistent with his generally ameliorative approach to Belmont, Lawrence Danson, in *The Harmonies of "The Merchant of Venice"* (New Haven: Yale University Press, 1978), 101, assumes "in charity" that Portia "refers less to [Morocco's] skin than to his temperament and habits of mind." Danson fails to notice that Portia has already used "complexion" to refer unambiguously to Morocco's color.

9. Does Portia test Bassanio or does she hint at the correct solution of the riddle? Perhaps she does both. Two critics have subtly discussed numerous possible hints in Portia's speeches before Bassanio chooses: Albert Wertheim, "The Treatment of Shylock and Thematic Integrity in *The Merchant of Venice*," *Shakespeare Studies* 6 (1970): 79–81; Harry Berger, Jr., "Marriage and Mercifixion in *The Merchant of Venice*," *Shakespeare Quarterly* 32 (1981): 157–59. Berger judiciously remarks that, "having encouraged us to wonder, the script never gives us enough evidence to resolve the issue with confidence." It is possible, of course, that Bassanio too eagerly wishes for "answers for deliverance" (38) and Portia therefore decides in the end to leave him to his own resources. If, however, the song contains a further, more decisive hint, the question becomes, who provides it? The National Theatre Company's 1970 production of the play suggests that Nerissa is of help. The notion is plausible, both because Nerissa, wishing to marry Gratiano, has a motive for helping Bassanio, and because 1.2 shows Portia carefully conveying her preference for Bassanio to Nerissa. It is perhaps pertinent to note that in *Il Pecorone*, one of Shakespeare's sources, a sympathetic lady-in-waiting provides the Bassanio figure with the hint needed to win the bride.

10. Berger, "Marriage and Mercifixion," 161, makes a similar observation. He also anticipates my argument about Portia's emerging resolve to secure her marriage and eliminate Antonio's threat to it.

11. The play's editors are not all agreed that the Salerio who arrives in Belmont is the same Salerio who is joined with Solanio elsewhere in *The Merchant*; for the textual problem posed by the numerous spellings of names either similar or identical to Salerio and Solanio's, see The New Shakespeare *Merchant*, 100–104.

12. Ralph Berry acutely discusses this passage in "Discomfort in *The Merchant of Venice*," *Thalia: Studies in Literary Humor* 1, no. 3 (1978–79): 13.

13. New Arden *Merchant*, lvii. Cf. Brown's remarks in *Shakespeare and His Comedies*, 2d ed. (London: Methuen & Co., 1962), 68.

14. *The Plays of William Shakespeare* (1765); reprinted in *Johnson on Shakespeare*, ed. Sherbo, 7:227.

15. The meaning "adjourn" is provided in Alexander Schmidt's *Shakespeare Lexicon*, 3d ed. (1902; reprinted as *Shakespeare Lexicon and Quotation Dictionary*, New York: Dover Publications, 1971), 1:351. The gloss, based on a dubious parallel with *Cor.* 2.1.76, seems forced to me. Nineteenth-century scholarship on the puzzle posed by the duke's calling upon Bellario is summarized by Horace Howard Furness in his New Variorum *Merchant* (Philadelphia: Lippincott Co., 1888), 4.1.110n.

16. Nevill Coghill, "The Basis of Shakespearian Comedy" (1950); reprinted in *Shakespeare Criticism: 1935–1960*, ed. Anne Ridler (Oxford: Oxford University Press, 1970), 215–20. For a more recent account along similar lines, see Ruth M. Levitsky, "Shylock as Unregenerate Man," *Shakespeare Quarterly* 28 (1977): 58–64.

17. In the New Arden *Merchant*, 4.1.379n, Brown glosses "in use" as "in trust" and specifically excludes the possibility that Antonio "would give or receive interest." Nevertheless, the Furness Variorum and more recent editions of the play, including *The Riverside Shakespeare*, 4.1.380–85n, acknowledge the ambiguity of this phrase and of the entire passage.

18. Moody, *Shakespeare: "The Merchant of Venice*," 44.

19. I preserve the punctuation of the Quarto and Folio; modern editors sometimes add a comma in the second line, after either "offend" or "himself."

20. Berry, *Shakespeare's Comedies*, 14.

21. The word *friend*, when not used to one warmly regarded, can be equivocal in Renaissance English. See p. 120 and Lawrence Stone, *The Family, Sex and Marriage in England*, 97.

22. For a sensitive discussion of the developing pessimism in this passage, see Grudin, *Mighty* Opposites, 67–68.

23. Rabkin (*Shakespeare and the Problem of Meaning*, 18) notices that Lorenzo's speech is contradicted both by Portia's ensuing ruse and by his own past actions: "'treasons, stratagems, and spoils' characterizes his exploits at least as accurately as it does those of Shylock."

24. Fiedler, *Stranger in Shakespeare*, 135.

ROBERT ORNSTEIN

The Merchant of Venice

Like most Shakespearean comedies, *Errors*, *Love's Labor's*, and *Two Gentlemen* do not achieve their dramatic resolutions until very near the end of their concluding scenes. *The Merchant* and *A Dream* have a somewhat different dramatic structure. Their climactic moments of conflict occur in their fourth and third acts respectively, and all antagonism and discord are resolved before their fifth acts begin. In both plays the last act is a long graceful coda in which the triumph of love is celebrated by a dramatic entertainment or charade, with witty gibes and affectionate teasings, with music and poetry.

Few endings in the comedies are as relaxed and as playful as that of *The Merchant*. The dialogue is charming; the heroes and heroines are attractive and appealing. Every obstacle that lay in the paths of the lovers has been removed, and as further proof that fate smiles, the news comes that Antonio's ships have come safely to port so that once again he is a prosperous merchant of Venice. Since other comedies end in less cheerful and harmonious ways, it may seem ungrateful to question the resolution of *The Merchant*, but the delight of its last scene depends, not on a transformation of discord into harmony, but rather on a denial that any price has been paid for the happiness of those who gather on the steps of Portia's mansion. This denial makes their gaiety seem somewhat amnesiac, for they have no thought of Shylock; they

From *Shakespeare's Comedies: From Roman Farce to Romantic Mystery*, pp. 90–118, 255–56.
Copyright © 1986 by Associated University Presses.

do not mention his name, though they speak of the rich Jew from whom Jessica "stole," who has become the unwilling benefactor of his daughter and son-in-law. It is as if Shylock the man had never existed, had never fathered Jessica, and had never cried out to Antonio and Salerio and Solanio about the indignities they heaped upon him. The heroes and heroines have come through the crisis of Shylock's murderous hatred unscathed and unaltered— and there's the rub, because those who have watched in the audience have been moved and perhaps disturbed by the nature of the victory that the last scene celebrates, and their memory of Shylock and the courtroom scene is still immediate and vivid. The joy of the final scene might be more satisfying if it were tinged with regret or if it included one touch of sorrow. But to wish for this complexity of tone is to wish that Shakespeare's characters were different in nature—or is it to wish that Shakespeare did not share the blindered attitudes of the Venetians to the alien Jew?

To some *The Merchant* is a reminder that Shakespeare was necessarily a man of his age, one who accepted its fundamental biases because it would never have occurred to him to question them. E. E. Stoll has no doubt that Shakespeare conceived of Shylock as a buffoon and comic villain because Jews were condemned and anathematized by Church doctrine, accused through the centuries of inhuman crimes, portrayed as bloodthirsty in legend and folktale, and despised throughout Christian society.[1] As an alien minority they were barely tolerated in the best of times and made the targets of official extortions, recurrent pogroms, and occasional wholesale massacres. The sorry history of Jew hatred does not, however, support Stoll's claim that Shylock is to be equated with conventional stereotypes of Jewish villainy. The villainous Jew can be found in novellas like *Il Pecorone*, but he is remarkably absent from the great literature of the Renaissance, and especially from the great literature of Renaissance England. He does not appear in any of the extant comedies or tragedies of Kyd, Greene, Dekker, Chapman, Jonson, Tourneur, Webster, Middleton, and Ford. The only villainous Jew portrayed in Elizabethan drama before Shylock is Marlowe's Barabas, and Barabas serves for much of *The Jew of Malta* as a stalking horse for Marlowe's scathing satire on Christian greed and hypocrisy before he achieves a degraded grandeur as a murderous Machiavel. The only other dramatic portrait of a Jew that precedes Shylock appears in Wilson's *Three Ladies of London* (1583), and there the Jew is not a snarling monster but rather noble and forgiving. In other words, Shylock is not one of many similar anti-Semitic dramatic portraits that can be explained by reference to Elizabethan prejudice against Jews. He exists, it would seem, because Barabas exists, because Shakespeare was inspired by *The Jew of Malta* to write his own play about a Jew and his daughter. If Shakespeare reduced the complexity of Marlowe's protagonist to a simple anti-Semitic caricature, he was almost unique among Elizabethans to use his art in this way.[2] Shall we believe that the dramatist who portrayed the black Othello as a noble heroic figure could not imagine a Jew as possessed of human feeling or deserving of understanding and sympathy? If this is so, we have mistook him all this while—his was not the most universal of minds.

The beginning of wisdom about *The Merchant* is a recognition that historical scholarship cannot establish what Shylock is or has to be and it cannot dictate our response to him.[3] The attempt to reduce Shylock to the bloodthirsty usurer of *Il Pecorone* is especially ironic in view of the astonishing transformation of source materials that takes place in *The Merchant*, which turns a cynical and somewhat sordid tale of Italianate cunning into a greatly poetic, romantic comedy; it also makes the despised moneylender a great dramatic figure, equal in importance to the romantic hero and heroine. Like many other novellas, *Il Pecorone* tells of intrigue, lust, and greed. Its hero, Giannetto (Bassanio) is a little soiled in the working; he lies to his benefactor to get money to obtain a rich wife, and when he finally outwits and marries her, he forgets for a time his benefactor's terrible plight. The Lady of Belmont is not a virginal maiden but rather a scheming, mercenary widow who offers to wed any man who can bed her, and by drugging the wine of her suitors wins the forfeit of their wealth. If the Lady of Belmont can turn into Portia, and Gianetto into the gentle Bassanio, it is conceivable that the Jewish moneylender may also become a nobler figure than he is in Shakespeare's source.

Errors, as we have seen, also significantly alters the tone of its source, *Menaechmi*, by eliminating its cynical assumptions and values and by making its characters more attractive and sympathetic. But the dramatic world of *Errors* closely approximates the bourgeois milieu of *Menaechmi*, whereas the dramatic world (or worlds) of *The Merchant* bears no resemblance to the tawdry novella world of *Il Pecorone*. For Shakespeare creates in Belmont and Venice a sense of splendor that is unique in the comedies, an imaginative realization of the magnificence of Renaissance Italy without any trace of Italianate corruption. To Belmont come the greatest princes of the world, for Portia is a rich and beautiful prize that inspires mythic comparisons. She is the golden fleece for which argonauts risk their chance of future happiness in marriage. She is another Virginia, a newfound land that offers the spendthrift gallant a second chance to recoup his estate. Feminine, delicate, graced with music and poetry, Belmont is the ideal setting for a romantic quest but Portia is not to be won by sighing protestations, aubades, and love poems. Who would win her must make hazard of himself, accept the fairytale challenge of the three caskets, and prove his worthiness in a trial of mind and heart that is redolent of many legendary testings of the purity and dedication of questing heroes.

Superficially Belmont is opposed as well as juxtaposed to Venice, a world in which men compete for profit and commercial advantage, in which ordinarily they risk only their capital—and their seamen's lives—in hope of the fabulous wealth to be gained by trade with Africa and Asia. Yet money and contract are as significant forces in Belmont as in Venice because Portia is immensely rich and the terms set down for winning her are as specific as those in any commercial transaction, even to stipulation of the forfeit that will be exacted should the wooer fail to achieve his objective. The law that protects the sanctity of commercial contracts in Venice also protects the right of Portia's deceased father to determine by will the way that his ducats and his daughter may be obtained. Conversely, Venice is not merely a trading center like the busy ports of Holland and Germany. She is a great maritime republic whose influence extended throughout the known world, whose argosies returned with silks and spices and treasures bartered for, or ransacked from, the fabled cities of the Mediterranean. The queen of the Adriatic, Venice was celebrated for its music and painting, its exquisite glasswares, splendid palaces, and churches.[4]

The dialogue of *The Merchant* makes clear the opulence of Venice, whose merchants are aristocratic in manner as well as means. The chaffering of the marketplace is heard only in the scenes with Shylock; otherwise the streets of Venice are the places where friends meet to talk and pass the time, to give and accept invitations to dinner and festive evenings. Great merchants like Antonio do not spend anxious hours in counting houses, for their risks are spread over many enterprises and a single loss cannot disable their estates. With such security, Antonio can indulge his generous instincts and be gracious to those less fortunate. He can look tolerantly on Bassanio's prodigality, which has made him as much Antonio's dependent as his bosom friend. Such wealth also breeds a kind of ennui, for Antonio lacks a challenge or goal to excite his interest. He has no taste for extravagant expenditure and he does not speak of his commercial successes with the pleasure Shylock takes in describing his cunning "thrift." It would be a mistake, however, to exaggerate Antonio's sadness or to take seriously Gratiano's boisterous rebuke of Antonio's "lifelessness"—"why should a man whose blood is warm within, / Sit like his grandsire, cut in alabaster?" Although life seems to have passed Antonio by, he does not regret bygone days or lost friends; it is unlikely that he ever heard the chimes at midnight. He takes a modest pride in his sobriety, even as he apologizes for it. By choice or by accident he is older than his companions; and by calling attention to his sadness, he invites and enjoys their somewhat envious solicitude and ragging. His affection for Bassanio, however, is not consciously selfish, and he takes a genuine if vicarious pleasure in advancing his younger friend's prospects.

Some who think that Shylock is a nasty caricature of a Jew are ready to compensate for Shakespeare's anti-Semitism by turning Antonio into a closet homosexual whose love of Bassanio is greedy and possessive.[5] Others, too polite to inquire into Antonio's sexual preferences, nevertheless speak of Antonio and Portia as rivals for Bassanio's love, although Antonio presses Bassanio to accept his aid in the quest of Portia's hand in marriage. Surely an Antonio who wished to monopolize Bassanio's affections could find an excuse not to provide money for the venture in Belmont, given the fact that all his wealth was engaged at present and he had to borrow money to lend it to Bassanio. Without a moment's hesitation, however, he sends Bassanio off to obtain the loan and insists on taking the loan from Shylock over Bassanio's objection. To all but Shylock, Antonio is the noblest of men, one who does not brag of his wealth or lecture others on the need for thrift. A pompous man would not have accepted Gratiano's raillery with such good humor. When Gratiano advises him not to fish "with this melancholy bait / For this fool gudgeon, this opinion," Antonio responds with smiling humor; he will grow a talker for this gear.

Antonio's love of Bassanio hints of qualities in the latter that may not be immediately apparent, although from the beginning Bassanio stands apart from the other Venetians who surround Antonio. Awed by Antonio's wealth, Salerio and Solanio would like to have Antonio's gallies and the anxieties about their safety they humorously ascribe to him; they would like to worry about tempests when they cool their tea with a breath or fear jagged rocks when they go to church and look at stone monuments. Bassanio is not, like them, excited by the thought of such great wealth. He has a gift for friendship, not only with the sober Antonio but also with the madcap Gratiano, who is ready to gibe at any pretense or cant. He likes Gratiano even though he knows his limitations. After hearing Gratiano's advice to Antonio not to be a stuffed shirt, Bassanio sums up his friend's wisdom: he speaks "an infinite deal of nothing." These are not the words of a shallow prodigal or one incompetent to manage his own life. Indeed, no one suggests that Bassanio is spendthrift in his tastes or extravagant in his entertainments. He bears not the slightest resemblance to the gaming, wenching, decayed gentlemen who appear in the Jacobean comedies of Shakespeare's contemporaries.

If we listen carefully to Bassanio, we will appreciate those virtues that win the love and regard of Antonio and Portia. He is soft-natured rather than improvident; tender-hearted, not irresponsible; and more indulgent of others than himself. Although he has no money, he takes Gobbo into his service because Gobbo wishes to leave Shylock's employ, and although he knows that Gratiano's brashness may jeopardize his venture in Belmont, he will not deny Gratiano's request to accompany him. He is not good at keeping money, either his own or his wife's. He wishes to give the three thousand ducats that were meant for Shylock to the young judge who saved Antonio, even though the judge desires no fee. Having no head for business, he has nothing to show for the monies he borrowed before from Antonio, and it is clear that he will always need generous friends if he does not marry an heiress. This is not to say, however, that the need for money oppresses Bassanio or that he brands himself a fortune hunter. He is not inspired to woo Portia as Petruchio is inspired to woo Kate, by talk of her dowry. Like Claudio and Benedick in *Much Ado*, he has a sensible interest in his future wife's estate, but he speaks less of Portia's wealth than Sebastian speaks of Olivia's gifts in *Twelfth Night*. Calculations of profit and loss are not Bassanio's forte; his appeal to Antonio for additional funds is almost childlike in its naïveté and in its shame-faced hesitancies. His parable of arrows lost and found is innocent enough, but not germane to the case and far more appropriate to a schoolboy than a Venetian nobleman. The money he spent will not be found again; it does not lie like an arrow in the underbrush waiting for the keen-eyed archer to find it. If his present venture follows the path of his earlier ones, his failure is assured. Although eager to present himself as a practical man, Bassanio unfolds a business prospectus for Antonio that is a tale out of Mother Goose, one that would draw laughter from any impartial entrepreneur. He does not disclose all the risks of this venture, for though it is true that Portia looked it him in a way that tokened her affection, she is not able to follow her heart. Everything depends on Bassanio's ability to solve the riddle of the caskets. Yet he is honest enough in detailing the odds against him. He speaks of the suitors who flock to Belmont from every nation, and he confesses that he has only a presentiment that he will succeed where many others have failed. His little homilies and indirections are not clumsy attempts at evasion; they reveal how painful it is to ask for more money when he has been unable to repay previous loans.

Antonio is annoyed that Bassanio does not immediately ask for the money he needs because that hesitancy makes some small question of Antonio's generosity. He does not sympathize with—or understand—Bassanio's need to "wind about his love with circumstance"; nor does he realize that his readiness to allow Bassanio to make "waste of all I have" must pain his unsuccessful friend. Such generosity is as insensitive as it is noble, for while he is insulted by Bassanio's hesitancy, he will not allow Bassanio any vestige of manly pride. Moments like these leave no doubt that it is better to give than to receive, and it is much easier to be able to give than to have to receive. Later in the play Antonio will discover how burdensome the debt of gratitude can be; here he is too accustomed to his role as benefactor to appreciate Bassanio's feelings, and because of that role Bassanio cannot be his equal in friendship, for the older man has the power money bestows while the younger man must accept his generosity knowing that he will probably be unable to repay what is loaned to him. Jessica can take what she needs (or wants) from Shylock without hesitation or shame at stealing from her father. Bassanio finds the gift of love burdensome even when freely offered because he would have the sense of worth that is denied the dependent.[6]

The power that Antonio's wealth gives him over his younger friends is matched by the power that Portia's father exerts over her life through the instrument of his will, which stipulates how she can be won. Like Antonio, Portia is very rich, and, so she says, weary of this great world. Nerissa has heard these sighing complaints before and rebukes them with gentle humor and sound philosophy even as Gratiano, her future husband, rebuked Antonio's melancholy. Portia's reflections on life reveal that she is as witty and perceptive as the heroines of *Love's Labor's*, but more obviously romantic in temperament; although she has, like them, a keen eye for the follies of men, she gives her heart ardently and completely to the man who deserves her love. Her pleasure in her femininity appears in her plaintive reference to her "little body" and she enjoys her role as the beauteous heiress whom all desire at the same time that she complains that she cannot choose whom she will marry. A few pious sentences from Nerissa about her father's virtue are sufficient to curb these rebellious thoughts, even though Portia has just before observed that good sentences are ineffectual when the will rebels. Her situation is that of the fairy-tale heroine who languishes in a tower and can be released only by a lover's courage and ingenuity—a sleeping beauty who can be awakened by a lover's kiss. As such, she should have long golden hair and a passive disposition. But she is not helpless or docile; even before she defeats Shylock, she is clearly a match for any man in insight and shrewdness.

The characterization of Portia is a triumph of artistic inspiration over ordinary logic, for how can she be both the princess in the tower and the confident, adventurous clever wench of folklore who defeats a cunning ogre? Only an unconventional woman could dominate the masculine arena of the law court, but only a conventional dutiful woman would submit to her father's will and not bend an article of it to assure her own happiness. Whereas the heroine in *Il Pecorone* is all of a piece, a cunning contriver in Belmont and in Venice, Portia is rich in seeming contrarieties, a heroine who is eager to assume a traditional role as adoring wife, and yet one who is confident of her ability to defeat Shylock when all others have failed. Despite the fairy-tale aura of the caskets, her situation is not radically different from that of Silvia or other heroines whose choice of husband is subject to a father's will and to the proprieties that dictate the nature of maidenly behavior. She waits to be wooed as women have always waited because modesty and caution forbid her to be too forward. Like any well-bred gentlewoman, Portia's freedom is circumscribed by her position in society. She must marry well, even if that means marrying some dolt with a title and money; she cannot follow her heart unless she is willing to sacrifice the opinion of the world.

One cannot imagine Beatrice waiting patiently in Belmont for a Benedick to arrive while a dozen dismal suitors try their luck at winning her. One doubts also that she would have allowed a great inheritance to quell her independent spirit. On the other hand, one cannot imagine Beatrice, for all her bristling independence, venturing forth as Portia does to rescue Antonio, for in a moment of crisis she turns to Benedick to champion Hero's cause and complains that she is not a man. Portia does not chafe at her circumstances, because even as she scrupulously obeys the dictates of her father's will, she seems to command her fate and does not seem to dread the possibility of being won by some lucky boor. She views her current suitors with cool amusement and describes with mocking satire their chasings after fashion, their rudenesses, and lack of breeding. She is relieved that the Frenchman, Englishman, Scot, German, and Neopolitan have left without risking the choice of the caskets, but her pulse quickens at Nerissa's praise of Bassanio and she hesitates only a moment before admitting her interest in him.

Portia enters the play immediately after Bassanio's glowing description of her. Shylock, who is to be her adversary, enters unannounced, as it were; there is not the slightest anticipation that Bassanio's need for money will involve him with a hated Jewish moneylender. If Shylock is immediately identified as a Jew by his clothing and manner of speech, he is not immediately typed as a cunning villain. Bassanio is not afraid of Shylock and nothing he says intimates that out of necessity he is dealing with a blood-sucking usurer. He walks on stage with someone who is obviously unlike the other Venetians in dress and mien, not with a villain who, sotto voce, gloats over the prospect of yet another victim. If anything, Shylock seems more concerned about the safety of his capital than the prospect of a handsome return. His slow, repetitious consideration of the terms of the proposed loan is the familiar hesitation of a businessman who does not want to seem too eager to close a deal. Where a confidence man would pretend an affable indifference to the terms to allay his victim's suspicions, Shylock is all caution, pedantic in his enumeration of the risk involved, even to the explanation of what he means by land rats and water rats. He exaggerates nothing in hope of greater usury. He readily admits that Antonio, whom he detests, is a "good man"—that is, financially sound. He knows precisely what ventures Antonio is presently engaged in, and, after consideration, he acknowledges that they do not imperil his worth: "I think," he concedes, "I may take his bond." This does not sound like a man who is ready to risk all to be revenged but rather one who has no taste for the risks that Antonio ordinarily assumes. He would not squander his ventures abroad, and he cannot, as a hated alien, afford the luxury of denying loans, even to his enemies.

Of course, Shylock is not all business. His pauses, seeming forgetfulness, and repetitions prolong the pleasurable moment when a Christian must wait upon his answer, and the moment is doubly pleasurable because Bassanio is so eager, so anxious for the loan, ready even to invite Shylock to talk with Antonio over dinner, an invitation that Shylock feels he can scornfully refuse. The luxury of contempt is not one he can usually afford; what he can assert is his right to make up his own mind. When Bassanio assures Shylock that he can take Antonio's bond, Shylock replies, "I will be assured I may. / And that I may be assured, I will bethink me." If Shylock's careful consideration of the bond and his readiness to express his repugnance at Christian ways ("I will not eat with you, drink with you, nor pray with you") are supposed to identify him as an unscrupulous but artful dissimulator, they do not succeed; and one must wonder why Shakespeare does not remove any doubt of Shylock's wickedness in the asides Shylock utters. The worst Shylock reveals about himself is that he hates Antonio bitterly and, if he could, he would "feed fat the ancient grudge" he bears him. That Shylock even now hungers to tear the flesh from Antonio's breast is dubious. His figure of speech is a conventional expression of hatred similar to Beatrice's desire to eat Claudio's heart in the marketplace. To see the half-mad Shylock of the courtroom scene in the Shylock who discusses terms with Bassanio is as mistaken as to see the Iago who senselessly murders his wife at the close of *Othello* in the petty cheat and confidence man who brags of his duplicity to Roderigo in the opening scene of the play. Iago's progress from swindling to murderous conspiracies is paralleled by Shylock's progress from a proud, successful businessman to the defiant outcast who whets his knife on the sole of his shoe, indifferent to everything but the satisfaction of his blood-lust. We can say that, like Iago's, Shylock's descent into villainy actualizes what is latent in his nature so long as we keep in mind that the same can be said of Macbeth when he murders Duncan and of Hamlet when he murders Polonius.

Because Portia is utterly convincing as a character, so too is the fairy tale of the caskets that hold the key to her future. Because Antonio and Shylock are completely convincing as characters, they persuade us that intelligent, practical men can agree to the horror of the "merry bond," which stipulates a forfeit of human flesh if the loan is not repaid. The agreement would present no problems if Antonio were ignorant of Shylock's hatred or if he were desperate for funds and had no choice but to accept whatever terms Shylock demands. But no, Antonio is not hard-pressed; he borrows only because he wishes to underwrite Bassanio's venture in Belmont, and he agrees to the bond with full knowledge of Shylock's hatred—indeed, only moments after he and Shylock have openly expressed their loathing of one another. That enmity is one of the more fascinating puzzles of the play because Shylock is not an obvious bloodsucker; he does not resemble the grasping usurers of the Jacobean stage who brag of their nefarious extortions, who foist off worthless commodities on foolish heirs and trick them into signing away their estates.[7] What rate of interest Shylock usually charges is never revealed, and we never learn what rate he intended to charge Bassanio because just when he is at the point of naming the rate, he launches instead into a recital of the wrongs and abuses he has endured from Antonio.

Is that not bizarre behavior for a diabolical villain? Does one lay a cunning snare for an enemy by reminding him of the reasons one has to loathe him? Not a fawning hypocrite who pretends friendship and love, Shylock has learned the necessity of cringing before Venetians, as he does in his first words to Antonio, but he would rather point out the contradictions and cruelty of Antonio's behavior than close a loan at advantageous terms. He could, in fact, have concluded the terms with Bassanio, contingent on Antonio's signature, but he wants to speak to Antonio before he makes the loan, knowing of course that Antonio would prefer to say nothing to him in these circumstances. If Antonio were a voice for moderation and reasonableness in commercial transactions, we could judge from his loathing how exorbitant Shylock is in his money-lending. But Antonio is not revolted by exorbitant rates; he objects to the charging of any interest on loans, even though in Venice as elsewhere in Renaissance Europe, borrowing money at interest was a customary business practice, which was tolerated though not officially "allowed" in Shakespeare's England.[8] Antonio's revulsion against interest is an extreme form of idealism, one which the Catholic church could expound but which had no meaning in the burgeoning commercial world of Elizabethan England, where venture capital was an economic necessity and public playhouses were constructed with funds obtained in the form of interest-bearing loans.[9]

Antonio's condemnation of interest is not echoed by any other Venetian and does not appear to be customary or universal. He is able to champion an outworn ideal because he is wealthy enough to be generous, and he practices his generosity within a small circle of Venetian friends and acquaintances. Now he stands on very slippery ground; wanting to be generous to Bassanio and morally superior to Shylock, he finds it unbearable to have to chaffer with the moneylender he despises. He salves his conscience, however, by announcing that he would not lend or borrow money for interest in his own behalf; "yet to supply the ripe wants of my friend, / I'll break a custom." Since he has no compelling reason to violate his sacred principle, he must convince himself that he is not stooping to an abhorred practice. The solution is to make Bassanio his "damned soul," even though it was Antonio who unhesitatingly decided to borrow the money Bassanio needed. His selflessness declared, he feels justified in continuing to revile Shylock. Indeed, precisely because his moral situation is slippery, he must be unbending in his scorn. He is the kind of idealist who demonstrates the purity of his conviction by his uncompromising contempt for those who believe otherwise. His high-mindedness and his championing of a universal moral principle free him from any need for civility to Shylock, and yet one cannot imagine him making interest-free loans to foreigners or aliens; his "universal" principle assumes a world of Venetians and Christians, a world without Jews or Turks.

Enjoying Antonio's discomfort, Shylock prolongs the negotiations; brushing Bassanio aside, he forces Antonio to deal with him face to face, one successful businessman to another. His pride in his success blinds him to the ugliness of defending sharp practice by citing the story of Jacob. He does not speak as one who wants kinder treatment from Venetians; indeed, he can hardly hope to educate Antonio, who rated him, called him misbeliever and cut-throat dog, spat on his beard and his Jewish gabardine, and kicked at him as "you spurn a stranger cur / Over your threshold." He has been allowed his place on the Rialto because he is needed and because he has accepted his humiliations as a good Jew (or a good nigger) should, without ever attempting to talk back, much less strike back. Now he would lift his head and talk plainly to these Christians, who make use of him or abuse him as their occasion warrants:

> . . . moneys is your suit.
> What should I say to you? Should I not say,
> "Hath a dog money? Is it possible
> A cur can lend three thousand ducats?" Or
> Shall I bend low and in a bondman's key,
> With bated breath, and whisp'ring humbleness,
> Say this:
> "Fair sir, you spet on me on Wednesday last,
> You spurn'd me such a day, another time
> You call'd me dog; and for these courtesies
> I'll lend you thus much moneys"?
>   (1.3. 119–29)

That Shylock has not exaggerated is made clear by Antonio's furious response:

I am as like to call thee so again,
To spet on thee again, to spurn thee too.
   (1.3. 130–31)

It is bad enough that Antonio has come to the Jew to borrow money at interest. It is intolerable to him that Shylock should expose the false assumption
that supports his high principle. That is to say, how can the generosity of
friendship be accepted as a norm of commercial dealings when all men are
not friends and when Antonio, like the other Venetians, is incapable of
treating Shylock like a fellow human being? Since he cannot ask Shylock
to lend money gratis as to a friend, his only alternative is to ask Shylock to
"lend it rather to thine enemy, / Who if he break, thou mayst with better
face / Exact the penalty." What a mind this is! Antonio cannot admit the
possibility that lending money is a business transaction, not an act of friendship, and therefore should earn a reasonable profit for the lender. But he
can turn his idealism inside out to justify his present actions: if interest-free
loans are the appropriate arrangement between friends, then loans at interest
are an appropriate arrangement between enemies. Who could ask for a more
high-minded conclusion?

Shylock, of course, is not morally superior to Antonio. The abuse he has
endured has not made him patient or compassionate. His awareness of the
hypocrisy of Christians does not prevent him from using his religion to justify a personal vendetta: "Cursed be my tribe," he whispers, "If I forgive him."
He fawningly rejects Antonio's suggestion that they deal with one another as
enemies. He would be friends, he says; he would have Antonio's love, forget
past insults, and lend him money without interest. Shylock's manner is cunning and hypocritical; his motive, however, is far from clear. He cannot hope
that Antonio will break the merry bond because the sum in question is trifling
in comparison with Antonio's wealth. Only a fool would dream of catching
Antonio on the hip in this transaction, though the dream must give Shylock
greedy satisfaction. He can also enjoy the fact that Antonio responds as if the
offer of friendship were genuine, even though the terms of the forfeit express
a sickening hatred. If Antonio were more principled—or more sensitive—he
would refuse Shylock's offer; he agrees to it, however, because it allows him
to take the Jew's money and keep his idealism unsullied. It also allows him to
tell himself that his steadfast adherence to principle has improved the Jew's
character. Not fearing the possibility of forfeiture, he says that the Jew grows
kind while Shylock rolls his eyes at the suspiciousness of Christians, whose
bad dealings teach them to doubt the motives of others.

At this moment Bassanio's nobility asserts itself. Although he needs
the money and has more compelling reason than Antonio to deceive himself

about this merry bond, he would not have Antonio seal to it for him. He likes not "fair terms and a villain's mind," but Antonio pushes aside his fears with assurances about his ability to repay the loan. When Shylock exits, Antonio remarks to Bassanio that "The Hebrew will turn Christian; he grows kind," a statement that borders on the fatuous and could be made only by one whose high principle is insulated from reality. He can patronize Shylock knowing that his hatred is impotent; the loan will be repaid, and if it were not, the despised Jew would not dare to take his savage forfeit.

Unless we believe that Shylock knows in advance what Antonio is going to think and say, we cannot believe that the merry bond is a calculated stratagem, for it is Antonio who first suggests that the loan be signed to as an act of hatred between enemies. Shylock, who takes pride in his business acumen, never gloats over his success in this matter or congratulates himself on deceiving those Christians. In his next appearance, he makes no reference to the "ensnaring" of Antonio either in dialogue or soliloquy. He speaks to Jessica only of his scorn for Christian prodigality and idle amusements. Alone with his daughter, Shylock reveals a claustrophobic contempt and suspicion of the Christian world in which he lives. His soul is not great with evil desires, it is petty in its aspirations and satisfactions. By instinct he is joyless and acquisitive, and both traits have been exacerbated by his outcast role in Venetian society. He is capable of at most a grudging affection for Launcelot Gobbo, who is leaving his household to enter Bassanio's service. "The patch," he confesses, "is kind enough, but a huge feeder / Snail slow in profit." Gobbo knows that such responses do not bespeak a fiendish mind. When he debates with himself whether to leave Shylock, he calls his master "a kind of devil," nay, "the very devil incarnation," yet his conscience, he says, tells him to stay with Shylock while the fiend tempts him to go. Either Gobbo is all confusion or there is a suggestion that loyalty to a Jew has some meaning. The unhappy Jessica also contemplates leaving her father to marry Lorenzo; she is both ashamed to be her father's daughter and ashamed to be disloyal in thought and deed, but her struggle of conscience is, if anything, more shallow than Gobbo's.

Jessica's elopement by torchlight into a Venetian carnival is not a quintessentially romantic adventure, for she is not a Julia or a Hermia who hazards all for love. She helps herself to her father's money and jewels to finance a honeymoon with Lorenzo, and she is as casual in spending Shylock's money as she is lighthearted in taking it. Portia's situation parallels Jessica's; her response to it is totally different. She keeps faith with the terms of her father's will and she makes certain that those who try the riddle of the caskets understand precisely what they stand to lose and win. Her welcome to Morocco and Arragon is correct if not cordial. Like Venice, Belmont opens its gates to visitors from every nation and Portia treats all with official courtesy. All have the same opportunity to win her, but they are far from equal in her judgment. She assures the Prince of Morocco that despite his dark complexion he stands "as fair / As any comer I have looked on yet / For my affection." This is tactful and politic (he may, after all, guess rightly) but not quite sincere, for she had earlier said to Nerissa, "If he have the condition of a saint and the complexion of a devil, I had rather he should shrive me than wive me," a casual joke of course, but the kind that only those with fair complexions make. When Morocco fails the test of the caskets and departs, Portia sighs with relief,

> A gentle riddance. Draw the curtains, go.
> Let all of his complexion choose me so.
>   (2.7. 78–79)

This is not a Desdemona who could find a Moor's visage in his mind; she is very much a product of her society, as she will demonstrate in her treatment of the defeated Shylock. Before Bassanio arrives, she regards all her suitors as foreigners who can be described with the usual canards about their national characteristics.

Complexions are also at issue in the choice of the caskets: one of bright gold, another of gleaming silver, and the third of sullen lead. To choose rightly is to win a beauteous heiress; to choose wrongly is to forfeit one's chance to marry anyone. Since the task requires an ability to solve the riddles of the inscriptions and to assay the silent messages of the caskets, no fool need apply. On the other hand, if the choosing were merely a test of intelligence or worldly shrewdness, the fairy-tale quest would lose its romantic aura. To win Portia, a suitor must have the right motive as well as an ability to see through false appearances; he must love her for herself and understand the intrinsic connection between loving and hazarding.

Morocco and Arragon choose sensibly and wrongly according to their individual bents and unwitting needs. It is almost inevitable that Morocco choose the gold casket because, despite Portia's assurances, he knows the way Europeans look on dark-skinned races and cannot admit the possibility that he is inferior to them. In greeting Portia he proclaimed the worth of his blood and courage and announced that he would not change his hue except to "steal" her thoughts. Yet when he mulls over the inscription on the silver casket, "Who chooseth me shall get as much as he deserves," he wonders if his desert "may not extend so far as to the lady." He immediately dismisses this thought as "a weak disabling" of himself but he has neither the wit nor the self-confidence to make an unconventional choice. It is necessary for him to identify himself with all the world and therefore choose "what many men desire." His reward is a death's-head and a scornful message about false seemings and foolish judgments that befits his shallow calculation that nothing less than gold could be worthy of this "angel" Portia. He does not convict himself of greed; he is too ordinary, however, to transcend the crass values expressed in his meditation on the decorum of noble tombs and the appropriate coinage for Portia's semblance.

Arragon comes closer to solving the riddle of the caskets. He knows that gold, which promises what many men desire, is often a snare, for the many are often a fool multitude that judge by outward appearances. His reflections are impressive in their way, and his choice of silver a logical enough deduction from his premises. Since he will not "jump with common spirits," and since it is hubristic to aim above one's deserts, he chooses the silver casket, but not before he delivers a shrewd commentary on the inequities of a world in which true merit is often ignored while title and wealth are often "derived corruptly." Does Arragon deserve a portrait of a blinking idiot and a sneering bit of doggerel about foolish judgments? If it is folly to hope that one will be rewarded according to one's deserts, it is folly also to hope for justice on earth. Arragon lacks imagination, not shrewdness. He is blind to the hint of the lead casket that love involves a hazarding of self as well as a gaining of desire. He chooses very sensibly and, therefore, not well. Even so, Portia's response seems unfeeling: "O, these deliberate fools, when they do choose, / They have the wisdom by their wit to lose." The way that clever men outsmart themselves amuses her here, as it will again in the trial scene and afterward.

Arragon's defeat sets the stage for Bassanio's arrival and testing, which comes even as Antonio's losses and Shylock's frenzy at Jessica's elopement are preparing the way for the horror of the forfeit in Venice. Ill fortune can bring a successful merchant to his knees; it is less probable, however, that the improvident Bassanio, whose other ventures failed, will be able to solve the baffling riddle of the caskets. Even Portia, who loves and cherishes Bassanio before he proves his worthiness in the trial of the caskets, is fearful that he may choose wrongly, and that fear shakes her customary poise. Her willingness to declare her love before he chooses is a lovely touch of incaution that testifies to the depth of her feeling. When she speaks of her desire to keep him a month or two in Belmont before he risks the test, her lines are as hesitant and her thought as indirect as Bassanio's when he had to ask Antonio for money:

> There's something tells me (but it is not love)
> I would not lose you, and you know yourself,
> Hate counsels not in such a quality.
> But lest you should not understand me well—

And yet a maiden hath no tongue but thought—
I would detain you here some month or two
Before you venture for me.
    (3.2. 4–10)

Despite her fears, she will not give in to the temptation to teach him how to choose, though some have found a cunning hint of the solution to the riddles in the lyrics of the song that is sung while he ponders his choice.[10] But if she is going to be false, she would be a fool to risk losing Bassanio by using so indirect a hint. Where Jessica says it is a heinous sin to be ashamed of her father and elopes with crammed pockets, Portia will be a faithful daughter whatever the consequence. She must have confidence in Bassanio's wisdom as well as her father's because if he cannot by himself solve the riddle, he is not worthy to be her husband. As Bassanio pauses before the caskets, she tries to allay her fears by mock-heroic imaginings. He is her Alcides about to slay the sea monster; she is Hesione saved from death. She will have music sound while he chooses so that he may swan-like die, "fading in music," if he loses. If successful, he will be greeted with flourishes like a new-crowned monarch and with the dulcet music that awakens a bridegroom on his wedding day. Love quickens what is best and brightest in Portia's spirit; for the first time she is not in command of the situation and having frankly confessed her love and vulnerability, she tempers her anxiety with humorous self-irony.

What was before a contest of wits between Portia's father and her suitors becomes now a meeting of true minds. "If you love me," she says to Bassanio, "you will find me out." To find her requires innocence as well as worldly wisdom, a sense of the ideal in love that is unspoiled by knowledge of the tawdriness of most of the prizes of the world. Since Portia imagines herself a virgin sacrifice, Bassanio must rise to heights of mythic heroism: he must be like Oedipus before the Sphinx or Alexander facing the Gordian knot. His ability to match Portia's wordplay about treason and confession augurs well of their future together and of his ability to succeed where Morocco and Arragon have failed. He approaches his task with a wariness that at first seems limited to commonplace prudence. He will not be taken in by false appearances because he knows that corrupt pleas, religious errors, vice, and cowardice can be masked by pleasing shows. As he continues to assess the choices, however, prudence gives way to poetic insight. The thought of a woman's false hair—golden locks taken from a corpse—connects human vanity and meretricious beauty to the lesson of the death's-head. There is no thought of himself, not a single "I," in Bassanio's lines until his mind is made up, then he swiftly rejects "gaudy gold, / Hard food for Midas," and silver "pale and common drudge / 'Tween man and man." Intuition rather than reason guides his choice of "meager lead," whose "paleness moves [him] more than eloquence." Fearing lightness, that which is easily acquired, he chooses the "threatening" heaviness, the sadness of lead, on which he hazards all. The ability to see beneath appearances that made Bassanio recoil from Shylock's merry bond is here confirmed. He is wise enough to doubt all but love itself, which is not mocked by time and death as are the prizes for which other men hazard all.

Opening the casket, Bassanio is dazzled by the beauty of Portia's image, yet not so dazzled that he forgets that this prize is itself an appearance cunningly contrived. The scroll bids him claim his lady with a loving kiss, as Morocco or Arragon would have done if either had succeeded. Before he did not calculate what he deserved; now he will not claim his bride unless she offers herself, and so he turns to Portia to give and to receive; he will not think that she is his unless she ratifies his victory. Thus at the moment that supposedly reduces Portia to the victor's prize, Bassanio releases her from bondage to her father's will and allows her freely to choose her husband. The other romantic comedies end when the obstacles to love have been overcome or are dissolved. Here love triumphs without the customary rituals and trials of wooing, and yet Portia's and Bassanio's speeches are the fullest realization in the comedies of the ideal of romantic love. The Petrarchan conceits that fell so easily from the lips of Proteus, Valentine, Lysander, and Demetrius echo briefly in Bassanio's admiration for Portia's portrait; then they gave way to the lovely simplicity of their mutual vows.

Only a skilled actress can convince us that the poised, witty Portia of the first scenes is the anxious, vulnerable, ardent bride-to-be of the casket scene who speaks of herself as an unpracticed maiden, happy in her innocence and ability to learn, and who commits herself to be schooled by "her lord, her governor, her king." If this surrender of self is an artful pretense, it is a gratuitous one, however, because Bassanio does not solicit it with manner or words. He does not play Petruchio in a way that would tempt her to play at being the Kate of the last scene of *The Shrew*. Rather than conceiving of himself as Portia's lord, he describes her loving words to him after he has chosen the right casket as "some oration fairly spoke / By a beloved prince." Portia does not speak like Kate; she speaks like Juliet of the immeasurable bounty of her love, and being more worldly than Juliet she attempts to express that yearning in arithmetical figures:

> I would not be ambitious in my wish
> To wish myself much better, yet for you
> I would be trebled twenty times myself,
> A thousand times more fair, ten thousand times more rich,

> That only to stand high in your account,
> I might in virtues, beauties, livings, friends,
> Exceed account.
>   (3.2. 151–57)

The joy of the occasion, which increases when Nerissa and Gratiano tell of their love and desire to marry, is brief, for Jessica, Lorenzo, and Salerio enter with news of Antonio's peril. If any doubt of Bassanio's nobility remained, it is erased by his response to Antonio's letter. He makes no attempt at self-justification; he does not tell how he recoiled from Shylock's proposal of the merry bond and told Antonio not to seal to it. He needed the money and he allowed Antonio to brush aside his fears. He confesses that when he told Portia he had nothing, he spoke falsely because in truth he "was worse than nothing"; he was the penniless man who allowed his dearest friend to engage himself to a mere enemy to feed his means. Portia is as generous as Bassanio is honest. She would have Shylock paid double or triple the sum owed to him; more important, she immediately chooses to subordinate her rights and desires as Bassanio's bride to his obligation to Antonio. She would have him leave for Venice before they have enjoyed their wedding night, for she knows that he could not lie by her side with a quiet soul while Antonio is in mortal danger. On the surface, at least, Antonio's letter is more generous still because it makes no claim on Bassanio; although he faces a terrible death, Antonio would not have Bassanio return to Venice if it were inconvenient.

> "Sweet Bassanio, my ships have all miscarried, my creditors
> grow cruel, my estate is very low, my bond to the Jew is forfeit;
> and since in paying it, it is impossible I should live, all debts are
> clear'd between you and I, if I might but see you at my death.
> Notwithstanding, use your pleasure; if your love do not persuade
> you to come, let not my letter."
>   (3.2. 315–22)

Can Antonio imagine that Bassanio will refuse the pathetic appeal implicit in his words? The very thought that Bassanio might prefer to "use [his] pleasure" is mean-spirited. Antonio was annoyed when Bassanio hesitated to ask for more money because that hesitation seemed to question Antonio's willingness to give all. Yet he does not see the insult implicit in the suggestion that Bassanio might be too busy to visit him in his time of extremity. This is a man who slenderly knows himself and will not see that his extreme of self-abnegation must lacerate Bassanio's already tormented conscience.[11]

Shylock, of course, is infinitely more repellent in his gloating over Antonio's plight. He will not heed any appeal for mercy, he says, because he has sworn an oath in heaven to have his bond, and of course religious vows take precedence over earthly considerations. Shylock's pleasure in having his enemy in his power is understandable. It is richly satisfying to cast away his fawning manner and openly express his contempt for the Christian even as he makes Antonio's insults the excuse for his inhumanity: "Thou call'dst me dog before thou hadst a cause, / But since I am a dog, beware any fangs." What is astonishing is the surprise of the Venetians at Shylock's fury, for Solanio and Salerio continue to bait him in the street and jeer at his misery even after learning of Antonio's losses. They brag to him of their role in Jessica's elopement and find his sorrow and anger at her "rebellion" a subject for coarse joking. When Shylock ominously warns, "Let Antonio look to his bond," they cannot believe that he will demand the terrible forfeit. It is not that they grant him any shred of human feeling; they simply cannot imagine that the hated outcast, the comic butt, will strike back at those who torment him. How could the buffoon who cried out in the streets for justice, for his ducats and his daughter without a sense of shame, be dangerous? The Christians laughed when he spoke of Jessica as his "own flesh and blood." They stole from him a child who was his collop, his flesh; should he not now tear away a pound of flesh from the bankrupt Antonio? It is ironic that Shylock's memorable assertion of his humanity should come at the very moment that an inhuman purpose is becoming fixed in his mind, but this irony does not lessen the force of Shylock's outcry. By now he is beyond caring about the Venetians' opinion, beyond wanting their recognition of him as a fellow human. He has tried to live with them, swallowed their insults, and put on a false geniality when the occasion demanded, but no longer. Now he will be himself with them—or rather he will be a new, terrible self—the very incarnation of the inhuman Jew of anti-Semitic legend. His is the hopeless self-destructive rage that burns down ghettos and that justifies a society's contemptuous view of its niggers. Having written off his daughter as an irretrievable loss, Shylock thinks only of the money she stole that he may yet recover. Thus he is made frantic by reports of the sums Jessica has already squandered:

A diamond gone, cost me two thousand ducats in Frankford!
The curse never fell on our nation till now, I never felt it till
now. Two thousand ducats in that, and other precious, precious
jewels. I would my daughter were dead at my foot, and the
jewels in her ear! Would she were hears'd at my foot, and the
ducats in her coffin!
    (3.1. 83–90)

This is Job turned burlesque comedian, wringing his hands over *his* turquoise that he had of Leah. He consoles himself with the fantasy that with Antonio gone, he can "make what merchandise I will" in Venice. But even if this outcome were possible—and it is not—the thought of profit is not uppermost in Shylock's mind, for he will not take nine thousand ducats for a pound of Antonio's flesh.

When Solanio and Salerio jeered at Shylock's misery, he claimed that he learned from Christians how to revenge a wrong. In the courtroom, however, he does not claim that the injuries done to him entitle him to mutilate and kill Antonio. He claims only that his bond is legal and cannot be abrogated. At least half-aware that his blood-lust is inhuman, he does not argue that his cause is good or just or even rational; instead he insists on the privilege of his "humor" as if his desire for Antonio's lifeblood were comparable to the harmless eccentricities and phobias of other men, some of whom cannot abide cats or pigs or bagpipes:

> So can I give no reason, nor I will not,
> More than a lodg'd hate and a certain loathing
> I bear Antonio. . . .
>   (4.1. 59–61)

Earlier he would not listen to Antonio because he would not be made "a soft and dull-eyed fool, / To shake the head, relent, and sigh." By the trial scene, however, he can listen to any appeal unmoved; he is even amused by the impotent rage of the Venetians. He answers Bassanio patiently, without vituperation; he responds to Gratiano's stream of invectives with smirking indifference. He affably counsels this "good youth" to repair his wit lest it fall to cureless ruin.

> Till thou canst rail the seal from off my bond,
> Thou but offend'st thy lungs to speak so loud.
>   (4.1. 139–40)

If Portia had known Shylock she might have been less confident of success when she set out in disguise for Venice, but then she does not assume that she alone will be able to save Antonio's life. She does not hasten to confront Shylock and thereby perform the task that rightly belongs to Bassanio. She enters the courtroom only after the others have failed to change Shylock's mind or find a way to prevent his murderous purpose. She necessarily wears a disguise to plead in a court of law, which is open only to men, and she is content to leave the court in disguise once she has accomplished her purpose.

Portia's disguise, like her talk of a religious pilgrimage, is a convention of romantic fabling, not a confirmation of a devious nature. She is nowhere more attractive than in her response to the threat to Antonio's life. She immediately gauges Bassanio's devotion to Antonio, and she knows he would be shattered by grief and remorse if Antonio were to die. Knowing that Antonio's plight must take precedent over her rights she does not pretend to be self-sacrificing, as Antonio does. It is for Bassanio's sake and for their future happiness that she sends him off, and she goes too because in rescuing Antonio, she rescues Bassanio from a life of regret. Splendidly composed in this crisis, she gives her household over to Lorenzo and gives specific instructions to Balthazar, her messenger to Doctor Bellario. When Lorenzo praises her selflessness in sending Bassanio to Venice, she replies that since Antonio must be very like Bassanio to be his "bosom lover," she is doing little enough to purchase "the semblance of my soul / From out the state of hellish cruelty!" Although this is modest enough, Portia catches the tincture of self-flattery in her explanation and adds, "This comes too near the praising of myself." Where Julia blushed at the thought of wearing a codpiece, Portia looks forward to pretending to be a man, knowing that many cowards and braggards make the same pretense. Her host of suitors have taught her much about the foibles of men and she will use that knowledge when she confronts Shylock.

Portia's dialogue with Nerissa about their trip to Venice, and Shylock's clashes with the Duke, Bassanio, and Gratiano prepare the way for a climatic battle of wits between them. Some would find a clash of principles as well as personalities in the courtroom scene. Shylock they see as an embodiment of Hebraic legalism and Portia as a spokesman for the New Dispensation of Christian mercy.[12] This allegorical interpretation would be more convincing if Shylock, like Angelo in *Measure for Measure*, argued the necessity of strictness in the application of the law. What Shylock claims is only the right to "humor" his hatred of Antonio by taking the forfeit that his bond and Venetian law allow. The theological overtones and Morality echoes of Angelo's debate with Isabella are lacking in Portia's clash with Shylock because Antonio is not, like Claudio, a sinner who has broken the moral and divine law and must die if his offense is not forgiven. Antonio faces a horrible death because the law of contracts in Venice (and all the world) takes precedence over humane sentiments. As Antonio knows, the law is the law, and its course cannot be denied by the Duke, even if the law permits one man to have a lien on another man's flesh. As Shylock points out, what difference is there between having the right to a pound of human flesh and owning a man outright, as the Venetians own their slaves?

Allegorical interpretations of *Measure for Measure* are reductive because they erase the drama of human personality and motive in the memorable scenes between Isabella and Angelo. Allegorical interpretations of the trial scene in *The Merchant* are distorting because Portia does not have a profound belief in the ethic of mercy any more than Shylock has a profound belief in the sanctity of law. Imbued with spiritual ardor the novice Isabella would have Angelo reach up toward the mercifulness of God, whose grace saved erring man from the just wages of his sins. Portia is too comfortable in her worldliness and too great a respecter of legalities to make impassioned pleas for mercy or to question the validity of human judgments. She believes in the sanctity of contracts even when, as in the case of her father's will, they restrict her own freedom. Just as she specified the conditions under which she may be won, she spelled out to Bassanio the contract of love that is symbolized by the gift of her ring, one that is based on customary notions of equity and speaks of the penalties that will be exacted if the agreement is broken. Of course she does not live by strict measurement of rights and wrongs. With strangers like Morocco and Arragon she is coolly impartial in behavior; with those whom she knows and loves she is unstinting in her generosity. Her appeal to Shylock for mercy is eloquent, but measured rather than impassioned in tone. She knows she cannot ask the Jew to follow the example of Christ; she can only remind him that mercy is an attribute of God and becomes the kings of this world better than their crowns. When he brushes aside the appeal, she asks him to be merciful only once again.

Her manner suggests that despite the terrible circumstances she enjoys her encounter with Shylock, another deliberate fool who is found to defeat himself with shallow wit. Thus while she holds the trump card—her knowledge of Venetian law—she is willing to humor Shylock and disarm him by allowing him to think that she fully supports his claim to Antonio's flesh. Bassanio would have her wrest the law in this instance, and "to do a great right, do a little wrong," but she is above such casuistries, which allow many an error to "rush into the state." From the beginning she grants the legality of Shylock's position, examines the bond and finds it forfeit, and bids Antonio prepare his bosom for Shylock's knife. Her style is brisk and efficient, her only concerns practical ones: Is there a balance to weigh the flesh? Is there a surgeon to stop Antonio's wounds lest he bleed to death? Her manner is so convincing that when at the last moment she abruptly turns Shylock's legalism against him, he is too astonished to speak, much less think of a counter to her somewhat fantastic argument. By delaying the blow until the very last moment, she not only stuns Shylock but also erases all doubt that he intended to kill Antonio. Shylock's hypocritical legalism is sickening: he will pay for no surgeon because he does not find that minimal decency stipulated in the bond. Antonio is nobler in his resignation, and also somewhat lifeless. He speaks of death as sparing him from the lingering misery of an impoverished age, and he is again unctuously selfless in his farewell to Bassanio:

Give me your hand, Bassanio; fare you well.
Grieve not that I am fall'n to this for you;
. . . .
Repent but you that you shall lose your friend,
And he repents not that he pays your debt.
   (4.1. 265–79)

In his eagerness to salve Bassanio's conscience Antonio subtly revises the past. When he brushed aside Bassanio's objections to the merry bond, he said, "Why fear not, man; I will not forfeit it." He did not assume that Bassanio would repay the loan although Bassanio was to receive the money from Shylock. He would not have Bassanio mourn for him, only suffer a lifetime of agonizing remorse.

Portia's judgment that Shylock cannot take less than a pound of Antonio's flesh or spill one drop of his blood is absurdly literalistic but exactly what Shylock's hypocritical legalism deserves: he is deterred from taking his inhuman forfeiture by the fear of losing his own life. He told Solanio and Salerio that if they prick a Jew he bleeds; now he must tremble lest in cutting Christian flesh it bleed. Yet at the joyful moment when Shylock is confounded and Antonio saved, the tone of the scene begins to change as Portia's manner with Shylock changes. Is there a reason to warn him not to shed "one drop of Christian blood"? Would Jewish or Turkish blood be less precious in the eyes of the law? The mention of *Christian blood* would not be significant if the phrase did not evoke ancient tales of ritual slaughter of Christians by Jews. Following Portia's lead, Gratiano begins to bait the confused Shylock with his own words as Salerio and Solanio had baited him about Jessica's elopement. When Portia cites the law that is directed against aliens who seek the life of a Venetian citizen, it becomes clear that Venetian justice is not blind; it makes distinctions between those who are Venetians and those who are not.

The only mercy Gratiano offers Shylock is the freedom to hang himself. Others are more kind. The Duke pardons his life before he asks it and suggests that contrition will reduce the state's share of the wealth Shylock must forfeit to a fine. Antonio would allow Shylock to keep half his wealth, and he promises to use the other half in his business only until Shylock dies, when it will be deeded to Jessica. But Portia, who eloquently spoke for mercy to Shylock, shows no pity to her fallen adversary. She does not allow Shylock to take his principal in lieu of the forfeit although Antonio and Bassanio do not object. When the Duke speaks of reducing confiscation to a fine, she warns him not to overstep his authority. He can speak, she says, "for the state, not for Antonio." After Antonio has proposed to give his share of Shylock's wealth to Jessica and Lorenzo, provided that Shylock turn Christian and leave all he owns at his death to his daughter, Portia asks, "Are you contented, Jew? What dost thou say?" Without another word to Shylock she orders the clerk to draw up a deed of gift. Far nobler than the Lady of Belmont in *Il Pecorone*, Portia is also far more vindictive to her defeated foe. In *Il Pecorone* the Jew, thwarted of his evil purpose, tears up the bond and leaves the court. Portia could allow Shylock to do this, but instead she insists that he face the full penalties of Venetian law. If Antonio, who faced Shylock's knife, can be compassionate, why must Portia now stand for the severity of the law? Of course, Antonio's mercy is itself legalistic. Perhaps he and the others believe that a coerced baptism will save Shylock's immortal soul—that it will be better for him to die a sham Christian than a "heathen" Jew. No doubt some in Shakespeare's audiences grew moist-eyed at the prospect of Shylock's forced conversion, but many others, both Protestant and Catholic, must have shared their queen's conviction that it is tyrannical to enforce religious conscience. The Marian persecutions were not that distant and forced conversions were part of the horror of the Spanish Inquisition. Although Elizabethan laws against overt Catholic worship were severe, and Puritan zealots were harshly dealt with, Elizabeth, with good reason, was reluctant to open windows into her subjects' souls or to pry into their private convictions, for bloody religious conflicts were tearing apart France and Germany and the shock of the Saint Bartholomew's Day massacre of Huguenots was still a vivid memory.

The forced conversion of Shylock is all the more interesting because religion does not seem to be a powerful force in Venice. Antonio and his friends do not seem more devout as Christians than Shylock is as a Jew. He uses his Jewishness as an excuse for personal vindictiveness; they carry their religious convictions so lightly that we scarcely know they exist. Their speeches are graced with the conventional pieties of those who live comfortably in this world and do not worry very much about their eternal destinies. Solanio can joke about the stones of a church making a merchant fear that his ships may founder on a rocky shoal. Portia shrewdly observes that "it is a good divine that follows his own instructions." When she tells Lorenzo that she and Nerissa are leaving for a monastery where they will "live in prayer and contemplation" until their husbands return from Venice, we smile even before we know her true purpose because we cannot imagine her giving her days and nights over to pious meditations. She speaks of shriving only in a jest about Morocco's dark complexion, and she would not be scandalized by Gobbo's jokes about religion. He tells Jessica that she will be damned for being a Jew's daughter. She protests that she will be saved by her Christian husband, but Gobbo points out that many conversions to Christianity will have an injurious effect on the Venetian economy by raising the price of hogs and that will dampen the zeal to convert the Jews. Declaring her father's house is hell,

Jessica will turn Christian, not because she believes in the Savior but because she loves Lorenzo and hates her life with Shylock.

Not accustomed to agonizing over spiritual matters, the Venetians will not agonize over Shylock's immortal soul or state of grace; his Christianity may be sham, but it is enough that they have conferred a spiritual benefit on him by opening up the possibility of redemption. Portia can have no regrets about her treatment of Shylock because she knows him only as the monster of the courtroom. She did not witness Antonio's abuse of him; she was not present when Salerio and Solanio jeered at his misery. If Shylock spoke again at the trial of the indignities Antonio heaped on him, or if he gave in the courtroom the speech about the humanity of Jews he made to Solanio and Salerio, we would judge Portia's behavior differently. Whether she would be more compassionate to Shylock if she shared an audience's knowledge of his mistreatment by Venetians, one cannot say. Bassanio, Antonio, and the Duke do not murmur at Portia's insistence that he be punished, and others find Shylock's misery merely ludicrous. Once she has dealt with Shylock, Portia is as generous as before with those of her circle. She refuses Bassanio's offer of three thousand ducats and accepts Antonio's gratitude with lovely humility:

> He is well paid that is well satisfied,
> And I, delivering you, am satisfied,
> And therein do account myself well paid.
> My mind was never yet more mercenary.
> I pray you know me when we meet again;
> I wish you well, and so I take my leave.
>   (4.1. 415–20)

Would that Antonio were capable of this unostentatious generosity.

The gentle Bassanio begs forgiveness for attempting to pay the young judge and asks Portia to take some personal remembrance as a tribute, not a fee. Since he expressed his willingness during the trial to sacrifice his wife as well as himself to save Antonio, Portia can, in good conscience, test his loyalty to the bond they swore together in Belmont. Casually she asks for Antonio's gloves and then for Bassanio's ring, a commonplace request in an age when rings were given as tokens of affection and gratitude. Having set no limit to his efforts to save Antonio, Bassanio is too embarrassed now to confess that he did not quite mean what he said. Unable to say that the ring is too precious to be parted with, he declares that it is too trifling a gift. When Portia persists he squirms, hedges, and finally explains why he cannot part with the ring. She should be delighted by his response and let the matter go, but the challenge

of obtaining the ring intrigues her, and she makes one last inspired assault on
Bassanio's convictions:

> And if your wife be not a mad woman,
> And know how well I have deserv'd this ring,
> She would not hold out enemy for ever
> For giving it to me.
> (4.1. 445–48)

Those who dislike Portia speak of her cunning attempt to manipulate
and dominate Bassanio by tempting him to break his vow. But if domination
were her goal, she had only to remove her disguise to make Bassanio feel
overwhelmingly obligated to her. What is at issue over the ring is the same
question of generosity and indebtedness that arose when Bassanio discussed
his need of money with Antonio in the first scene of the play. Bassanio, who
has accepted the generosity of Antonio and Portia, is also able to accept the
generosity of the young judge even though he is uncomfortable and somewhat ashamed. Antonio, who wondered why Bassanio could not easily accept
repeated gifts of money, is unable to accept the generosity of the young judge
because he is accustomed to giving, not receiving, and he finds the acceptance
of generosity too burdensome. If he were more sensitive to the feelings of
others, he would respect Bassanio's fidelity to his vow, but then if he were
more sensitive to the feelings of others, he would not have spat on Shylock's
beard. It takes more generosity of spirit than Antonio possesses to accept a
gift outright. Even though Portia has already exited, Antonio appeals to Bassanio to part with his ring, and Bassanio cannot again say no.

The comedy of the ring episode brings the trial scene to a happy conclusion and provides an emotional transition from the rancor of the courtroom
to the peacefulness of Belmont, to which the heroes and heroines will soon
return. Because of Portia's witty handling of the chagrined Bassanio, Jessica
does not walk out on stage immediately after Shylock has been crushed to
join Lorenzo in a charming love duet. They enter after Portia has received
Bassanio's ring and after she and Nerissa have planned their comic revenge
on their luckless husbands. Ignorant of the bitterness and vituperations of
the trial, Jessica and Lorenzo enjoy the beauty of the night and add to it the
beauty of their poetry. Although somewhat shallow and unscrupulous, at least
about taking Shylock's money, they are capable of fine sentiments and tender
feelings. Perhaps when Jessica sold her father's treasured ring for a monkey,
she did not know the ring was a gift from her dead mother; perhaps she could
not believe her father could be attached to a gift from his dead wife, though
she knew well enough his love of her. In any event, her charming duet with

Lorenzo does not alter our sense of their limitations because untroubled by pangs of conscience, they joke about Jessica stealing from the wealthy Jew with her unthrift love. Lorenzo's memorable description of the heavens and the music of the spheres expresses a refinement of sensibility, not a spirituality of attitude. He describes the "floor of heaven" as if it had been fitted by Venetian craftsmen, "thick inlaid with patens of bright gold." He speaks of angels singing "to the young-eyed cherubins," as if he were describing a beautiful fresco. In the best of possible worlds, the irresponsible and improvident will be dull as clods. In Shakespeare's dramatic world as in ours, shallow, improvident and self-absorbed persons can be charming conversationalists, connoisseurs of fine wine, and lovers of art.

To appreciate Jessica and Lorenzo's charm is not to say that they deserve Shylock's money because they have an appreciation for fine things while he is miserly and incapable of enjoying his money. If this argument holds, we must agree with the reasoning of Victorian factory owners, who justified paying starvation wages on the ground that workers would probably squander additional wages on gin. When Nerissa tells of the "special deed of gift" that Shylock signed leaving all his possessions to Lorenzo and Jessica, Lorenzo exclaims, "Fair ladies, you drop manna in the way / Of starved people." The age of miracles has apparently not ended so far as Venetians are concerned, for God still watches over his chosen people. It might be difficult for Portia to prove in a court of law that Shylock plotted against Antonio's life by offering a loan under terms that Antonio called kind and "Christian" and willingly sealed to, but in any event Shylock's hatred of Antonio has ensured Jessica's material prosperity, and that is the kind of providence that matters to Lorenzo.

All the news in the final scene of *The Merchant* is joyful. Jessica and Lorenzo are provided for; Antonio learns that his ships have come safely to port. Portia and Nerissa, Bassanio and Gratiano are safely home and can enjoy their belated wedding night. The only bar to future happiness is the failure of Bassanio and Gratiano to keep their marriage rings, a failure in which their wives are implicated. Since no wrangling or discord between the lovers occurred before their betrothals, some affectionate teasing and mock accusations are not out of place. Having taught Shylock the dangers of a hypocritical literalism in the trial scene, Portia now pretends to be more literal-minded than Shylock in identifying her truth to Bassanio with his possession of her ring. Whoever owns the ring, she declares, is her husband and has the right to possess her. With Nerissa, she refuses to believe any preposterous tales about rings given to a young judge and his clerk. Bassanio swears that if Portia understood why he surrendered her ring, she would not be angry. She replies that no man would be so unreasonable as to want the ring after Bassanio had explained its sacred meaning. Perhaps she means what she says, because men can reason the need to keep or part with wedding rings but women will not acknowledge a debt greater than the vow of marriage. Or at least, one cannot imagine Portia surrendering her wedding ring to relieve a friend of a sense of obligation.

Ideally, love does not traffic with wills and estates; ideally it is unmindful of wealth or the color of a skin or religious preference. In Venice and Belmont, however, love cannot be blind to such considerations, and contracts of marriage, like many other contracts, necessarily deal with the ownership of property and dowries as well as the obligations of love and fidelity. This does not mean, however, that the sanctity of wedding vows is mocked by crass considerations. Behind Portia's pretended literalism is a belief in the literalness and absoluteness of wedding vows, which do not admit of sentimental gestures, sensible compromises, and accommodations to circumstance. Love is not love that alters when it alteration finds, and therefore Bassanio had no right to part with Portia's ring nor Portia the right to use his "infidelity" as the excuse for her own bending. *The Merchant* does not pose the higher law of love against the quid pro quo of worldly bonds because the bond of love is in itself transcendent, a world-without-end bargain that is an act of faith in another. Once again Antonio offers to be bound for Bassanio's sake. Portia relents, and with the threat of infidelity exorcised, all ends well for the lovers and their dear friend.

Dissatisfied with that conclusion, Sir Laurence Olivier ended a fine television production of *The Merchant* with a close-up of a pensive Jessica reading over Shylock's deed of gift to her and Lorenzo, as if she were troubled at the last by her father's fate and even a bit regretful of her abandonment of him. This note of sadness was moving in its way but false to the character of Jessica and to the mood of the final scene. It did not clarify Shakespeare's artistic intention or improve upon it. It was a sentimental gesture that Olivier felt obliged to make because religious bigotry still plagues the world four hundred years after the composition of *The Merchant*. There is no reason to sentimentalize Jessica when thousands of immigrant children have, like her, felt estranged from parents whose foreign speech and ways seemed embarrassing and stultifying. In the past century thousands of American children have fled their old-world parents to become part of the American present and future. The "problem" of the final scene is not rooted in Shakespeare's failure to see Jessica, Lorenzo, and the others as we see them. The problem lies in our unwillingness or inability to accept the portraits Shakespeare draws of both the Jew and his Christian enemies. We want Portia and Antonio and Jessica to be more understanding of Shylock because they have so many attractive qualities. Or we want to be more certain that Shakespeare was aware of their limitations even though our sense of their limitations is created by the changes Shakespeare made in his source materials. It bothers us that having raised a cynical tale of intrigue and sordid motive to the level of great poetic drama, Shakespeare does not grace the ending of *The Merchant* with noble insight and recognitions. But such recognitions would hardly be appropriate when the climactic agon of the play pits Portia's cleverness against Shylock's, rather than the ethic of love and generosity against an inhuman legalism. After Gratiano's Jew-baiting, Portia's unrelenting attitude to Shylock, and the "mercy" of an enforced conversion, any final realization of Shylock's tortured humanity by the Venetians would be a last-minute revision of their characters. If the ending of *The Merchant* troubles, it does so because it is absolutely true to the preceding action, even though it is not "as we would like it."

Those who believe that Shylock was supposed to be a buffoon, a killjoy, and a ritual scapegoat whose expulsion makes possible the happy ending suggest that Shakespeare erred in making Shylock too human and sympathetic a figure. If the humanity of Shylock is an artistic error or miscalculation, however, it is one that Shakespeare was peculiarly prone to, for not long after *The Merchant* he was to make the same error again in the final scene of *2 Henry IV*, in which Henry rejects Falstaff; and not long after that, he was to repeat this very miscalculation in the unpleasant humiliation of Malvolio by Feste and Toby. Is it reasonable to assume that Shakespeare made the same significant artistic error three times? Or does the error lie in critics' attempts to reduce his complex art to simplistic ritual patterns that presume a denial of human sympathy to this character or that?[13]

The cheerfulness of the final scene of *The Merchant* is very like the cheerfulness of the final scene of *Henry V*, in which the dread anxiety that preceded the battle of Agincourt, the moral issues raised by the English soldiers around the campfire, and the slaughter of the French are wiped completely from the King's mind. Brushing aside Burgundy's pleas for an end to the devastation of France, Henry demands recognition of his "just" rights because the mercy he urged on his adversaries has no claim on him, and his only interest is to woo Katherine for his bride. The victory he has won has not enlarged his sympathies any more than Portia's victory has enlarged hers. Although Henry speaks of the French nobility as his brothers, his emotional attachments are limited to the happy few, the English band of brothers who stood together against great odds, indeed, whose devotion to one another was inspired by the threat of the foreign enemy. In a similar way the devotion of the characters to each other in *The Merchant* is inspired by the threat of the alien Shylock, and their identification with one another depends in part on an awareness of their difference from the many outsiders who are drawn to Venice and Belmont. Their insular world is limited to those of similar taste and breeding who look like them, dress like them, and pray like them. If that insularity breeds narrowness and arrogance, it also makes possible the solidarity of the group, its traditional civilities, and capacity for altruism. For centuries, after all, the little republic of Venice had defended its freedom and independence and extended its power and influence because it took pride in its unique heritage and place among the states of the world. Similar ideals of civic virtue inspired the American colonists, the happy few who stood against the power of Britain and founded a nation based on the principle that all men are created equal, but who reserved to themselves the right to keep slaves—that is, to own human flesh—provided the flesh was dark-complected and duly purchased. The mercy Antonio offers to Shylock is a solution to the problem of despised and feared minorities, but one doubts that baptism will make Shylock Christian and Venetian enough to be welcomed at Belmont, even if like Jessica, he grows ashamed of ever having been a Jew.

Notes

1. See the discussion of anti-Semitism in medieval and Renaissance Europe in E. E. Stoll's *Shakespeare Studies* (New York: G. E. Stechert, 1942; first edition 1927), 269–90.

2. Stoll mentions four Elizabethan plays that have anti-Semitic portraits of Jewish usurers apart from Marlowe's and Shakespeare's (*Shakespeare Studies* 272). His footnotes reveal, however, that two of these villains are not identified as Jews, and at least two are modeled after Shylock.

3. See Lawrence Danson's critique of Stoll's assumptions in *The Harmonies of "The Merchant of Venice"* (New Haven: Yale University Press, 1978), 133–34.

4. For a contrary view see Leggatt, who draws a sharp contrast between Belmont and Venice, which he calls a "world of need" (*Shakespeare's Comedy* of Love, 125).

5. See Danson's astute criticism of this view of Antonio (*Harmonies*, 34–36).

6. The desire of the receiver of generosity to be worthy of the gift is memorably expressed in George Herbert's religious poetry, especially "Love III."

7. For a portrait of a villainous usurer in later drama, see Sir Giles Overreach in Massinger's *A New Way to Pay Old Debts*. The malevolent Overreach has little in common with the Shylock of the first three acts.

8. Although Elizabethan law theoretically forbid all usury, severe penalties were set only for rates higher than ten percent, and commercial loans were a common business practice in Shakespeare's age.

9. See E. K. Chambers, *William Shakespeare: A Study of Facts and Problems* (Oxford: 1930) 2: 65–66.

10. Supposedly Portia gives away the answer to the riddle of the caskets by the song which rhymes "bred," "head," and "nourished" to draw Bassanio's attention to "lead."

11. The self-pitying tone of Antonio's letter is mirrored in the extreme self-abnegation of Sonnet 71, "No longer mourn for me." Some critics rejoice in the saintliness of attitude expressed in the sonnet, but its total denial of psychological

reality, its hyperbolic command that not one tear be shed, seems to me to cry out for ironic interpretation.

12. See Nevill Coghill, "The Basis of Shakespearian Comedy," *Essays and Studies* (1950): 1–28. More intricate and ingenious in Barbara K. Lewalski's "Biblical Allusion and Allegory in *The Merchant of Venice*," *Shakespeare Quarterly* 12 (1962): 327–43.

13. It is almost commonplace for critics to suggest that Shakespeare made an artistic mistake in allowing Shylock to become too human and deserving of an audience's sympathies; see Barber, *Shakespeare's Festive Comedy*, 190–91; Nevo, *Comic Transformations*, 136ff. Palmer, on the other hand, notes the splendid comic balance of the portrait of Shylock, *Comic Characters*, 87.

HARRY LEVIN

A Garden in Belmont:
The Merchant of Venice, 5.1

Comedy, at its most typical, has generated an urban and bourgeois—not to say a mercantile—atmosphere, in keeping with the sharpness of its satiric tone. Shakespeare transcends that pattern by characteristically harking back to nature and by sounding what C. L. Barber has taught us to call a festive note. Money gets mentioned less often in Shakespeare's other and later plays than in his fledgling adaptation from Plautus, *The Comedy of Errors*. Within its classical tradition love was envisaged as a casual, if not a venal, relationship. Conflicts tended to develop between the pantaloon or *senex iratus*, the angry old man clutching his moneybags, and the young lovers abetted by servants cleverer than their masters. Comedy in Shakespeare's romantic vein, which embraces a good many heterogeneous elements, tends to seek and find a retreat amid the countryside, in some green world or pastoral surrounding where mundane complications may be happily resolved. Such is the vitalizing influence of the forest in *A Midsummer Night's Dream* and *As You Like It*, of the Bohemian sheepcote in *The Winter's Tale*, and of the enchanted island in *The Tempest*. The respective comic spheres of city and country are uniquely interlinked in *The Merchant of Venice*. In *The Tempest*, *The Winter's Tale*, *As You Like It*, and *A Midsummer Night's Dream*, the vicissitudes of rustication set aright the discontents of court. The court that holds jurisdiction over *The Merchant of Venice*, of course, is not regal but legal.

From *Shakespeare and Dramatic Tradition: Essays in Honor of S. F. Johnson*, edited by W. R. Elton and William B. Long, pp. 13–31. Copyright © 1989 by Associated University Presses.

97

That does not make it any less dramatic, inasmuch as England's central institution, the law, has incidentally served as a matrix for the drama. Among its original sponsors were lawyers at the Inns of Court, who produced the first English tragedy, *Gorboduc*, where the dumb shows were made vocal by the parleys of opposing counsels. It could not have been an accident that the first English comedy, *Fulgens and Lucres*, was self-characterized in juridical terminology as a "process." A trial, being a verbal agon before an audience, presents a kind of theatrical performance. Dramatists were apt in exploiting its possibilities, and very notably the Jacobeans, who rose to such climactic courtroom scenes as Jonson's in *Volpone* and Webster's in *The White Devil*. Shakespeare had his own reasons for bypassing the notorious arraignment of Prince Hal, and he showed a particular sympathy for trials in which the defendant was a woman and a queen: Hermione and Katherine of Aragon. But circumstance could not have provided him with a more striking confrontation of values, styles, and personalities than what takes place in the fourth act of *The Merchant of Venice*. Given the suspense relieved by such a climax, anything that followed ran the danger of anticlimax. Spectators have been known to walk out after the exit of Shylock, and there have been productions wherein the fifth act was drastically curtailed or else omitted altogether.

Critics with an eye to more modern stages, like Gustav Freytag and Harley Granville-Barker, have been inclined to view Shakespearean drama as inherently a three-part form. Its pseudo-classical five-act structure, which seems to have been rather unevenly superimposed, means more in print than it does in the theater, though its amplitude could have licensed the playwright to double and redouble his plot. Even so, since its denouements can be foreseen quite early, particularly in the comedies, the story-line may slacken after the third act. Slack can be taken up by directly completing the story and thereupon devoting the fifth act to a divertissement, as in *A Midsummer Night's Dream*. The situation would be much the same in *Love's Labor's Lost*, if Shakespeare had not overturned it with a last-minute shock. In *The Tempest* he postpones the conclusion by eking out the fourth act with a masque. In *The Merchant of Venice* the predicated business has virtually terminated with the courtroom scene. He employs a brief aftermath to plant his motivation for the sub-subplot of the last act, the displacement and replacement of the rings. Without this contrivance there would be no action left; and despite it there have been actors, audiences, and commentators who have regarded the rest as a superficial and expendable letdown. Act 5 may be less of a "graceful winding up," in Hazlitt's phrase, than it is—in A. W. Schlegel's—"a musical afterpiece."

Generally, Shakespeare's underplots move parallel to his main plots, as with the revenge of Laertes in *Hamlet* or the sons of Gloucester in *King*

Lear. In the comedies, where the theme so repeatedly involves wooing, the couples are reduplicated at different levels: Bassanio and Portia never far from Gratiano and Nerissa, the four transversely paired as knight and squire or mistress and waiting-woman, plus Lorenzo and Jessica on a plane connecting the two plots. Those two plots are aligned with an antithetical series of contrasts between the pettifogging commercialism of Venice and the leisurely grace of Belmont, between man's justice and woman's mercy, between adversary and amatory relations, hatred versus love. In yoking such antitheses together, Shakespeare took the risk of letting Shylock run away with the play, just as Falstaff jeopardizes the equilibrium of *2 Henry IV.* The pound of flesh and the three caskets are even-handedly balanced in the subtitle of the first quarto. The title role is hardly that of a hero, though it has sometimes been confused with Shylock's; as a matter of fact, the entry in the Stationers' Register appends an alternative title, "the iewe of Venyce." The merchant Antonio speaks no more than 188 lines, less than Bassanio (339), Shylock (361), and Portia (578), who comes fourth after Rosalind (721), Cleopatra (670), and Imogen (591) among Shakespeare's most articulate heroines.

Shylock's part, then, is not much longer than Bassanio's and much shorter than Portia's; he appears in but five of the twenty scenes. A succession of histrionic stars managed to extend it by acting out and sentimentalizing the episode reported by Solanio and Salerio in choric mockery: his outcry on returning from the banquet to discover that Jessica has eloped and taken some of his hoard along. The stellar potentialities in the conjunction of Shylock and Portia gained this play an outstandingly rich history of performance, more frequent during certain periods than any other Shakespearean vehicle with the exception of *Hamlet.* Yet it seems to have gone unperformed through the seventeenth century, possibly because its mixed emotions were unpalatable to neo-classical tastes. In Viscount Lansdowne's mangled and coarsened version, *The Jew of Venice* (1701), Shylock has to be played as a comic butt—a twist which prompted Shakespeare's first editor, Nicholas Rowe, to confess that he thought the personage had been "design'd Tragically by the Author." Rowe's perception of "a savage Fierceness and Fellness" would be realized by Charles Macklin, who preempted "the Jew / That Shakespeare knew"—as Pope put it—for almost fifty years. That archvillain would be romanticized by nineteenth-century Shylocks from Edmund Kean to Henry Irving, whose "patriarch of Israel" provoked the derision of Bernard Shaw.

Heinrich Heine's testimony might have betrayed some hereditary bias, but he claimed to have witnessed a blonde Englishwoman weeping sympathetically over the downfall of Shylock and consequently ranked *The Merchant of Venice* among Shakespeare's tragedies. An increasing pathos in the interpretation could be correlated with a broadening tolerance for Jews.

Shylock's hard heart would be softened to a maudlin degree in the Yiddish theater, and Arnold Wesker has recently attempted to depict him in amicable collusion with Antonio. Nonetheless it must be noted that, ever since Hitler made so catastrophic an issue of antisemitism, the play has figured less prominently in both the repertory and the classroom. Meanwhile scholars like E. E. Stoll, considering historical attitudes toward ethnicity and usury, had recaptured an image of the Jewish moneylender that Shakespeare knew—or rather, did not know, since there had been no English Jewry for 300 years. Out of the stereotypes he created a curmudgeon, sinister and grotesque by turns, yet a human being. Swinburne, confounding Shylock with Lear, could proclaim him "more sinned against than sinning." Where could the balance between those states be determined, if not in a lawcourt? He has been on the defensive after the elopement: "If you prick us, do we not bleed" (3.1.64)? He takes the offensive before the tribunal: "Hates any man the thing he would not kill" (4.1.67)?

The poetic justice of the hearing is accentuated by a vernacular echo. It was Shylock, hatching his machination, who soliloquized about Antonio: "If I can catch him once upon the hip ..." (1.3.46). It is Gratiano, after the switch in judgment, who gloats and jeers: "Now, infidel, I have you on the hip" (4.1.334). It brings home the irony of hoisting the engineer in his own petard, when Portia—her plea for compassion having fallen upon deaf ears—resorts to a legalism more literal-minded than Shylock's. Vengeance has been his seething and mounting objective: revenge against racial persecution, revenge against financial rivalry, revenge against a twofold personal loss. Shakespeare would be coming to closer grips with that barbaric motive in probing Hamlet's compunctions. Ethically *The Merchant of Venice*, like *The Atheist's Tragedy*, is an antirevenge play. G. L. Kittredge used to maintain that Shakespeare portrayed no villain so malign but that he had a case, and it is the losing case for Shylock that makes the play so controversial. There are wavering moments when the Christian comedy might almost have turned into a Jewish tragedy, observed the Variorum editor, charting the shifts of interpretative sympathy. But the sexual game, the light-hearted banter, and what Coleridge termed "the lyrical movement" of act 5 would be heartlessly *de trop* if we recognized Shylock as the protagonist.

Sir Arthur Quiller-Couch believed that it had been underrated, that it constituted "the most delightful part of the play." Though act 4 is unquestionably the showpiece, its high tensions call for a resolution. Where the urbanized lagoons of Venice are precincts of sharp practice, which Jonson would elaborate in *Volpone*, the bucolic terra firma of Belmont represents "a place where life is heightened," according to Anne Barton. Temperamentally and geographically it borders on *Twelfth Night*: "This is Illyria, Lady." Portia's villa is a haven lighted by the chromatic glow of Veronese, after the hustle and bustle of the Rialto. Shakespeare commutes in artful alternation from the one locale to the other: twelve of the scenes are set in Venice, eight in Belmont. Venice repairs to Belmont in the wake of the suitors' "secret pilgrimage" (1.1.120). The successful suit of Bassanio, with an undertone of ambiguity, is compared to the Argonauts' mythical quest for the golden fleece (1.1.170; 3.2.241). Moving in the opposite direction, Belmont makes an incursion into Venice when Portia goes to the rescue; penetrating that ambience as a dea ex machina, she must assume the guise of a man and a barrister. Her juristic exploit cannot be scrutinized very professionally. The terms of the bond, like those of her father's will, as Granville-Barker has pointed out, are the stuff of fairy tales. "Shylock is real while his story remains fabulous."

Shakespeare's "all-combining mind"—the formulation is Henry Hallam's—could have found his themes of extortion and courtship already combined in what seems to have been his principal source, a novella from *Il Pecorone*, the collection of tales by Ser Giovanni Fiorentino. The tale about the pound of flesh and the loophole for avoiding that penalty had been told many times in the European Middle Ages and can be traced as far afield as the *Mahábhárata*. But the lady of Belmonte in the Italian romance is a rich widow who must be successfully bedded and who has a stratagem for staving off all except the last of her swains. Shakespeare obviously needed something more courtly and more presentable on the stage. Within Giovanni's framework, held together by the Venetian loan, he substituted a folktale that again had many far-ranging analogues and was probably familiar to him through its inclusion in the *Gesta Romanorum*. Among those fascinated by the three caskets was Freud, who predictably saw them as symbols of women's bodies and hence analogous to the judgment of Paris and other myths that hinge upon triple choices. The paradox that allows the basest metal to form a receptacle for the prize fits in well with a recurrent Shakespearean theme, the distinction between appearance and reality, moralized in such maxims as "All that glisters is not gold" or "O, what a goodly outside falsehood hath!" (2.7.65; 1.3.102).

In the *Gesta Romanorum* the chooser of the golden casket is promised "that he deserveth," and it is the silver one which promises "that his nature desireth." In the lottery of Portia's destiny the moral symbolism has been reversed; gold is associated with desire and silver with desert (2.1.15). The inscription on the leaden casket in the old fable reads: "Who so chooseth me shall finde that God hath disposed to him." Such religious quietism differs profoundly from the Marlovian challenge that ultimately attracts Bassanio: "Who chooses me must give and hazard all he hath" (2.7.9). Quiller-Couch, remarking that "a predatory young gentleman such as Bassanio would not have chosen the leaden casket," begs the question; for a character necessarily consists of whatever he does and says, and this is Bassanio's most important act or statement. True, he started out by speaking as a fortune hunter, anxious to wive it wealthily in Belmont like Petruchio in Padua. But Belmont, unlike Padua, is fabulous terrain. Broaching his intention to restore his depleted fortunes, he mentions Portia's inheritance, her beauty, and her virtue in that order (1.1.161–63). Though it may be a long shot, he is truly a gambler. So is Antonio, whose ventures threaten to be much unluckier than his friend's, since—having wealth and life itself to lose—it is he who gives and hazards all he has, both his purse and his person.

It has been speculated that when Portia welcomes Bassanio, she reveals the password: "pause a day or two / Before you *hazard* . . ." (3.2.1 f.). This is of a piece with the tempting conjecture that the cautionary song "Tell me where is fancy bred," which accompanies his appraisal, hints at the proper choice through its rhymes with "lead": "bred," "head," and "nourished" (63–65). Portia, however, though she frankly confesses her preference for Bassanio, is sworn to silence on the sphinxlike riddle by the conditions of her father's will—a document almost as stringent as Shylock's bond. In her poignant awareness of each casket's responding message, she must constrain strong feelings while the Princes of Morocco and Aragon are going through the rite. They have been preceded by at least half a dozen, as we learn from the witty and sophisticated prose of her expository scene with Nerissa, where the candidates are reduced to caricatures of their several nationalities. Paternal stricture not only condemns them to dismissal, but forbids them the consolation of marriage elsewhere. It stretches the long arm of coincidence when Bassanio, the third suitor whom we witness, is both the first she has liked and the first to opt for lead. The gamble is moralized by his expressed distrust of "outward shows" (73). Yet under the circumstances, and in view of the alternatives, she seems even luckier than he.

Small wonder that when the casket disclosed her fate, one of the famous Portias, Ellen Terry, kissed it and sprinkled rose leaves. The complexity if not the inconsistency, the moods and changes of her character have aroused diverse opinions. Portia was "not a very great favourite" with Hazlitt; she was "the most perfect of [Shakespeare's] creations" for H. H. Furness. Her name refers us back to Cato's daughter, Brutus's wife, a Roman model of perfection (1.1.166). Since it is she who solves a dilemma baffling to everyone else, she is demonstrably the most intelligent person in the courtroom. Yet, while ardently accepting Bassanio as "her lord, her governor, her king," she has described herself as "an unlesson'd girl, unschool'd, unpractic'd" (3.2.165, 159). Unlike Jessica, who is embarrassed about enacting a breeches part, she exuberantly throws herself into the garb and bearing of a lawyer. Like Saint Joan—Shaw's, not Shakespeare's—she can enter a man's world and straighten out its confusions. Her chats with Nerissa are acutely critical of the male sex. Yet, under her "father's imposition," this brilliant woman can neither choose nor refuse her future husband (1.2.26). Such apparent contradictions lend the role a matchless range: enchantress, chatelaine, gossip, hoyden, jurisconsult, prankster, lady-love. It offers the actress, as Hamlet does the actor, an opportunity to play many parts and to dominate the cast.

The amenities of Belmont harbor no escape from the extortions of Venice. Bassanio has no sooner passed his test and been certified as the Lord of Belmont by Portia's ring, than Salerio arrives posthaste with the news of Antonio's jeopardy, and the plots converge in the second scene of act 3. Amid the goings and comings and the adverse reports from high seas, the three-month contract has fallen due all too suddenly. Lorenzo and Jessica have likewise gravitated to Portia's sanctuary and will become its temporary lord and lady during her absence. Here too they will recounter Launcelot Gobbo, whose defection parallels Jessica's—from Shylock's "sober house" to the "shallow fopp'ry" of the merrymakers (2.5.35 f.). Launcelot had introduced himself with the kind of set piece made popular by the clown of Shakespeare's troop, Will Kempe, recalling the farewells of Launce and his dog in *The Two Gentlemen of Verona* and foreshadowing the Porter's monologue in *Macbeth*. Like the Porter, Gobbo acts out a little morality play, in this case a dialogue between Conscience and the Devil. The ethical quandary is complicated because his conscience bids him stay, while the fiend exhorts him to depart—from a house which Jessica will identify with hell (2.2.1 ff.; 2.3.2). When they meet at Belmont he rallies her about her conversion, jesting that it will help to "raise the price of hogs" (3.5.24).

Playing the preacher, he has been threatening her with the scriptural doom for "the sins of the father," unless she plead bastardy (1 f.). He had anticipated her unfilial trickery by an initial trick upon the elder Gobbo, who—notwithstanding his blindness—recognized his "own flesh and blood" (1.2.92). Shylock is bated by Antonio's friends for his repeated lament over the lovers' getaway: "My own flesh and blood to rebel!" (3.1.34, 37, 38 f.). In his vindictive code of an-eye-for-an-eye, this could be a providential avengement upon his scheme to exact the pound of Antonio's flesh, while neglecting the blood. Jessica's rejection may be contrasted with Portia's acceptance of her defunct father's legalisms. Rather than undergo the ordeal of the caskets, Lorenzo has merely to catch the casket of jewels tossed down by Jessica (2.6.33). Shylock's immediate reactions, as reported, verge on sheer bathos. Since he equates his daughter with his ducats, and her apostasy with his precious stones, the Venetian boys seem justified in jeering at his outcries (3.8.15 ff.). When we see and hear him at first hand, he is oscillating grotesquely between grief over his losses and joy over Antonio's, equating his lost diamond with the curse upon his race, and calling simultaneously for the return of the booty and for Jessica's demise (3.1.85–90). These monetary reductions cannot seriously have been meant to engage our sympathies.

Yet, when he learns that Jessica has frivolously bartered away his turquoise ring for a monkey, Shakespeare accords him one touch of common humanity, wryly voiced: "... I had it of Leah when I was a bachelor. I would not have given it for a wilderness of monkeys" (121–23). For an instant we are startled by a glimpse of Shylock as a loving husband, even as we glimpse the ghost of a dutiful daughter in Lady Macbeth's hesitation at Duncan's fatal bedside: "Had he not resembled / My father as he slept, I had done't." Jessica has been criticized severely as a minx, a shameless hussy, the most undutiful of daughters, and Lorenzo has fared no better for supposedly leading her astray. Thematically she reverses the dark legend of the Jew's daughter, utilized to decoy Christian youths toward their ritual murder, which flowers into a miracle in the narration of Chaucer's Prioress or the ballads about Saint Hugh of Lincoln. Shakespeare had a nearer precedent in Marlowe's *Jew of Malta*, where Abigail revolts against her plight, is converted to Christianity, and becomes one of her father's innumerable victims. Barabas, the latter, can be taken as the cynical measure of Shylock's credibility, since his monstrous vendetta is wholly animated by the lust for gold and for the power it confers. His amoral and esthetic paean—"O girl! O gold! O beauty! O my bliss!"—is grimly echoed by Shylock's jeremiad over his daughter and his ducats.

Jessica would suffer by comparison with the pathetic Abigail, if *The Merchant of Venice* were a tragedy. But since it was framed to be a comedy, albeit with a difference, she need not be blamed for surviving to grace the charmed circle of Belmont. Since Shakespeare has treated her sympathetically, we ought not to treat her antipathetically unless we are prepared to censure him. When her prototypes—in works of fiction that must have influenced him—help themselves at the expense of their usurer-fathers, they are turning ill-gotten gains into merited dowries. Her scriptural precursor was Rachel, in the book of Genesis, stealing the paternal effigies. Jessica's flight is essentially a liberation and not a desertion, though it may not seem to be so in the light of latter-day broad-mindedness. From a strictly historical viewpoint, she has been an infidel, born and bred outside the one true faith, and therefore ineligible for salvation. Yet the Christians seem to accept her as an *anima naturaliter christiana*; and Gratiano, with a pun on *Gentile*, declares her "a gentle, and no Jew" (2.5.51). Her baptism, the prerequisite of marriage to Lorenzo, will assure her progress through this world into the next. Such presumptions may not jibe with ours, and certainly do not accord with Shylock's. Antonio's high-minded stipulation, that "he presently become a Christian," is not likely to have been received as a spiritual favor (4.1.387).

With due respect for intellectual background, we should not overstress it to the neglect of dramatic foreground. In characterizing a Jewish outlook and idiom, Shakespeare drew concretely on the Old Testament here and there. But it asks for too much from Belmont, in any excepting the most loosely general terms, to argue that act 5 is imbued with the spirit of the New Testament. A current tendency of criticism, and of production as well, seeks to invest even Shakespeare's lighter comedies with an aura of solemnity. Though *The Merchant of Venice* is by no means light in its implications, it still adheres to the nature of the comic genre by indulging the pleasure principle, which is destined to enjoy the final triumph. Though Jessica and Lorenzo cannot be absolved from the taints of frivolity and extravagance, these are qualities that thrive in the purlieus of high comedy. Lorenzo's metaphor, "For the close night doth play the runaway," has been acted out in the haste of their miniature balcony scene (2.6.47). United with her in the security and serenity of Portia's country estate, he will retrospectively evoke that runaway evening:

> In such a night
> Did Jessica steal from the wealthy Jew,
> And with an unthrift love did run from Venice
> As far as Belmont.
>   (5.1.14–17)

The verb *steal* is his ambiguous acknowledgment that, in their stealthy departure they have burglarized Shylock's ghetto dwelling. And Jessica, in her gently mocking rejoinder, linking crime and religion with love in a metaphysical conceit, will take note of Lorenzo's gallantry, "Stealing her soul with many vows of faith" (19).

The bitterest blow to fall upon Shylock has been their "unthrift love." Wider than the religious distance between them is the opposition between that inveterate miser and this pair of spendthrifts who can lavish fourscore of his austerely hoarded ducats upon a single frolicsome occasion. Comedy, opposed to the asceticism of hoarding, sides implicitly with the hedonism of spending: with the handout as opposed to the hold-in. Liberality, in Aristotelian ethics, is defined as a mean between the extremes of avarice and prodigality. Prodigality, though rather a vice than a virtue, can be construed as the amiable weakness of beautiful people. Bassanio has embarked upon his speculative adventure because his debts have become "something too prodigal" (1.1.129). Shylock tolerates his hospitality, contrary to ethnic principles, so that he may ambiguously and ominously "feed upon / The prodigal Christian" (2.5.14 f.). Antonio, when facing his apparent losses at sea, is prematurely and unjustly stigmatized by Shylock as "a bankrout, a prodigal" (3.1.44

f.). Gratiano, embroidering on the parable, has likened the fortunes of love to those of a maritime enterprise:

> How like a younger or a prodigal
> The scarfed bark puts from her native bay,
> Hugg'd and embraced by the strumpet wind!

This fickle metaphor proceeds to veer about and present, for a crucial interval, a portent of failure:

> How like the prodigal doth she return,
> With over-weather'd ribs and ragged sails,
> Lean, rent, and beggar'd by the strumpet wind!
>   (2.6.14–19)

There can and will be further and happier fluctuations in the long run. The wind, ancillary to the bitch-goddess Fortune, will change again. In the mean time enough has been adumbrated to prepare the way for a season of homecoming, forgiveness, and fatted calf.

The setting for that reunion has been located by most editors in "the avenue before Portia's house"—*avenue* in its horticultural aspect. Theobald would specify "a Grove or Green place"; and the script makes clear that the resident lovers are waiting there to welcome the returning parties on, we might well imagine, a terrace of some sort. A garden, we are never allowed to forget, symbolizes the conceptual norm of Shakespeare's imagery. "Our bodies are our gardens," says Iago. Flowers provide an emblematic language for Ophelia's madness, weeds for Lear's. A literal gardener, in *Richard II*, propounds an allegorical object lesson in statecraft for "our sea-walled garden," England. The Wars of the Roses break out when Yorkists and Lancastrians angrily pluck their floral emblems in the Temple Garden. Jack Cade's rebellion peters out when the rebel leader is run to earth in a peaceful Kentish garden. The Duke of Burgundy points a concluding moral in *Henry V*: vanquished France is "this best garden of the world," whose cultivation should bring peace and plenty—a hopeful prospect not to be attained. Since it is past nightfall in Portia's garden, no attempt is made to describe the foliage; when Oberon evoked the wild thyme and nodding violets on the bank where Titania lay asleep, the resulting sensation was as tactile and olfactory as it was visual. Here the main problem for Shakespeare was to convey an impression of nighttime while the performance was taking place in the daytime.

It may have neutralized disparities for Lorenzo to begin the scene by observing "The moon shines bright" (5.1.1). This is the starting point of the lyrical nightpiece together, "In such a night as this ... ," invoking classic myths of moonlit assignations. Its counterpart in *Romeo and Juliet* is an *aubade*, the duet between lovers parting at dawn, under the dialectical patronage of the lark and the nightingale. The literary examples cited by Lorenzo and Jessica, which derive from Chaucer and Ovid, prove to be more ominous than encouraging. Troilus and Cressida would become the most problematic of Shakespeare's couples. Pyramus and Thisbe he had lately been reducing to burlesque in *A Midsummer Night's Dream* and transmuting into tragedy in *Romeo and Juliet*. Dido, if she was one of Cupid's saints, had become a martyr. Medea was a *femme fatale* with a fearsome record, whose nocturnal rendezvous with Jason was not a tryst but a spell of ghoulish witchcraft. When Berlioz was writing his libretto for *The Trojans*, he would stray from its Virgilian source to his cherished Shakespeare and base the lyrics for his love duet on this exchange of Jessica's and Lorenzo's. Since the singers are Dido and Aeneas, they cannot instance themselves, but they can invoke—more appropriately than Thisbe and Medea—Venus and Diana. One set of role models is twice called upon. "In such a night," Lorenzo whispers,

> Troilus methinks mounted the Troyan walls
> And sigh'd his soul toward the Grecian tents,
> Where Cressid lay that night.
>   (3–6)

This is much less auspicious than the operatic allusion, since she has betrayed him with Diomedes, and he is full of jealousy and sorrow, whereas Aeneas pictures the lover awaiting his beloved in the joyous expectation of fulfilment:

> Par une telle nuit, fou d'amour et de foie,
> Troïlus vint attendre aux pieds des murs de Troie
> La belle Cresside.

The auspices look better, but the outcome will be tragic, whereas the omens in *The Merchant of Venice* are passing clouds in a benevolent sky. When Rosalind, disguised as a pert youth, instances "the patterns of love" in *As You Like It*, she too cites Troilus along with the equally ill-starred Leander. Her sardonic point is that, although they died, it was "not for love." Love may be a universal experience, but it can be less exalting than such romantics as Orlando naively profess. So Jessica and Lorenzo, having striven to "out-night" one another, terminate their litany with an exchange of good-humored mutual reservations (23). Functionally, as the stagewise

Granville-Barker could show, their antiphonal stanzas have sustained the continuity while Portia and Nerissa were changing back from lawyers' robes to feminine attire.

Jessica and Lorenzo are symmetrically interrupted by the messenger Stephano, with his alibi for the arrival of Portia after her pretended pilgrimage, and by the redomesticated Gobbo, mimicking the posthorn that has heralded the coming of Bassanio. There is a brief interlude of anticipation, filled by Lorenzo:

> How sweet the moonlight sleeps upon this bank!
> Here will we sit, and let the sounds of music
> Creep in our ears. Soft stillness and the night
> Become the touches of sweet harmony.
> (54–57)

What stays visible, upward not earthward, is seen in configurations of darkness and light: the sky and the stars, "the floor of heaven" and the "patens of bright gold" (58, 59) that shine through it. These are synesthetically transposed into aural images; and if the singing of angelic choirs is inaudible to mortal ears, like the music of the spheres, corporeal musicians can be summoned to "wake Diana with a hymn" (66). The moon—another amorous predecessor, sleeping with Endymion—must by now have discreetly passed behind a cloud (109). The intensive lyricism of this act, composed wholly in verse, with sound effects and an orchestral nocturne, makes it an appropriate sounding board for Shakespeare's tribute to "the sweet power of music" (79). Jessica's confession, "I am never merry when I hear sweet music," contributes to the bittersweet mood of the play (69). And Lorenzo's ensuing eulogy draws upon both Orphic and Pythagorean traditions to affirm the civilizing functions of harmony and to portend a harmonious resolution. Some of the critics' efforts to put him down as a mere wastrel should be weighed against his humane criterion:

> The man that hath no music in himself,
> Nor is not moved with concord of sweet sounds,
> Is fit for treasons, stratagems, and spoils . . .
> Let no such man be trusted.
> (83–88)

Shylock happens to be such a man, who, in his suspicion of the masked revellers, has admonished Jessica against "the drum / And the vile squealing of the wry-neck'd fife" (2.5.29, 30). And though for him the bagpipe exemplifies an irrational dislike, it could likewise represent the harsh cacophony of his own temperament (4.1.49, 56).

The scenes at Belmont, on the other hand, are counterpointed by melodious fanfares and enhanced with musical accompaniment at two turning points: Bassanio's decision and Portia's reentry. It is significant that although Shakespeare fondly and frequently alludes to music throughout his work, he uses the word itself in *The Merchant of Venice* more often than anywhere else: fifteen times, eleven of them in the last act alone. Browsing through Professor Spevack's concordance affords a convenient and suggestive method of tracing Shakespeare's thematic concerns, as they have been verbally orchestrated. Among the other words we note that reach their highest frequency in this play are *Jew* (69 times), *bond* (39), *ring* (38), *choose* (35), *judge* (24), *flesh* (23), *Christian* (22), *forfeit/forfeiture* (19), *casket* (13), and *hazard* (11). The incidence is high with *law* (19), *justice* (15), and *mercy* (13), yet not as high as in *Measure for Measure*, where comparable issues are at stake (29, 26, and 16 respectively). All of these are key words instrumental to the plot, denoting its situations and interactions. The excessive repetition of the brusque monosyllable *Jew*, rasping across the rift that divides the dramatis personae, emphasizes the alien status of Shylock and the routine contempt of his interlocutors. But the iteration of *music* comes as an extra embellishment, not less welcome because it transposes the mode.

After the discords of Venice we arrive at the concord of Belmont. The Venetian masque was hastily dropped with the suburban flight of act 2; the celebration over the offstage marriages in act 3 had to be put off for the litigation of act 4. Ordeals are duly overtaken by revels, with the grand finale of act 5, carrying out the mischievous scenario that Portia has spontaneously devised while pursuing her legal career. Day is the time for affairs of business, night for escapades of imagination. It is dark when she enters, but not too dark, no more than "the daylight sick" (5.1.124). Her colloquy with Nerissa, like the preceding repartee of Jessica and Lorenzo, trips along from images of light to those of sound. Relativistic comparisons—beginning with the moon and the candle, moving on to the lark and the crow and other birds, and culminating in the day and the night—lead into a brittle sequence of sententious quips.

> How far this little candle throws his beams!
> So shines a good deed in a naughty world.
>   (90 f.)

This motif of glimmering through the darkness, figuratively as well as physically, pervades the entire scene. "Everything in its season" is the burden of her remarks, signalizing both the round of the seasons and their seasoning effect upon those who have weathered them (107 f.). Gradually she is discerned and greeted by Lorenzo, just as the trumpet announced the entrance of Bassanio's party. Gradually picking up her train of thought, he hails her with a trope of solar brilliance. She acknowledges the standard compliment with a standard quibble on *light*, connoting loose behavior as well as illumination, and thereby interjecting a coquettish hint of marital infidelity (129–31).

He proceeds to introduce the guest of honor, Antonio, who has celebrated his acquittal by crossing from Venice to Belmont: "the man ... / To whom I am so infinitely bound." Bassanio has always been *attached* to Antonio; moreover, he is now doubly *indebted* to him, in the deepest conceivable sense; and Portia's reply adds a trenchant reminder of the contract in the recent law case:

> You should in all sense be much bound to him,
> For as I hear he was much bound for you.
>   (134–37)

The energy of the monosyllables is reinforced by the parallellism of the lines, the catchword occupying the same position in both and controlling the transposition from "him" to "you." We are reminded of Shylock's laconic and equivocal answer to Bassanio at the very outset: "Antonio shall become bound, well" (1.3.6). At the height of his pride, when he had all but succeeded in fatally binding Antonio, Shylock rebuffed Bassanio's appeal by asserting his own independence: "I am not bound to please thee with my answers" (4.1.65). His insistence on the bond reechoed through the court, accentuated by that device which the rhetoricians term *epistrophe*, the repeated locution at the end of a line. "Is it so nominated in the bond" (259)? Could any rhetorical question have been more implacable? Shylock's household wisdom was summed up when he ordered Jessica to shift the doors:

> Fast bind, fast find—
> A proverb never stale in thrifty mind.
>   (2.5.54 f.)

But, for better and worse, she will not bind and he will not find. He has no more luck in shutting out the world, in holding Jessica and his goods bound fast, than he will have in entrapping Antonio. She has not loved her father, as Cordelia loves Lear, "according to my bond"; she rejects, like Goneril and Regan, "the bond of childhood," her family ties; yet Jessica's recoil has been warranted by overriding considerations.

Portia's gracious reception of Antonio is cut short by the farcical outburst between Nerissa and Gratiano. As the young lawyer Balthazar, she
has demanded Bassanio's ring for her fee. Gratiano has been his emissary in
reluctantly yielding it up; and his corresponding transaction with Nerissa,
as the sham law clerk, has been effectuated behind the scenes. It is fit-
ting—and it builds up the humorous progression—that Portia should stand
above the battle judiciously, until Gratiano's self-defense exposes her mis-
placed confidence in Bassanio. His effort to allay her mock-suspicion sets
them off on what might be called a blank-verse *pas de deux*. "Sweet Portia,"
he pleads,

> If you did know to whom I gave the ring,
> If you did know for whom I gave the ring,
> And would conceive for what I gave the ring,
> And how unwillingly I left the ring,
> When nought would be accepted but the ring,
> You would abate the strength of your displeasure.

Since she is actually the person to whom he gave the ring, she well knows
for whom and for what it was given, and with what reluctance. It is he who is
ironically unaware that she knows, that she was the civil doctor, and that she
has the ring—whose erstwhile disappearance is deftly stressed by the terminal syllables in a rising succession of conditional clauses. But she can also
out-ring him, epistrophe for epistrophe, as fluently as she has outmatched
the spokesmen of masculine jurisprudence:

> If you had known the virtue of the ring,
> Or half her worthiness that gave the ring,
> Or your own honor to contain the ring,
> You would not then have parted with the ring.
>   (192–202)

Momentarily it seems as if Shakespeare were inviting the director to become
a choreographer. The dancing is more formal in the finales of many other
comedies, and the Elizabethan theater regularly featured song-and-dance
afterpieces known as "jigs." But I recall a eurythmic blocking of this passage
where Portia turned her back and promenaded the stage, followed at several
paces by Bassanio, each of them taking a single step per line and pausing
at every repetition of ring. At a more psychological level, the gamesman-
ship resembles the last-act manoeuvres in *The Marriage of Figaro*, another

garden scene at night both in the comedy of Beaumarchais and the opera
of Da Ponte and Mozart, where the men are absurdly hoodwinked by the
mistaken identities of the women.

Gratiano has operated as a zany to Bassanio, the jocular subaltern who
goes through the same motions as his mentor with a parodic exaggeration.
From the beginning he elected to "play the fool," when Antonio declared his
own part to be "a sad one" upon the world's stage (1.1.79). Bassanio rebuked
that "skipping spirit" for being "too wild, too rude, and bold of voice" (2.2.187,
181). Gratiano's conversational style, "an infinite deal of nothing," bears a
generic resemblance to that of Shakespeare's other free-speakers: Mercutio,
Berowne, Benedick, and in another key Hotspur (1.1.112). In Gratiano's *con-
tretemps* with Nerissa, he parries her suspicions about the missing ring by
describing its recipient—herself in her disguise—as "a little scrubbed boy"
(5.1.162). Her tactic is to push the accusation, which no one could appreciate
better than she, that this boy was a woman: "The clerk will ne'er wear hair
on's face that had it" (144). Portia's equivocations to Bassanio go farther, and
express a resolve to get even by a reciprocal adultery: "I'll have that doctor for
my bedfellow"—that doctor being, in actuality, her virginal self (233). Nor
does she deny herself anything in saying: "By heaven, I will ne'er come in
your bed / Until I see the ring" (190 f.). Such conjugal tests continually and
increasingly bring home to us the awareness that these marriages have yet to
be consummated, that bed lies ahead.

It is Antonio, Antonio unbound, lone bachelor in the presence of three
couples newly united by "love's bonds," who intervenes to halt the flirtatious
charade (2.6.6). Typically, he characterizes himself as "th'unhappy subject of
these quarrels" (5.1.237). It was he who opened the play on a note of sadness:
"In sooth I know not why I am so sad" (1.1.1). In linking his free-float-
ing anxiety with the fortunes of his ships at sea, Salerio and Solanio then
painted an incidental picture of his mercantile position. That might well have
served to diagnose a justifiable premonition, but Antonio rejected the motive,
as he did the suggestion of love. Conscious of his moody role, like Jaques,
who would expatiate upon their simile of the *theatrum mundi*, he cultivates
a special melancholy of his own. Among his cohort of friends, who warmly
attest his moral and fiscal worth, he reserves a unique affection for Bassanio.
"I think he only loves the world for him," Solanio remarks (2.8.50). When
Antonio philosophically accepts the unrelenting decree, he addresses his farewell to Bassanio, requesting him to tell his new wife about it,

And when the tale is told, bid her be the judge
Whether Bassanio had not once a love.
    (4.1.276 f.)

This is the point at which Bassanio, seconded by Gratiano as usual, wishes that his wife could be traded for Antonio's life, prompting dryly appropriate comments from Portia and Nerissa and a caustic aside from Shylock reflecting against his new son-in-law: "These are the Christian husbands" (295). Portia—who is the judge right now—has beforehand, on the basis of Lorenzo's report, accepted Antonio as "the bosom lover of my lord" (3.4.17). Modern readers have sometimes scented a homosexual relation. That supposition would not explain why Bassanio courted Portia, or why Antonio backed the courtship so generously. "Greater love hath no man than this . . ." But the mortal sacrifice envisioned by the Gospel of Saint John altogether transcended sexuality. Though Antonio is not a saint, he seems to live vicariously, ready to die for the happiness of another. *The Merchant of Venice* does not strain the issue of love versus friendship, as do *The Two Gentlemen of Verona* and the *Sonnets*, though it may put some strain on our credulity.

Yet if we suspend our disbelief in the vagaries of male impersonation, we ought not to balk too much at milder improbabilities. Shakespeare had the convention of boy actors so well in hand that he liked to mock it, and Portia gayly seizes the chance to burlesque the other sex: "these bragging Jacks" (3.4.77). Helena, her opposite number in *All's Well That Ends Well*, likewise scores a professional success, after disguising herself as a physician, and wins her errant husband's ring through a less innocent wile than Portia's, the bed-trick. The loan of a ring was among the traditional devices for misunderstanding in *The Comedy of Errors*. Jessica's romance with Lorenzo is colored with touches of the carnivalesque. Since the actual wooing of Portia must be conducted as a ceremonial, there has been little opportunity for open flirtation until this final episode. Portia has been more and more effectually in charge, pulling all the strings like Rosalind in *As You Like It*. Nominally she may have deprecated herself as an unschooled girl and made Bassanio lord and master of her person and property with the gift of the ring. But—mistress of it once more—she makes a fool of him by her fifth-act joke, after having outwitted the males by her fourth-act verdict. There should be no feminist capitulation for her, as there was for Katherina in *The Taming of the Shrew*.

When Antonio pleads with Portia, offering "to be bound again" as security for his friend, she precipitates the denouement by producing the bone of contention (5.1.251). It is she who presides over the recognition scene, clearing up the misunderstandings and handing out the prizes. Antonio's argosies have come safe to harbor after all, though how she obtained the good news will remain her secret forever. And, when Nerissa informs Jessica and Lorenzo of Shylock's bequest, Lorenzo's response is becomingly biblical: "Fair ladies, you drop manna in the way / Of starving people" (294 f.). Threats of cuckoldry are dissolved in jests, for Bassanio and Gratiano, with the disclosure that their shadowy rivals have been their own wives incognito. Within two hours the night—such a night!—will be over. To suggest that these lovers might just as well stay up through another day, and thus delay the consummation further, is no more than teasing. Conventionally, the happy endings of comedy have been formalized by revelry, by feasts or dances with a mating or betrothal in view: from the *gamos* of Aristophanes, with its phallic procession, to the tutelary blessing of the god Hymen for the four assorted couples in *As You Like It*. Here, since the weddings have already taken place, it is high time for the privacy of the bridal chamber.

There, between the postponed embraces, the spouses can complete their "inter'gatories," mutually filling in the details by reverting metaphorically to the cross-questioning of the courtroom (298). As they retire into the villa, two by two, extinguishing the candles in the garden, Antonio remains the lonely celibate, observably less at home in Belmont than in Venice. Like the melancholy Jaques—and not unlike the unpartnered Bunthorne in *Patience*—he is the odd man out, who must conclude: "I am for other than dancing measures." The dialogue has waxed increasingly erotic, charging the air with double entendres, and the saltiest diction has been Gratiano's. Under the misapprehension that Nerissa may have regained the ring by dalliance with her alter ego, he has sworn to "mar the young clerk's pen" (237). Revelation is metamorphosis; that boy—it transpires—was a girl, his girl; and his attitude shifts from aggressiveness to protectiveness. Yet he lapses, with his ultimate couplet, into another genital innuendo:

Well, while I live I'll fear no other thing
So sore, as keeping safe Nerissa's ring.
    (306 f.)

In this context it might not be improper to remember the fabliau of Hans Carvel's ring. That became available in English through the ribald poem of Matthew Prior, adapted from the *Contes* of La Fontaine; but it could be read during the Renaissance in versions by Rabelais, Ariosto, and others; and it is one of those facetious anecdotes that was bound to be passed along by word of mouth. Therein an old and cold jeweller takes a young and promiscuous wife. He is advised by the Devil how to curb her promiscuity: by permanently keeping his third finger encircled within her. Gratiano, to be sure, may imply that there are other and better ways of accomplishing that purpose. Shakespeare's own high-spirited wordplay loses no occasion for reminding us that men are males, that women are females, and *vive la différence!* The last word is the key word that brings us back to the digital symbol of the conjugal bond. The ring itself, the tie that binds, has also been proposed as a legal fee, in a milieu where ducats are worth their weight in daughters and where a pound of flesh could be the contractual consideration for three thousand ducats. Thus, as Barbara Lewalski has argued on other grounds, "The ring episode is, in a sense, a comic parody of the trial scene."

In concern over Portia's and Nerissa's rings, we have nearly forgotten Leah's ring and what it signified to her husband if not her daughter. Why have these revels been staged, if not to put Shylock out of our minds, to awaken us from the throes of a nightmare? Yet, with Shakespeare, the query always lingers: which is the reality, which the dream? Shylock the killjoy must be scoffed out of court; Shylock the spoilsport must be exorcised from the realm of comic euphoria. We ought not to sentimentalize this self-chosen scapegoat. Olivia can afford a soft valediction for Malvolio in *Twelfth Night*: "He hath been most notoriously abus'd." But he must go, and go he does, impenitently and ineffectually vengeful: "I'll be reveng'd on the whole pack of you." We waste no grief on him—why so much grief over Shylock? "He doesn't cast a shadow sufficiently strong," in Edwin Booth's opinion, "to contrast with the sunshine of the comedy." Other actors, however, have tried to exalt him into a tragic hero. Erich Auerbach would situate him at the borderline, an odd pariah originating in farce, voicing certain humanitarian ideas that have acquired a deeper resonance during later centuries, yet finally capitulating as a "duped devil" ("geprellter Teufel") before the "careless Olympian serenity" ("achtlos olympische Heiterkeit") of fairytale motifs and tender blandishments.

"To make him a tragic hero . . . ," Auerbach has written, "clashes with the whole dramatic economy." Others would contend that, through the figure of Shylock, such a clash is built into the drama. Dr. Johnson praised "the union of two actions in one event." So did Bertolt Brecht, though from quite another dramaturgical standpoint. Unity, which Brecht might not have emphasized, depends on Shylock's total exclusion from act 5. He is not even named, except for Portia's mention of "the rich Jew" and the reversion of his fortune "after his death" (292 f.). Yet, because the characterization has conveyed so powerful an impact, his shadow has continued to haunt the sunny purlieus of Belmont. In the French adaptation performed by the actor-director Firmin Gémier, Shylock chilled the honeymoon by making an untimely reappearance in Portia's garden. To his conventional attributes—the hooked nose, the forked beard, the red curls, the jewelled fingers, the pantaloon's cap, the tribal gabardine—Gémier added a hangman's noose. The intrusion was an unwarrantable distortion, but it all too heavily underlined a besetting Shakespearean point: that happiness, in one way or another, is seldom unconnected with suffering. Joy cannot be unconfined, when such joylessness can still be humanly instigated. But to pursue that insight, as Barber suggested, would require an additional play.

And significantly, in spite of its carefully planned conclusion, this play has given rise to a train of sequels, most of them dedicated to the vindication of Shylock. A sense of unfinished business seems to have led the Irish playwright St. John Ervine to a disillusioning postlude, *The Lady of Belmont*, wherein—though Shylock makes a painless financial comeback—the wedded lovers succumb to boredom or resort to adultery ten years afterward. Maurice Schwartz, in *Shylock and His Daughter*, grounded upon a post-Nazi Hebrew novel, relocated characters within the ghetto of Venice and tried to work out an uneasy reconciliation. One of the objections to comedy, and to most fiction, is that real human beings can never count on living happily ever after. Since this truism is intimated by *The Merchant of Venice*, it looks beyond its genre. Some may perceive in it, with W. H. Auden, "as much a problem play as one by Ibsen or Shaw." Such approaches, while sharpening its focus, have narrowed its range. Granted, the problems it raises for us were too easily, and factitiously, solved by the ideologies and conventions of Shakespeare's day. His gift for humanizing and intensifying his subject matter projected it into an unforeseeable future, so that we can now look back at it and consider it timely. By the same token, it is subject to continuing vicissitude, and no problem it broaches can expect a final solution.

TONY TANNER

Which Is the Merchant Here? And Which the Jew?: The Venice of Shakespeare's Merchant of Venice

see how yond justice rails upon yond simple thief. Hark in thine ear: change places, and handy-dandy, which is the justice, which is the thief?

(*King Lear* IV.vi.151–4)

When Portia, disguised as Balthasar, "a young and learned doctor", enters the Court of Justice in *The Merchant of Venice*, her first, business-like, question is "Which is the merchant here? And which the Jew?" (IV.i.173) It is an astonishing question. We know that Shylock would have been dressed in a "gaberdine", because, we are told, Antonio habitually spits on it. This was a long garment of hard cloth habitually worn by Jews who, since 1412, had been obliged to wear a distinctive robe extending down to the feet. Shylock would have been, literally, a 'marked' man (in a previous century he would have had to wear a yellow hat). Antonio, a rich merchant who, we are again told, habitually comes "so smug upon the mart" (where 'smug' means sleek and well-groomed, as well as our sense of complacently self-satisfied), is more likely to have been dressed in some of the 'silk' in which he trades (look at the sumptuously dressed Venetian merchants in Carpaccio's paintings to get some idea). It would have been unmissably obvious which was the merchant and which was the Jew. So, is that opening question just disingenuousness on Portia/Balthasar's part—or what?

The first act is composed of three scenes set in the three (relatively) discrete places, or areas, each of which has its distinct voices, values, and concerns.

From *Venetian Views, Venetian Blinds: English Fantasies of Venice*, edited by Manfred Pfister and Barbara Schaff, pp. 45–62. Copyright © 1999 by Editions Rodopi B.V.

Together, they make up the world of the play. I will call these—Rialto Venice; Belmont (Portia's house, some indeterminate distance from Venice; probably best thought of as being like one of those lovely Renaissance palaces still to be seen in the Veneto); and Ghetto Venice (Shylock's realm: the word 'ghetto' never appears in the play, and, as John Gross has pointed out, Shakespeare makes no mention of it. But the name *Ghetto Nuovo* (meaning New Foundry) was the name of the island in Venice on which the Jews were, effectively, sequestered (and from which the generic use of 'ghetto' derives); and, clearly, Shylock lives in a very different Venice from the Venice enjoyed by the confident Christian merchants. Hence my metaphoric use of the name for what, in Shakespeare, is simply designated as 'a public place'). The opening lines of the three scenes are, in sequence:

In sooth I know not why I am so sad.
It wearies me, you say it wearies you . . .

By my troth, Nerissa, my little body is aweary of this great world.

Three thousand ducats—well.

Sadness and weariness on the Rialto and in Belmont; money matters in the Ghetto. Is there any inter-connection? Can anything be done?

Antonio speaks first, which is quite appropriate since *he* is the 'Merchant' of the title—not, as some think, Shylock. Had Shakespeare wanted Shylock signalled in his title, he could well have called his play *The Jew of Venice*, in appropriate emulation of Marlowe's *The Jew of Malta* (1589), which was playing in London in 1596 when Shakespeare (almost certainly) started his own play, and which he (most certainly) knew and, indeed, deliberately echoed at certain key points (of which, more by and by). But Shylock is a very different figure from Barabas, who degenerates into a grotesque Machiavellian monster. In fact, Shylock only appears in five of the twenty scenes of the play; though he is, overwhelmingly, the figure who leaves the deepest mark—'incision' perhaps (see later)—on the memory. He shuffles off, broken, beaten, and ill—sadder and wearier than anyone else in Venice or Belmont—at the end of Act Four, never to return. But, while the triumph and victory belong unequivocally to Portia, it is the Jew's play.

However, Antonio is our merchant, and very Hamlet-ish he is, too. He sounds an opening note of inexplicable melancholy:

But how I caught it, found it, or came by it,
What stuff 'tis made of, whereof it is born, I am to learn . . . (I,i,3–5)

We might later have a guess at at least some of the 'stuff' it is made of, but for now Salerio and Solanio (another of those effectively indistinguishable Rosencrantz-and-Guildenstern couples Shakespeare delights in—it offers another 'which-is-which?' puzzle in a lighter key), try to commiserate with him and cheer him up. And in their two speeches, Shakespeare—breathtakingly—manages to convey a whole sense of mercantile Renaissance Venice. Of course, they say, you are understandably worried—"your mind is tossing on the ocean"—about your "argosies" (a very recent English word for large merchant ships, coming from the Venetian Adriatic port of Ragusa—and also used in Marlowe's play). Salerio, packing all the pride and confident arrogance of imperial, incomparable Venice into his lines, imagines those ships as "rich burghers on the flood", or "pageants [magnificent floats in festival and carnival parades] of the sea", which

> Do overpeer the petty traffickers
> That cursy [curtsy] to them, do them reverence,
> As they fly by them with their woven wings. (I,i,12–14)

Other sea-faring traders are "petty traffickers": Venetian merchants, attracting and exacting world-wide admiration and deference, are something quite superbly else. Solanio chimes in, evoking a merchant's necessary anxieties about winds, maps, ports, piers, and everything that, he says, "might make me fear / Misfortune to my ventures"—'ventures' is a word to watch. Salerio develops the theme, imagining how everything he saw on land would somehow remind him of shipwrecks:

> Should I go to church
> And see the holy edifice of stone
> And not bethink me straight of dangerous rocks,
> Which touching but my gentle vessel's side
> Would scatter all her spices on the stream,
> Enrobe the roaring waters with my silks—
> And in a word, but even now worth this,
> And now worth nothing? (I,i,29–36)

"But now a king, now thus", says Salisbury when he watches King John die, pondering the awesome mortality of kings (*King John* V,vii,60). In this Venice, there is much the same feeling about the loss of one of their argosies, monarchs (or burghers—it was a republic) of the sea as they were. And what a sense of riches is compacted into the lines imagining spices scattered on

the stream, and waves robed in silk—an image of spilt magnificence if ever
there was one.

It is important to note Salerio's reference to "church ... the holy edifice
of stone". In one of those contrasts dear to artists, the stillness and fixity of the
holy edifice of stone is to be seen behind the flying ships on the tossing oceans
and flowing streams––the eternal values of the church conjoined with, and
in some way legitimating, the worldly wealth-gathering of the sea-venturing,
transient merchants; the spiritual ideals sustaining the material practices. For
Venice was a holy city (the Crusades left from there), as well as the centre of a
glorious worldly empire. It was an object of awe and fascination to the Elizabethans. Indeed, as Philip Brockbank suggested, Venice was for Renaissance writers what Tyre was for the prophet Isaiah—"the crowning city, whose merchants
are princes, whose traffickers are the honourable of the earth" (*Isaiah* 23:8). But
Tyre was also a "harlot" who made "sweet music", and Isaiah prophesies that it
"shall commit fornication with all the kingdoms of the world" (Venice was also
famed, or notorious, for its alleged sensualities—in Elizabethan London there
was a brothel simply named 'Venice'). But, also this about Tyre:

> And her merchandise and her hire shall be holiness to the Lord:
> for it shall not be treasured nor laid up; for her merchandise shall
> be for them that dwell before the Lord, to eat sufficiently, and for
> durable clothing. (23:18)

Traditionally, religion is ascetic and preaches a rejection of worldly goods.
But here we see religion and the 'use of riches' creatively reconciled—and
by spending, not hoarding. As Tyre, so Venice. But there is, in *Isaiah*, an
apocalyptic warning—that God will turn the whole city "upside down" and
"scatter" the inhabitants—

> And it shall be, as with the people, so with the priest ... as with the
> buyer, so with the seller; as with the lender, so with the borrower;
> as with the taker of usury, so with the giver of usury to him. The
> land shall be utterly emptied, and utterly spoiled: for the Lord hath
> spoken this word. (24:2,3)

Ruskin would say that that was effectively what *did* happen to Venice. But that
is another story. The point for us here is that the Venetian setting of his play
allowed Shakespeare to pursue his exploratory interest in (I quote Brockbank)

> the relationship between the values of empire and those of the
> aspiring affections, human and divine; those of the City of Man

and those of the City of God … between the values we are encouraged to cultivate in a mercantile, moneyed and martial society, and those which are looked for in Christian community and fellowship; between those who believe in the gospel teachings of poverty, humility and passivity, and those who (as the creative hypocrisy requires) pretend to.

Returning to the play, Solanio says that if Antonio is not sad on account of his "merchandise", then he must be in love. Antonio turns away the suggestion with a "Fie, fie!". As it happens, I think this is close to the mark, but we will come to that. Here Solanio gives up on trying to find a reason for Antonio's gloom—

> Then let us say you are sad
> Because you are not merry; and 'twere as easy
> For you to laugh and leap, and say you are merry. (I,i,47–9)

And he leaves with Salerio, who says to Antonio—"I would have stayed till I had made you merry". 'Merry' is a lovely word from old English, suggesting pleasing, amusing, agreeable, full of lively enjoyment. "To be merry best becomes you," says Don Pedro to the vivacious Beatrice "for out o' question, you were born in a merry hour" (*Much Ado* II,i,313–4)—and we feel he has chosen just the right word. The princely merchants of Venice favour the word, for, in their aristocratic way, they believe in 'merriment'. It is an unequivocally positive word; it has no dark side, and carries no shadow. Yet in this play, Shakespeare makes it become ominous. When Shylock suggests to Antonio that he pledges a pound of his flesh as surety for the three thousand ducat loan, he refers to it as a "merry bond", signed in a spirit of "merry sport" (I,iii,170,142). The word has lost its innocence and is becoming sinister. The last time we hear it is from Shylock's daughter, Jessica in Belmont—"I am never merry when I hear sweet music" (V,i,69). After her private duet with Lorenzo, nobody speaks to Jessica in Belmont and these are, indeed, her last words in the play. It is hard to feel that she will be happily assimilated into the Belmont world. Something has happened to 'merryness', and although Belmont is, distinctly, an abode of "sweet music", a note of un-merry sadness lingers in the air.

* * *

When Bassanio enters with Gratiano, he says to the departing Salerio and Solanio, as if reproachfully, "You grow exceeding strange; must it be so?"

(I,i,67) It is a word which recurs in a variety of contexts, and it reminds us that there is 'strangeness' in Venice, centring on Shylock, whose "strange apparent cruelty" (IV,i,21) is some sort of reflection of, response to, the fact that he is treated like "a stranger cur" (I,iii,115) in Venice. And he is, by law, an alien in the city—the stranger within. Gratiano then has a go at Antonio—"You look not well, Signior Antonio" ("I am not well", says Shylock, as he leaves the play—IV,i,395: now the merchant, now the Jew. Sickness circulates in Venice, along with all the other 'trafficking').

> You have too much respect upon the world;
> They lose it that do buy it with much care.
> Believe me, you are marvelously changed. (I,i,74–6)

His scripture is a little awry here: what people lose who gain the whole world is the *soul*, not the world. A *mondain* Venetian's slip, perhaps. But we are more likely to be alerted by the phrase 'marvelously changed'. Shakespearian comedy is full of marvellous changes, and we may be considering what transformations, marvellous or otherwise, occur in this play. In the event, the 'changes' turn out to be far from unambiguous 'conversions'. Somewhere behind all these conversions is the absolutely basic phenomenon whereby material is converted into 'merchandise' which is then converted into money—which, as Marx said, can then convert, or 'transform' just about anything into just about anything else. It is perhaps worth remembering that Marx praised Shakespeare, in particular, for showing that money had the power of a god, while it behaved like a whore.

Jessica willingly converts to Christianity, hoping for salvation, at least from her father's house, but it hardly seems to bring, or promise, any notable felicity or grace. Shylock is forced to convert to Christianity—which, however construed by the Christians (he would thereby be 'saved'), is registered as a final humiliation and the stripping away of the last shred of his identity. When Portia gives herself to Bassanio, she says:

> Myself, and what is mine, to you and yours
> Is now converted. (III,ii,166–7)

and this is to be felt as a willing conversion, a positive transformation—just as she will, like a number of other heroines, 'change' herself into a man to effect some genuine salvation. Sad Antonio, it has to be said, is not much changed at all at the end—though his life has been saved, and his ships have come sailing in. Venice itself, as represented, is hardly changed; not, that is, renewed or redeemed—though it is a good deal more at ease with itself for having got rid of Shylock. If that is what it *has* done. One hardly feels that, as it were, the realm has been purged, and that the malcontent threatening the joy of the festive conclusion has been happily exorcised. The play does not really end quite so 'well' as that. It is not a 'metamorphic' celebration.

It is Bassanio's plea for financial help from Antonio that concludes the first scene, and the way in which he does so is crucial to an appreciation of what follows. He admits that he has "disabled mine estate" by showing "a more swelling port" than he could afford. 'Swelling port' is 'impressively lavish life-style', but I think we will remember the 'portly sail' of the Venetian argosies just referred to, also, no doubt, 'swollen' by the winds (cf the 'big-bellied sails' in *A Midsummer Night's Dream*). The Venetian princely way of life is both pregnant and distended—fecund and excessive. As Bassanio is, however inadvertently, recognising by using a key word: he is worried about his 'great debts':

> Wherein my time, something too prodigal,
> Hath left me gaged. (I,ii,1490–50)

Shylock calls Antonio a "prodigal Christian", and it was always a fine point to decide to what extent 'prodigality' was compatible with Christianity (think of the parables of the Prodigal Son, and the Unjust Steward), and to what extent it contravened it. It is one of those words which look two ways, pointing in one direction to the magnanimous bounty of an Antony, and in the other to the ruinous squandering of a Timon. Clearly, the munificent prodigality of Antonio is in every way preferable to the obsessive meanness and parsimony of Shylock. But there is a crucial speech on this subject, tucked away, as was sometimes Shakespeare's wont, where you might least expect it. Salerio and Gratiano are whiling away the time in front of Shylock's house, waiting to help Lorenzo in the abduction of Jessica. Salerio is saying that lovers are much more eager to consummate the marriage than they are to remain faithful ('keep obliged faith') subsequently. "That ever holds" says Gratiano:

> All things that are
> Are with more spirit chased than enjoyed.
> How like a younger or a prodigal
> The scarfed bark puts from her native bay,
> Hugged and embraced by the strumpet wind!
> How like the prodigal doth she return,
> With over-weathered ribs and ragged sails,
> Lean, rent, and beggared by the strumpet wind. (II,vi,12–19)

An apt enough extended metaphor in a mercantile society, and the Venetians must have seen many ship sail out 'scarfed' (decorated with flags and streamers) and limp back 'rent'. It may be added that Gratiano is something of a cynical young blade. But the speech stands as a vivid reminder of one possible fate of 'prodigality', *and* of marriage. Ultimately of Venice too, perhaps.

Bassanio, whatever else he is (scholar, courtier) is a 'prodigal', and he wants to clear his 'debts'. Antonio immediately says that "my purse, my person" (a nice near pun, given the close inter-involvement of money and body in this play) "lie all unlocked to your occasions" (I,i,139). This open liberality might be remembered when we later hear the frantically retentive and self-protective Shylock (a name not found outside this play) repeatedly warning Jessica to "look to my house ... lock up my doors ... shut doors after you" (II,v,16,29,52). The difference is clear enough, and need not be laboured. Antonio also positively invites Bassanio to "make waste of all I have" (I,i,157)—insouciantly negligent aristocrats like to practise what Yeats called 'the wasteful virtues'. The contrast with 'thrifty' Shylock, again, does not need underlining.

But Bassanio has another possible solution to his money problems; one which depends on 'adventuring' and 'hazard'.

> In Belmont is a lady richly left;
> And she is fair and, fairer than that word,
> Of wondrous virtues ...
> Nor is the wide world ignorant of her worth,
> For the four winds blow in from every coast
> Renowned suitors, and her sunny locks
> Hang on her temples like a golden fleece,
> Which makes her seat of Belmont Colchos' strand,
> And many Jasons come in quest of her.
> O my Antonio, had I but the means
> To hold a rival place with one of them,
> I have a mind presages me such thrift
> That I should questionless be fortunate! (I,i,161–176)

Antonio, all his wealth at sea, at the moment has neither "money, nor commodity"; but he will use his "credit" to get "the means". He will borrow the *money* from Shylock to finance Bassanio's quest of a second *golden* fleece. So it is that the seemingly discrete worlds of the Ghetto, the Rialto, and Belmont are, from the beginning, indeed, interinvolved.

Venice, as we have seen it and will see it, is overwhelmingly a man's world of public life; it is conservative, dominated by law, bound together by contracts, underpinned by money—and closed. Belmont is run by women living the private life; it is liberal, animated by love, harmonised by music and poetry ('fancy'), sustained by gold—and open. However cynical one wants to be, it will not do to see Belmont as "only Venice come into a windfall" (Ruth Nevo). It is better to see it as in a line of civilised, gracious retreats, stretching from Horace's Sabine farm, through Sidney's Penshurst, Jane Austen's Mansfield Park, up to Yeats's Coole Park. As Brockbank said, such places ideally offered "the prospect of a protected life reconciling plenitude, exuberance, simplicity and order." It was Sidney who said that "our world is brazen, the poets only deliver a golden", and you might see Belmont as a kind of 'golden' world which has been 'delivered' from the 'brazen' world of trade and money. Yes, somewhere back along the line, it is all grounded in ducats; but you must think of the churches, palaces, art works and monuments of the Renaissance, made possible by varying forms of patronage, and appreciate that the "courtiers, merchants and bankers of the Renaissance found ways of transmuting worldly goods into spiritual treasure" (Brockbank). Belmont is a privileged retreat from Venice; but, as Portia will show, it can also fruitfully engage with it.

In scene two, we are in Belmont, and Portia is weary. Partly surely, because she must be bored stiff with the suitors who have come hopefully buzzing round the honey-pot—the silent Englishman, the mean Scotsman, the vain Frenchman, the drunken German, and so on, as she and Nerissa amuse themselves discussing their different intolerabilities. But, more importantly, because she is under the heavy restraint of a paternal interdiction (familiar enough in comedy, though this one comes from beyond the grave). She has been deprived of *choice*—and she wants a mate. Then we learn from Nerissa about the lottery of the casquets, which she thinks was the "good inspiration" of a "virtuous" and "holy" man. We shall see. But we note that, in this, Belmont (in the form of Portia) is as much under the rule of (male) law as Venice. There are "laws for the blood" in both places, and they may by no means be "leaped" or "skipped" over (I,ii,17ff.). In other comedies, we see inflexible, intractable, unmitigatable law magically, mysteriously melt away or be annulled. Not in this play. Here, the law is followed, or pushed, to the limit—and beyond. Indeed, you might say that Belmont has to come to Venice to help discover this 'beyond' of the law.

And now, in scene three, we are in Shylock's Venice; and we hear, for the first time, what will become an unmistakable voice—addressing, as it were, the bottom line in Venice: "three thousand ducats—well". Shylock speaks in—unforgettable—prose, and this marks something of a crucial departure for Shakespeare. Hitherto, he had reserved prose for, effectively, exclusively comic (usually 'low') characters. With Shylock, this all changes. For Shylock is *not* a comic character. He has a power, a pain, a passion, a dignity—and, yes, a savagery, and a suffering—which, whatever they are, are not comic.

On his first appearance, Shylock establishes his 'Jewishness' by, among other things, revealing his adherence to Jewish dietary rules—"I will not eat with you, drink with you, nor pray with you" (I,iii,34–5). But when Antonio appears, Shylock reveals a darker side of his nature in an 'aside':

> I hate him for he is a Christian;
> But more, for that in low simplicity
> He lends out money gratis, and brings down
> The rate of usance here with us in Venice.
> . . .
> He hates our sacred nation, and he rails,
> Even there where merchants most do congregate,
> On me, my bargains, and my well-won thrift,
> Which he calls interest. Cursed be my tribe
> If I forgive him. (I,iii,39–49)

Shylock gives three good reasons for his hating of Antonio—insofar as one can have *good* reasons for hatred: personal, professional, tribal. This is interesting in view of his response during the trial scene, when he is asked why he would not prefer to have ducats rather than Antonio's flesh:

> So can I give no reason, nor I will not,
> More than a lodged hate and a certain loathing
> I bear Antonio . . . (IV,i,59–61)

His opening exchange with Antonio really defines the central concern of the play, and is crucial. He has already mentioned 'usance' ('a more cleanly name for usury'), 'thrift' (which means both prosperity and frugality—'thrift, Horatio, thrift'), and 'interest'. And 'usury', of course, is the heart of the matter. Any edition of the play will tell you that the law against lending money at interest was lifted in 1571, and a rate of 10% was made legal. Queen Elizabeth depended on money borrowed at interest, so did most agriculture, industry, and foreign trade by the end of the sixteenth century (according to R. H. Tawney). So, indeed, did Shakespeare's own Globe Theatre. Plenty of Christians lent money at interest (including Shakespeare's own father); and Bacon, writing "Of Usury" in 1625, said "to speak of the abolishing of usury is idle". Antonio, scattering his interest-free loans around Venice, is certainly an 'idealised' picture of the merchant, just as Shylock sharpening his knife to claim his debt, is a 'demonised' one. But Aristotle and

Christianity had spoken against usury, and there was undoubtedly a good deal of residual unease and ambivalence about it. Ruthless usurers were thus especially hated and abused, and since Jews were identified as quintessential usurious money-lenders, (and, of course, had killed Christ), they were available for instant and constant execration. This must certainly be viewed as a collective hypocrisy—one of those 'projections' by which society tries to deal with a bad conscience (not that Shakespeare would have seen many Jews in London; it is estimated that there were less than two hundred at the time). Shakespeare was not addressing a contemporary problem; rather, he was exploring some of the ambivalences and hypocrises, the value clashes and requisite doublenesses, which inhere in, and attend upon, all commerce.

The play is full of commercial and financial terms: 'moneys', 'usances', 'bargains', 'credit', 'excess' and 'advantage' (both used of usury and profit), 'trust', 'bond' (which occurs vastly more often than in any other play: curiously 'contract' is *not* used—Shakespeare wants us to focus on 'bond'), 'commodity' and 'thrift'. Launcelot Gobbo is "an unthrifty knave", while Jessica flees from her father's house with "an unthrift love". This last serves as a reminder that both here and elsewhere in Shakespeare the language of finance and usury could be used as a paradoxical image of love (happiness accrues and passion grows by a form of *natural* interest). You will hear it in Belmont as well as on the Rialto. When Portia gives herself to Bassanio, she, as it were, breaks the bank:

> I would he trebled twenty times myself,
> A thousand times more fair, ten thousand times more rich,
> That only to stand high in your account,
> I might in virtues, beauties, livings, friends,
> Exceed account. (III,ii, 153–7)

Rich place, Belmont; generous lover, Portia!

The absolutely central exchange occurs when Antonio and Shylock discuss 'interest', or 'borrowing upon advantage'. "I do never use it" declares Antonio (what is the relationship between 'use' and 'usury'? Another consideration.) Shylock replies, seemingly rather inconsequentially: "When Jacob grazed his uncle Laban's sheep. . . ." Antonio brings him to the point. "And what of him? Did he take interest?" Shylock seems to prevaricate: "No, not take interest—not as you would say / Directly int'rest" and then recounts the story from Genesis. This tells how Jacob tricked—but is that the right word?—his exploitative uncle, Laban: they agreed that, for his hire, Jacob should be entitled to any lambs, in the flocks he was tending, that were born "streaked and pied". Following the primitive belief that what a mother sees during conception has an effect

on the offspring, Jacob stripped some "wands" (twigs or branches), so that some
were light while others were dark, and "stuck them up before the fulsome ewes"
as the rams were impregnating them. In the subsequent event, a large number
of "parti-coloured lambs" were born, which of course went to Jacob. Nice work;
but was it also sharp practice? Or was it both, and so much the better? Or, does
it matter? Not as far as Shylock is concerned:

> This was a way to thrive, and he was blest;
> And thrift is blessing if men steal it not. (I,iii,86f.)

'Ewes' may be a pun on 'use'; and for Shylock, it is as legitimate to use ewes
in the field as it is to use usury on the 'mart'. Not so for Antonio:

> This was a venture, sir, that Jacob served for,
> A thing not in his power to bring to pass,
> But swayed and fashioned by the hand of heaven.
> Was this inserted to make interest good?
> Or is your gold and silver ewes and lambs? (88–92)

And Shylock:

> I cannot tell; I make it breed as fast. (88–93)

Antonio's last line effectively poses *the* question of the play. It was a line
often quoted, (or more often, slightly misquoted), by Ezra Pound in his
increasingly unbalanced vituperations against usury and Jews. The root
feeling behind it is that it is somehow *unnatural* for inorganic matter (gold,
silver, money) to reproduce itself in a way at least analogous to the natural
reproductions in the organic realm ("they say it is against nature for *Money*
to beget *Money*", says Bacon, quoting Aristotle). This enables Antonio to
reject Shylock's self-justifying analogy: Jacob's story does *not* "make interest
good", because he was having, or making, a "venture", and the result was,
inevitably, "swayed and fashioned" by—heaven? nature? some power not his
own. This, revealingly, was how Christian commentators of the time justified Jacob's slightly devious behaviour (as Frank Kermode pointed out)—he
was making a *venture*. Antonio's ships are 'ventures', and Bassanio is on a
venture when he 'adventures forth' to Belmont. It seems that the element
of 'risk' (= to run into danger) and 'hazard' purifies or justifies the act. As
'hazard' was originally an Arabian word for a gaming die, this would seem
to enable gambling to pass moral muster as well. Perhaps it does. Whatever,
there is seemingly *no* risk, as well as no nature, in usury. Shylock's answer,

that he makes his money "breed as fast", is thought to tell totally against him; and Bassanio's subsequent remark, "for when did friendship take / A breed for barren metal of his friend?" (I,iii,130–1), is taken to orient our sympathies, and values, correctly. But this won't quite do.

Because, like it or not, money most certainly *does* 'breed'. It may not literally copulate, but there is no way round the metaphor. Sigurd Burckhardt is the only commentator I have read who has seen this clearly, and he wrote: "metal ['converted' into money] is not barren, it does breed, is pregnant with consequences, and capable of transformation into life and art". For a start, it gets Bassanio to Belmont, and the obtaining of Portia and the Golden Fleece (or Portia *as* a golden fleece). And, as if to signal his awareness of the proximity, even similitude, of the two types of 'breeding', with the lightest of touches: when Gratiano announces he is to marry Nerissa at the same time as Bassanio marries Portia, Shakespeare has him add—"We'll play with them the first boy for a thousand ducats" (III,ii,214). You 'play' for babies, and you 'play' for ducats. Which also means that when Shylock runs through the streets crying "O my ducats! O my daughter!" (echoing Marlowe's Barabas who cries out "oh, my girl, my gold", but when his daughter *restores* his wealth to him), we should not be quite so quick to mock him as the little Venetian urchins. He may not use his money to such life-enhancing and generous ends as some of the more princely Venetians; but he has been doubly bereaved (which literally means—robbed, *reaved*, on all sides, *be*-).

Having mentioned that robbery, I will just make one point about the Jessica and Lorenzo sub-plot. However sorry we may feel for Jessica, living in a 'hell' of a house with her father; the behaviour of the two lovers is only to be deprecated. Burckhardt is absolutely right again: "their love is lawless, financed by theft and engineered by a gross breach of trust". Jessica "gilds" herself with ducats, and throws a casket of her father's wealth down to Lorenzo ("Here, catch this casket; it is worth the pains" II,vi,33—another echo-with-a-difference of Marlowe's play, in which Abigail throws down her father's wealth from a window, to her *father*). This is an anticipatory parody, travesty rather, of Portia, the Golden (not 'gilded') Fleece, waiting to see if Bassanio will pass the test of *her* father's caskets (containing wisdom, rather than simple ducats). He 'hazards' all; this couple risk nothing. They squander eighty ducats in a night—folly, not bounty. Jessica exchanges the ring her mother gave her father as a love-pledge, for—a monkey! They really do make a monkey out of marriage—I will come to their famous love duet in due course. Their's is the reverse, or inverse, of a true love match. It must be intended to contrast with the marriage made by Bassanio and Portia. This marriage also, admittedly, involves wealth—as it does paternal caskets; but, and the difference is vital, wealth *not gained or used in the same way*.

Those caskets! Shakespeare took nearly everything that he wanted for his plot (including settings, characters, even the ring business in Act V) from a tale in *Il Pecorone* (The Dunce), a collection of stories assembled by Giovanni Fiorentino, published in Italy in 1558—everything except the trial of the caskets. In the Italian story, to win the lady, the hero has to demonstrate to her certain powers of sexual performance and endurance. Clearly, this was not quite the thing for a Shakespearean heroine. So Shakespeare took the trial-by-caskets from a tale in the thirteenth-century *Gesta Romanorum*, which had been translated into English. Here, a young woman has to choose between three vessels—gold, silver, lead—to discover whether she is worthy to be the wife of the Emperor's son. All we need note about it is one significant change that Shakespeare made in the inscriptions on the vessels/caskets. Those on the gold and silver ones are effectively the same in each case—roughly, "Who chooseth me shall gain/get what he desires/deserves". But in the mediaeval tale, the lead casket bears the inscription *"Thei that chese me, shulle fynde [in] me that God hath disposid"*. Now, since the young woman is a good Christian, she could hardly have been told more clearly that this was the one to go for. It is, we may say, no test at all. Shakespeare changes the inscription to "Who chooseth me must give and hazard all he hath" (II,vii,9). This is a very different matter. Instead of being promised a placid and predictable demonstration of piety rewarded, we are in that dangerous world of risk and hazard which, at various levels, constitutes the mercantile world of the play. And to the prevailing lexicon of 'get' and 'gain' has been added the even more important word—'give'. One of the concerns of the play is the conjoining of *giving* and *gaining* in the most appropriate way, so that they may 'frutify' together (if I may borrow Launcelot Gobbo's inspired malapropism). "I come by note, *to give* and *to receive*", Bassanio announces to Portia (III,ii,140—my italics). Which is no less than honesty.

While she is anxiously waiting as Bassanio inspects the caskets, Portia says:

> Now he goes,
> With no less presence, but with much more love,
> Than young Alcides [Hercules], when he did redeem
> The virgin tribute paid by howling Troy
> To the sea monster. I stand for sacrifice;
> The rest aloof are the Dardanian wives,
> With bleared visages come forth to view
> The issue of th' exploit. Go, Hercules! (III,ii,53–60)

The "virgin tribute" was Hesione, and her rescue by Hercules is described in Book XI of Ovid's *Metamorphoses* (where it is preceded by stories concerning

Orpheus, who turned everything to music, and Midas, who turned everything to gold—they are both referred to in the play, and are hovering mythic presences behind it). Portia's arresting claim—"I stand for sacrifice"—resonates through the play; to be darkly echoed by Shylock in court—"I stand for judgment . . . I stand here for law" (IV,i,103,142). When she says "stand for", does she mean 'represent', or 'embody'; or does she imply that she is in danger of being 'sacrificed' to the law of her father, unless rescued by right-choosing Hercules-Bassanio? Or is it just that women are always, in effect, 'sacrificed' to men in marriage, hence the "bleared visages" of those "Dardanian wives"? Something of all of these, perhaps. In the event, it is Portia herself who, effectively rescues, or—her word—'redeems', not Troy, but Venice. Bassanio (courtier, scholar, *and* fortune-seeker) is, as we have seen, if not more, then as much Jason as Hercules. The point is, I think, that he has to be *both* as cunning as the one *and* as bold as the other. The 'both-ness' is important.

This is how Bassanio thinks his way to the choice of the correct casket:

> So may the outward shows be least themselves;
> The world is still deceived with ornament.
> In law, what pleas so tainted and corrupt,
> But being seasoned with a gracious voice,
> Obscures the show of evil? (III,ii,73–7)

This, *mutatis mutandis*, is a theme in Shakespeare from first to last—"all that glitters is not gold", and so on (II,vii,65). Bassanio is on very sure grounds in rejecting the gold and silver and opting for lead, *in the context of the test*. But—'ornament': from *ornare*—to equip, to adorn. Now, if ever there was an equipped and adorned city, it was Venice. It is aware of dangerous seas and treacherous shores, of course; but it is *also* a city of beauteous scarves, and silks and species—and what are they but 'ornaments' for the body and for food? Bassanio is an inhabitant and creation of an ornamented world, and is himself, as we say, an 'ornament' to it. So why does he win by *going through a show* of rejecting it? He wins, because he realises that he has to subscribe to the unadorned modesty of lead, *even while* going for the ravishing glory of gold. *That* was the sort of complex intelligence Portia's father had in mind for his daughter. Is it hypocrisy? Then we must follow Brockbank and call it "creative hypocrisy". It recognises the compromising, and willing-to-compromise, doubleness of values on which a worldly society (a society in the world) necessarily rests, and by which it is sustained. The leaden virtues, and the golden pleasures. Bothness.

Such is the reconciling potency of Belmont; and Portia seals the happy marriage with a ring. But, meanwhile, Shylock is waiting back in Venice for his pound of flesh, and he *must* be satisfied. Must—because he has the law on his side, and Venice lives by law; its wealth and reputation depend on honouring contracts and bonds—as Shylock is the first to point out: "If you deny [my bond], let danger light / Upon your charter and your city's freedom". Portia, as lawyer Balthasar, agrees: "There is no power in Venice / Can alter a decree established" (IV,i,38–9,220–1). "I stay here on my bond" (IV,i,241)—if he says the word 'bond' once, he says it a dozen times (it occurs over thirty times in this play—never more than six times in other plays). We are in a world of law where 'bonds' are absolutely binding. Portia's beautiful speech exhorting to 'mercy' is justly famous; but, as Burckhardt remarked, it is impotent and useless in this 'court of justice', a realm which is under the rule of the unalterable letter of the law. Her sweet and humane lyricism founders against harsh legal literalism. The tedious, tolling reiteration of the word 'bond' has an effect which musicians know as 'devaluation through repetition'. The word becomes emptier and emptier of meaning, though still having its deadening effect. It is as if they are all in the grip of a mindless mechanism, which brings them to a helpless, dumb, *impasse*; with Shylock's dagger quite legally poised to strike. Shylock, it is said, is adhering to the old Hebraic notion of the law—an eye for an eye. He has not been influenced by the Christian saying of St Paul: "The letter killeth but the spirit giveth life." For Shylock, the spirit *is* the letter; and Antonio can only be saved *by* the letter. It is as though Portia will have to find resources in literalism which the law didn't know it had.

And so, the famous moment of reversal:

> Tarry a little; there is something else.
> The bond doth give thee here no jot of blood;
> The words *expressly* are "a pound of flesh."
> Take then thy bond . . .
> Shed thou no blood, nor cut thou less nor more
> But just a pound of flesh. (IV,i,304–7, 324–5; my italics)

Ex-press: to press out. Portia squeezes new life and salvation out of the dead and deadly law—and not by extenuation or circumvention or equivocation. "How every fool can play upon the word!", says Lorenzo, in response to Launcelot's quibbles. But you can't 'play' your way out of the Venetian law courts. Any solution must be found within the precincts of stern, rigorous law. "The Jew shall have all justice . . . He shall have merely justice and his bond". (IV,i,320,338) And, to Shylock: "Thou shalt have justice more than thou desir'st". (315) Portia makes literalism yield a life-saving further reach. Truly, the beyond of law.

Life-saving for Antonio—and for Venice itself, we may say. But not, of course, for Shylock. He simply crumples; broken by his own bond, destroyed by the law he "craved". But prior to this, his speeches have an undeniable power, and a strangely compelling sincerity. Necessarily un-aristocratic, and closer to the streets (and the ghetto life back there somewhere), his speech in general has a force, and at times a passionate directness, which makes the more 'ornamented' speech of some of the more genteel Christians sound positively effete. Though his defeat is both necessary and gratifying—the cruel hunter caught with his own device—there is something terrible in the spectacle of his breaking. "I pray you give me leave to go from hence. I am not well" (IV,i,394–5). And Gratiano's cruel, jeering ridicule, with which he taunts and lacerates Shylock through the successive blows of his defeat, does Christianity, does humanity, no credit. Like the malcontent or kill-joy in any comedy, Shylock has to be extruded by the regrouping, revitalised community, and he is duly chastised, humiliated, stripped, and despatched—presumably back to the Ghetto. He is never seen again; but it is possible to feel him as a dark, suffering absence throughout the final Act in Belmont. And in fact, he does make one last, indirect 'appearance'. When Portia brings the news that Shylock has been forced to leave all his wealth to Jessica and Lorenzo, the response is—"Fair ladies, you drop manna in the way / Of starved people" (V,i,293–4). 'Manna' was, of course, what fell from heaven and fed the children of Israel in the wilderness. This is the only time Shakespeare uses the word; and, just for a second, its deployment here—at the height of the joy in Christian Belmont—reminds us of the long archaic biblical past stretching back behind Shylock—who also, just for a second, briefly figures, no matter how unwillingly, as a version of the Old Testament God, providing miraculous sustenance for *his* 'children' (a point made by John Gross).

But why did not Shakespeare end his play with the climactic defeat of Shylock—why a whole extra Act with that ring business? Had he done so, it would have left Venice unequivocally triumphant, which perhaps he didn't quite want. This is the last aspect of the play I wish to address, and I must do so somewhat circuitously. Perhaps Shylock's most memorable claim is:

> I am a Jew. Hath not a Jew eyes? Hath not a Jew hands, organs,
> dimensions, senses, affections, passion?—fed with the same food,
> hurt with the same weapons, subject to the same diseases, healed by
> the same means, warmed and cooled by the same winter and summer
> as a Christian is? If you prick us, do we not bleed? (III,i,55–61)

That last question, seemingly rhetorical (of course you do), but eventually crucial (Shylock seems to have overlooked the fact that if he pricks Antonio, *he* will bleed too), is prepared for, in an admittedly small way, by the first suitor to attempt the challenge of the caskets. The Prince of Morocco starts by defending the "shadowed livery" of his "complexion", as against "the fairest creature northward born":

> And let us make incision for your love
> To prove whose blood is reddest, his or mine. (II,i,6–7)

So, a black and a Jew claiming an equality with white Venetian gentle/gentiles (another word exposed to examination in the course of the play), which I have not the slightest doubt Shakespeare fully accorded them (the princely Morocco, in fact, comes off rather better than the silvery French aristocrat who follows him). And Morocco's hypothetical 'incision' anticipates the literal incision which Shylock seeks to make in Antonio. When Bassanio realises that Portia is going to ask to see her ring, which he has given away, he says in an aside:

> Why, I were best cut my left hand off
> And swear I lost the ring defending it. (V,i,177–8)

So, there may be 'incisions' made 'for love', from hate, and out of guilt. Portia describes the wedding ring as

> A thing stuck on with oaths upon your finger,
> And so riveted with faith unto your flesh. (V,i,168–9)

'Rivetting on' is, I suppose, the opposite of Shylock's intended cutting out; but, taken together, there is a recurrent linking of law (oaths, bonds, rings)—and flesh. The play could be said to hinge on *two* contracts or bonds, in which, or by which, the law envisions, permits, requires, ordains, the exposing of a part of the body of one party to the legitimate penetration (incision) by the other party to the bond. If that party is Shylock, the penetration/incision would be done out of hate—and would prove fatal; if that other party is Bassanio it should be done out of love—and give new life. Shylock swears by his 'bond'; Portia works through her 'ring'.

It should be noted that, in the last Act, when Bassanio is caught out with having given Portia's ring away to Balthasar, he stands before Portia as guilty and helpless as Antonio stood before Shylock. And, like Shylock, she insists on the letter of the pledge, and will hear no excuses and is not interested in mercy. Like Shylock too, she promises her own form of 'fleshly' punishment (absence from Bassanio's bed, and promiscuous infidelity with others). As with the word 'bond' in the court scene, so with the word 'ring' in this last scene. It occurs twenty-one times, and at times is repeated so often that it risks suffering the semantic depletion which seemed to numb 'bond' into emptiness. *Both* the word 'bond' and the word 'ring'—and all they represent in terms of binding/bonding—are endangered in this play. But the law stands—and continues to stand; bonds must be honoured or society collapses: there is nothing Bassanio can do. Then, just as Portia-as-Balthasar found a way through the Venetian *impasse*, so Portia-as-Portia has the life-giving power to enable Bassanio to *renew* his bond—she gives him, mysteriously and to him inexplicably, the same ring, for a second time. (She has mysterious, inexplicable good news for Antonio, too, about the sudden safe arrival of his ships.) A touch of woman's magic. For Portia is one of what Brockbank called Shakespeare's "creative manipulators" (of whom Prospero is the last). Like Vincentio (in *Measure for Measure*), she uses "craft against vice". She can be a skilful man in Venice (a veritable Jacob), and a tricky, resourceful, ultimately loving and healing woman in Belmont (a good Medea with something of the art of Orpheus—both figures invoked in the scene). She can gracefully operate in, and move between, both worlds. Because she is, as it were, a man-woman, as good a lawyer as she is a wife—more 'both-ness'; she figures a way in which law and love, law and blood, need not be mutually exclusive and opposed forces. She shows how they, too, can 'frutify' together.

The person who both persuades Bassanio to give away his ring, and intercedes for him with Portia ("I dare be bound again") is Antonio. He is solitary and sad at the beginning, and is left alone at the end. He expresses his love for Bassanio in an extravagant, at times tearful way. It is a love which seems to be reciprocated. In the court scene, Bassanio protests to Antonio that

> life itself, my wife, and all the world
> Are not with me esteemed above thy life.
> I would lose all, ay sacrifice them all
> Here to this devil to deliver you.

Portia, (she certainly does "stand for sacrifice"!), permits herself an understandably dry comment:

> Your wife would give you little thanks for that
> If she were by to hear you make the offer. (IV,i,283–8)

Perhaps this is why she decides to put Bassanio to the test with the ring. I do, of course, recognise the honourable tradition of strong male friendship, operative at the time. I also know that 'homosexuality', as such, was not invented until the late nineteenth century. I am also totally disinclined to seek out imagined sexualities which are nothing to the point. But Antonio is so moistly, mooningly in love with Bassanio (and so conspicuously uninvolved with, and unattracted to, any woman), that I think that his nameless sadness, and seemingly foredoomed solitariness, may fairly be attributed to a homosexual passion, which must now be frustrated since Bassanio is set on marriage. (Antonio's message to Bassanio's wife is: "bid her be judge / Whether Bassanio had not once a love", which implies 'lover' as much as 'friend'; revealingly, Antonio's one remaining desire is that Bassanio should witness the fatal sacrifice he is to make for him.) Even then, we might say that that is neither here nor there. Except for one fact. Buggery and usury were *very* closely associated or connected in the contemporary mind as unnatural acts. Shylock is undoubtedly a usurer, who becomes unwell; but if Antonio is, not to put too fine a point on it, a buggerer, who is also unwell, well. . . .

Perhaps some will find the suggestion offensively irrelevant; and perhaps it is. But the atmosphere in Venice-Belmont, is not unalloyedly pure. The famous love duet between Lorenzo and Jessica which starts Act Five, inaugurating the happy post-Shylock era—"In such a night . . ."—is hardly an auspicious one, invoking as it does a faithless woman (Cressida), one who committed suicide (Thisbe), an abandoned woman (Dido), and a sorceress (Medea whose spells involved physical mutilation), before moving on to a contemporary female thief—Jessica herself. I hardly think that she and Lorenzo will bear any mythological 'ornamenting'. And that theft has become part of the texture of the Belmont world. It is a place of beautiful music and poetry—and love; but with perhaps just a residual something-not-quite-right lingering from the transactions and 'usages' of Ghetto-Rialto Venice. (The very last word of the play is a punningly obscene use of 'ring' by Gratiano, the most scabrous and cynical voice in Venice—again, a slightly off-key note.) There is moonlight and candle-light for the nocturnal conclusion of the play, but it doesn't 'glimmer' as beautifully as it did at the end of *A Midsummer Night's Dream*. Portia says:

> This night methinks is but the daylight sick;
> It looks a little paler. 'Tis a day
> Such as the day when the sun is hid. (V,i,124–6)

A little of the circulating sickness has reached Belmont. The play is a comedy; but Shakespeare has here touched on deeper and more potentially complex and troubling matters than he had hitherto explored, and the result is a comedy with a difference. And, of course, it is primarily Shylock who makes that difference.

Now, let's go back to the beginning. "Which is the merchant here? And which the Jew?" It turns out to be a good question.

BIBLIOGRAPHY

Brockbank, Philip. "Shakespeare and the Fashion of These Times". *Shakespeare Survey* 16 (1963).

Burckhardt, Sigurd. "The Merchant of Venice: The Gentle Bond". *Journal of English Literary History* 29 (1962).

Gross, John. *Shylock. Four Hundred Years in the Life of a Legend*. London, 1992.

Kermode, Frank. "The Mature Comedies". In: Brown, J.R./B. Harris (eds.): *Early Shakespeare*. Stratford-upon-Avon Studies, 3. London, 1961.

Nevo, Ruth. *Comic Transformations in Shakespeare*. London, 1980.

Tawney, R. H. *Religion and the Rise of Capitalism*. London, 1926.

W. H. AUDEN

The Merchant of Venice

With memories of the horrors of the last ten years and forebodings about anti-Semitism, it is difficult to look objectively at a play in which the villain is a Jew. But we must, in order to understand it. In England in Shakespeare's day, English writers didn't know Jews, who had been expelled by Edward I in 1290 and not readmitted until the time of Cromwell. A few years before the play was written, there had been a law case in which Dr. Roderigo Lopez, a Portuguese Jew who was physician to the Queen, was tried and executed for treason—it was a frame-up. Whatever prejudice against the Jews existed among Elizabethans, it was not racial. Lorenzo marries Shylock's daughter—there is no thought of racial discrimination. The only racial remark in the play is made by Shylock, and the Christians refute it. Religious differences in the play are treated frivolously: the question is not one of belief, but of conformity. The important thing about Shylock is not that he is a Jew or a heretic, but that he is an outsider.

The Merchant of Venice is about a certain kind of society, a society that is related to and can't do without someone whom it can't accept. The Gentile Venetian society is a newborn bourgeois capitalist society, no longer feudal, not yet industrial. Feudal society is based on status by birth. In such a society, marriage must be arranged between the right people. But in *The Merchant of Venice* the issue is breeding, not inheritance. Jessica makes clear that though

From *Lectures on Shakespeare*, reconstructed and edited by Arthur Kirsch, pp. 75–85, 372–73. Copyright © 2000 by Arthur Kirsch for the notes and © 2000 by the Estate of W. H. Auden for lectures and writings by Auden.

she is "a daughter" to Shylock's "blood, / I am not to his manners" (II.iii.18–19), and Lorenzo shows his lack of prejudice in perceiving this and marrying her. Portia, too, has no racial prejudice. She explains to the Moor that were she not bound by the test of the caskets,

> Yourself, renowned Prince, then stood as fair
> As any comer I have look'd on yet
> For my affection.
> (II.i.19–21)

There is also no sense of a stratified class structure in the play: Gratiano, who marries Nerissa, Portia's maid, is treated as an equal by Bassanio and Antonio, and Nerissa is treated in the same way by Portia. There is a free choice in personal relationships. Even the choice of caskets is not an arrangement to provide a particular person for Portia, but a device to insure her marrying a person with a particular kind of character, someone capable of making her happy. The first four suitors announce that even if they win Portia by choosing the right casket, they won't insist that she marry them unless she is willing. This is not feudal. Feudal society has fixed obligations. In this play personal obligations are unlimited, as Antonio's conduct to Bassanio shows. Antonio tells Bassanio, when he is asked for help,

> You know me well, and herein spend but time
> To wind about my love with circumstance;
> And out of doubt you do me now more wrong
> In making question of my uttermost
> Than if you had made waste of all I have.
> Then do but say to me what I should do
> That in your knowledge may by me be done,
> And I am prest unto it.
> (I.i.153–60)

Bassanio displays the same limitless generosity when he rushes to Antonio without first lying with Portia, whom he has just won and married. Today there are no personal obligations in a laissez-faire society. In *The Merchant of Venice* you are free to form the personal relationships you choose, but your obligations are then enormous. There are few plays of Shakespeare in which the word "love" is used more frequently, and the understanding of love is not unlike E. M. Forster's in his essay "I Believe," in which he says, "if i had to choose between betraying my country and betraying my friend, I hope I should have the guts to betray my country."

There is an aesthetic awareness in all the characters in this play. Lorenzo shows it when he describes the moonlight to Jessica:

> How sweet the moonlight sleeps upon this bank!
> Here will we sit and let the sounds of music
> Creep in our ears. Soft stillness and the night
> Become the touches of sweet harmony.
> Sit, Jessica. Look how the floor of heaven
> Is thick inlaid with patens of bright gold.
>   (V.i.54–59)

Lorenzo also says that

> The man that hath no music in himself,
> Nor is not mov'd with concord of sweet sounds,
> Is fit for treason, stratagems, and spoils;
> The motions of his spirit are dull as night,
> And his affections dark as Erebus.
> Let no such man be trusted.
>   (V.i.83–88)

Lorenzo shows the same sensibility in all his other speeches, and an aesthetic consciousness is evident as well in Bassanio's descriptions of Portia and her wealth:

> Nor is the wide world ignorant of her worth;
> For the four winds blow in from every coast
> Renowned suitors, and her sunny locks
> Hang on her temples like a golden fleece,
> Which makes her seat of Belmont Colchos' strond,
> And many Jasons come in quest of her.
>   (I.i.167–72)

Portia's wish that music accompany Bassanio's choice of the casket shows and creates a similar aesthetic attentiveness:

> Let music sound while he doth make his choice;
> Then, if he lose, he makes a swanlike end,

Fading in music. That the comparison
May stand more proper, my eye shall be the stream
And wat'ry deathbed for him. He may win;
And what is music then? Then music is
Even as the flourish when true subjects bow
To a new-crowned monarch. Such it is
As are those dulcet sounds in break of day
That creep into the dreaming bridegroom's ear
And summon him to marriage.
    (III.ii.43–53)

Portia shows the same disposition in criticizing the various suitors she has not liked: the Neapolitan who boasts of his horse—gents don't boast—and the Count Palatine, who is gloomy, full of "unmannerly sadness" (I.ii.54)—one must be gay. Though gaiety must have a limit. At a lunch party in the south of France, during the Spanish Civil War, a voice pipes up, "Spain must be madly ungay this summer." The story goes that in the last war a Guards officer who was home on leave was asked what war was like, and answered, "So annoying—the noise, and the *people*." Again, in the last war, a friend of mine who went over the top and didn't shoot, took a rug and a book, was wounded, and lay comfortably and read until they came for him. Portia criticizes Monsieur Le Bon because "He is every man in no man" (I.ii.64–65)—one must be an individual and have a center, whether it is shown or not. She finds fault with Falconbridge because, though he tries, he's not chic, speaks no languages, and is "oddly . . . suited" (I.ii.79)—one mustn't be provincial. The Scottish lord, who "borrowed a box in the ear of the Englishman, and swore he would pay him again when he was able" (I.ii.84–86), is rejected for lacking esprit, being too dull. The Duke of Saxony's nephew, a drunken boor, is rejected because one must have good manners.

One must also be quite carefree and unpossessive. When Jessica joins this society, the first thing that upsets Shylock is that she spends four score ducats in one evening and buys a monkey for a ring. Be free with money, be imprudent, always gamble, and as in Gratiano's marriage, act on impulse. Bet on the first boy, always wagering money on chance. The Venetians are fashionably frivolous, and it is true that, like all frivolous people, they're also a little sad. In the opening lines of the play, Antonio says,

In sooth, I know not why I am so sad.
It wearies me; you say it wearies you;
    (I.i.1–2)

and he tells Gratiano,

I hold the world but as the world, Gratiano—
A stage; where every man must play a part,
And mine a sad one.
    (I.i.77–79)

Portia echoes him at the start of the second scene when she says, "By my troth, Nerissa, my little body is aweary of this great world" (I.ii.1–2). She treats the feeling more lightly than it in fact is in order not to bore people. Gratiano, a frivolous chatterbox, a Gentile opposite of Shylock, is a type of his society, and he's the only one who doesn't wish to pardon Shylock. Speaking at one point of Lorenzo's lateness, Gratiano says that chasing is more fun than catching: "All things that are / Are with more spirit chased than enjoy'd" (II.vi.12–13).

Unlike a feudal society, which is based on land, the basis of this society is money coming from speculative trade, not from production, as in an industrial society. It is possible to become suddenly rich or suddenly poor, and money has commodity as well as exchange value. As a moneylender, Shylock is guilty of usury. Antonio, when he asks for the loan from Shylock, says:

If thou wilt lend this money, lend it not
As to thy friends—for when did friendship take
A breed for barren metal of his friend?
But lend it rather to thine enemy,
Who if he break, thou mayst with better face
Exact the penalty.
    (I.iii.133–38)

The condemnation of the breeding of money by money goes back to Aristotle, and in Canto XI of the *Inferno*, Virgil castigates the moneylenders and associates them with sodomists:

Violence may be done against the Deity, in the heart denying
and blaspheming Him; and disdaining Nature and her bounty:
  and hence the smallest round seals with its mark both Sodom
and Cahors, and all who speak with disparagement of God in
their hearts.

Cahors was a center of non-Jewish usury and of misbelievers. Virgil also instructs Dante that Genesis "behoves man to gain his bread and prosper" and that "because the usurer takes another way, he contemns Nature in herself and in her follower, placing elsewhere his hope."

At the time *The Merchant of Venice* was written, however, these traditional attitudes against usury were breaking down. In an economy for direct consumption or barter borrowing, the borrowing of money is an exception, and money is not a commodity that one sells for a profit—which is how we would feel if we were asked for interest on the loan of a dollar from a friend. In a society where money becomes generally needed, a conflict arises between the abhorrence of usury and the necessity for it. The hypocrisy is that though moneylending will be condemned and the lender despised, men will still go to the moneylender. Shylock's argues that Laban's method of producing parti–colored sheep, though not "directly int'rest," "was a way to thrive, and he was blest; / And thrift is blessing, if men steal it not" (I.iii.78, 90–91). Antonio objects, saying,

> This was a venture, sir, that Jacob serv'd for;
> A thing not in his power to bring to pass,
> But sway'd and fashion'd by the hand of heaven.
> Was this inserted to make interest good?
> Or is your gold and silver ewes and rams?
>   (I.iii.92–96)

Nonetheless, Shylock's commentary on Laban's sheep was actually used by theologians trying to give interest canonical legality. Moneylending serves the need for ready cash. Because it is regarded as immoral, however, it is handed over to outsiders. The madame runs the brothel, but the senator still visits it. It's a bad situation for outsiders, who will go to a job from which they are not excluded, to the most lucrative job, but one that is socially condemned: moneylending.

Wealth in Venetian society depends upon speculation and exploitation. Shylock points this out when he justifies his possession of the pound of flesh by arguing from the Gentiles' unwillingness to free their slaves:

> What judgment shall I dread, doing no wrong?
> You have among you many a purchas'd slave,
> Which, like your asses and your dogs and mules,
> You use in abject and in slavish parts,
> Because you bought them. Shall I say to you,
> "Let them be free, marry them to your heirs!
> Why sweat they under burthens? Let their beds
> Be made as soft as yours, and let their palates
> Be season'd with such viands"? You will answer,
> "The slaves are ours." So do I answer you.

The pound of flesh which I demand of him
Is dearly bought, 'tis mine, and I will have it.
  (IV.i.89–100)

Within the charmed social circle of Venice and Belmont, all is love, affection, grace, wit, beauty, riches. The improper suitors are seen as outsiders. Shylock sums them up as an outsider par excellence. He is an outsider partly by religion, which is not too important, more a formal, social matter, and partly by profession, which partially reflects the extravagance of society itself. But he is an outsider chiefly by character, for which society is partly responsible, though social conditions are never quite enough to determine character. In contrast to the others, he's gloomy, priggish, and hates music. He enjoins Jessica not to listen to the masques:

What, are there masques? Hear you me, Jessica.
Lock up my doors; and when you hear the drum
And the vile squeaking of the wry-neck'd fife,
Clamber not you up to the casements then,
Nor thrust your head into the public street
To gaze on Christian fools with varnish'd faces;
But stop my house's ears—I mean my casements.
Let not the sound of shallow fopp'ry enter
My sober house.
  (II.v.28–36)

Shylock is too serious. He's not really more acquisitive than the other Venetians—they, too, clearly seek profit—but he is more possessive, he keeps his possessions to himself, and he does not value personal relationships. He is more concerned about his ducats and diamonds than his daughter, and he cannot imagine making a sacrifice to personal relations.

Why, there, there, there, there! A diamond gone cost me two
thousands ducats in Frankford! The curse never fell upon our
nation till now; I never felt it till now. Two thousand ducats in
that, and other precious, precious jewels. I would my daughter
were dead at my foot, and the jewels in her ear! Would she were
hears'd at my foot, and the ducats in her coffin! No news of them?
Why, so—and I know not what's spent in the search. Why, thou
loss upon loss! the thief gone with so much, and so much to find
the thief, and no satisfaction, no revenge! nor no ill luck stirring

but what lights o' my shoulders; no sighs but o' my breathing; no
tears but o' my shedding.
  (III.i.87–101)

Why does Shylock finally alienate our sympathy, even though we can
understand his wanting revenge? Part of the reason is that his revenge is in
excess of the injury—a characteristic of revenge plays. But he mainly alien-
ates our sympathy because he tries to play it safe and use the law, which is
universal, to exact a particular, personal revenge. A private quest for revenge
may have started a feud, but would be forgivable. What is not forgivable is
that he tried to get revenge safely. Shylock's unlimited hatred is the negative
image of the infinite love of Venetian and Belmont society, which proposes
that one should behave with a love that is infinitely imprudent. "Who chooseth me must give and hazard all he hath," the motto of the lead casket, is also
the motto of the play.

Legality is a problem in the play, as in *Measure for Measure*. A law is
either a law *of* or a law *for*. The law of gravitation is a law of, a description of
a pattern of regular behavior observed by disinterested observers. There must
be no exception and no caprice. Conformity is necessary for the law to exist,
for if an exception is found, the law has to be rewritten in such a way that
the exception becomes part of the pattern, for it is a presupposition of sci-
ence that events in nature conform to law—in other words, a physical event is
always related to some law, even if it be one of which scientists are at present
ignorant. Laws *for*, like human legislation, are patterns of behavior imposed
on behavior that was previously lacking in pattern. In order for the laws to
come into existence, there must be at least some people who don't conform
to them—there is no American law, for example, dealing with cannibalism.
Unlike laws *of*, which must completely explain how events occur, laws *for* are
only concerned with commanding or prohibiting the class of actions to which
they refer, and a man is only related to the law when it is a question of doing
or not doing one act of such a class. When his actions are not covered by law,
when alone in a room reading a book, for example, he is related to no law at
all. *The Merchant of Venice* shows that morals are not to be thought of as laws
of, that laws *for* can't account for all actions, and that ethics can't be based on
right, but must be based on duty.

How do we judge the means and ends of action? Utilitarian theory
doesn't consider the choice of means, but argues that utility and right are
identical. But why is a key "right" in opening a door and a bent wire "wrong"?
Kant and Fichte ask, what is your ethical duty if you know where A is, and
B, who intends to murder A, asks you where A is? If your assumption is that
you must tell the truth, then what? Kant argues that you must tell. Or, if your

assumption is that human life is sacred, then you don't tell. Duty is not what is conformable to right, but to what I owe. There is no refuge in generality, the choice is specific. There are no alternatives, the choice must be *mine*. And ought implies can. Antonio's sense of infinite obligation links utility and duty, as utility and right cannot be linked. Right states that a man should help friends, but doesn't explain why. Shylock thinks of duty upside down, and sees a one-to-one relation between action and intention. He tries to get Antonio. His mistake is that he tries to invoke the law and gets caught out. Laws are not adapted to particular ends, but deal with generalities. It's amazing that the Doge and others didn't realize that the bond involved bloodshed, but we have to accept that.

The question the play raises is, how shall I behave? I might assume that if I follow the rules, I'm okay, but Portia points out that obediences differ:

> Therefore, Jew,
> Though justice be thy plea, consider this—
> That, in the course of justice, none of us
> Should see salvation. We do pray for mercy,
> And that same prayer doth teach us all to render
> The deeds of mercy. I have spoke thus much
> To mitigate the justice of thy plea.
> (IV.i.197–203)

Portia, on the other hand, does trust to a legal generalization to free a man from an evil character:

> But in the cutting it if thou dost shed
> One drop of Christian blood, thy lands and goods
> Are, by the laws of Venice, confiscate
> Unto the state of Venice.
> (IV.i.309–12)

A shyster lawyer uses the same kind of argument. A "Profile" of the nineteenth-century New York criminal law firm, Howe and Hummel, in the *New Yorker*, describes how William F. Howe got one his clients off on a charge of arson. Howe arranged for a plea bargain on the charge of attempted arson, and when his client, Owen Reilly,

> came up for sentence, Howe arose and pointed out that the law provided no penalty for attempted arson. The court begged enlightenment. The sentence for attempted arson, Howe explained,

like the sentence for any crime attempted but not actually committed, was half the maximum imposed by law for the actual commission of the crime. The penalty for arson was life imprisonment. Hence, if the court were to determine a sentence for Reilly, it would have to determine what half a life came to. "Scripture tells us that we knoweth not the day nor the hour of our departure," Howe said. "Can this court sentence this prisoner at the bar to half of his natural life? Will it then sentence him to half a minute or to half the days of Methuselah?" The court agreed that the problem was beyond its earthbound wisdom.

By a similar kind of argument, Howe argued in 1888 that a convicted cop-killer, Handsome Harry Carlton, could not be executed. The Electrical Death Penalty law of that year had suspended hanging as of 4 June 1888 and installed electrocution as of 1 January 1889. Howe was able to argue that between June 4th and January 1st, murder was legal, since through the careless syntax of the bill, the law appeared to read that during that period there was no legal penalty for murder. And without a penalty, Howe said, there could be no crime. A higher court disposed of the problem, and Handsome Harry didn't get off, but for a while in New York murder seemed technically legal. Ergo, law is fundamentally frivolous, whereas a moral sense is serious. Hard cases make bad law. "Sell all thou hast and give to the poor" is a particular command, not a law.

Shylock is the outsider because he is the only serious person in the play. He may be serious about the wrong things, the acquisition of property, since property is itself a frivolous *thing*. In contrast, however, we have a society that is frivolous because certain gifts are necessary to belong to it—beauty, grace, wit, riches. Nothing that doesn't apply to everyone can be serious, and a frivolous society makes life a game. But life is not a game because one cannot say: "I will live if I turn out to be good at living." No, gifted or not, I must live. Those who cannot play a game can always be spectators, but no one can be a spectator of life; he must either live himself or hang himself. The Greeks, being aesthetes, regarded life as a game, i.e., as a test of inborn *areté*. The compensation for the chorus who could not play was to enjoy seeing the star players come one by one to a sticky end.

An aesthetically conceived society depends on the exploitation of the ungifted. A society constructed to be like a beautiful poem—as was imagined by some aesthetically-minded Greek political theorists—would be a nightmare of horror, for given the historical reality of actual men, such a society could only come into being through selective breeding, extermination of the physically and mentally unfit, absolute obedience to its Director, and a large slave class kept out of sight in cellars. The people in *The Merchant of Venice* are saved by their excess of love, which destroys the pattern of exclusiveness generated by self-love.

Whenever a society is exclusive, it needs something excluded and unaesthetic to define it, like Shylock. The only serious possession of men is not their gifts but what they all possess equally, independent of fortune, namely their will, in other words, their love, and the only serious matter is what they love—themselves, or God and their neighbor. The people in *The Merchant of Venice* are generous, and they behave well out of a sense of social superiority. Outside of them is Shylock, but inside is melancholy and a lack of serious responsibilities—which they'd have as farmers or producers, but not as speculators. They are haunted by an anxiety that it is not good sense for them to show.

The caskets are the key to the play. All the suitors are in the right social "set." Two of them do what the "set" does. The first chooses the gold casket, "to gain what many men desire," and inside is a death's head. Death is what the aesthete is most afraid of. The second suitor, seeking to "get as much as he deserves," chooses the silver casket, and inside is a portrait of a grinning idiot, the specter behind natural gifts. The third casket, which Bassanio must choose, is made of lead—common, universal, and unaesthetic—and it must be chosen with complete passion, for Bassanio must give and hazard all he has.

I am glad that Shakespeare made Shylock a Jew. What is the source of anti-Semitism? The Jew represents seriousness to the Gentile, which is resented, because we wish to be frivolous and do not want to be reminded that something serious exists. By their existence—and this is as it should be—Jews remind us of this seriousness, which is why we desire their annihilation.

Notes

This lecture has been reconstructed from notes by Arisen and Griffin. Auden discusses *The Merchant of Venice* in "Brothers and Others," *DH*, 218–37, and he wrote an article on the play, "Two Sides to a Thorny Problem," for *The New York Times*, 1 March 1953, section 2.

Page

139. "The only racial remark . . . Christians refute it.": This statement is neither persuasive nor clear. Auden may be referring to Shylock's assertion that he takes revenge "by Christian example" (III.i.73–74) and the Duke's statement in pardoning him: "That thou shalt see the difference of our spirit / I pardon thee thy life before thou ask it" (IV.ii.368–69).

139. "Religious differences . . . treated frivolously": For the connotations of Auden's use of the word "frivolous" throughout this lecture and in others, see *DH*, 429–32.

140. "The first four suitors": The first suitors, on the contrary, leave because they wish to win Portia "by some other sort than your father's imposition, depending on the caskets" (I.ii.113–15).

140. "Today there are . . . *laissez-faire* society.": Ansen's notes read, "Today there are no personal obligations in a *laissez faire* society, which comes round to status in totalitarian states."

140. E. M. Forster, "I Believe," in *I Believe*, ed. Clifton Fadiman (New York: Simon and Schuster, 1939), 81.

141. "aesthetic awareness": Auden's sense of the word "aesthetic" depends, in part, on Kierkegaard. See, e.g., "Equilibrium Between the Aesthetical and the Ethical in the Composition of Personality," *Either/Or*, 2:133–278; and *FA*, 172–74.

142. "At a lunch party . . .": After this sentence in his notes, Ansen inserts, with a caret, "Adrian and Francisco." This may be Ansen's interpolation, though his notes also suggest that Auden may have thrown it out to him as a hint during the lecture. In Part II of "The Sea and the Mirror," Adrian and Francisco say: "Good little sunbeams must learn to fly, / But it's madly ungay when the goldfish die," *CP*, 415. Ansen was writing a paper on "The Sea and the Mirror" at the time of this lecture. See also Fuller, *Auden: A Commentary*, 361.

142. "the noise, and the *people*": Auden also recounts this story in *ACW*, 383.

143. "back to Aristotle": *Politics* I. iv.

143. Dante, *Inferno*, Canto XI, *The Divine Comedy*, trans. Carlyle-Wicksteed, p. 68. In *DH*, 231, Auden quotes the same passage from the *Inferno*, and says about the collocation of Sodom and Cahors, which was known for its usurers, that it can "hardly be an accident that Shylock the usurer has as his antagonist a man whose emotional life, though his conduct may be chaste, is concentrated upon a member of his own sex."

146. "law *of* or a law *for* . . . at present ignorant": From Auden's review of Kierkegaard, *FA*, 177.

146. "Utilitarian theory . . . are identical.": Ansen's notes read, "Utilitarian theory doesn't consider the choice of means, put as caprice, but argues that utility and right are identical."

146. "Kant and Fichte ask": See, e.g., Immanuel Kant, "On a Supposed Right to Tell Lies from Benevolent Motives."

147. "A 'Profile'": Richard Rovere, "Profiles: 89 Centre Street: II, The Weepers," *The New Yorker*, 30 November 1946, 48–49.

148. "But life is not a game . . . hang himself.": From *SO*, 169.

148. "The Greeks . . . sticky end.": From *SO*, 170.

148. "A society constructed to be . . . cellars.": Details from *SO*, 178, and *DH*, 85.

149. "The only serious . . . their neighbor.": From *SO*, 168–69, and cf. *DH*, 431–32.

149. "behave well out of a sense of social superiority": After this sentence in his notes, Ansen writes, "can't be friends?" The context of the phrase is unclear.

149. "What is the source of anti-Semitism?": See *Auden as Didymus*, 42–44, and lecture and notes on *Richard III*. Auden also discusses Jewish seriousness, "the Jewish passion for truth," in "The Greeks and Us," reprinted in *FA*, 14.

PETER D. HOLLAND

The Merchant of Venice *and the Value of Money*

Anyone who reads or watches many Shakespeare plays grows accustomed to having to learn a new vocabulary for money. Marks, nobles, groats, crowns, pieces, shillings, pence, sovereigns and pounds—and that only covers some of the words used in the English histories. But we grow used to the notion that these terms are in a fixed or fixable relationship to each other. When in *Henry V*, Nim complains that Pistol has not paid him 'the eight shillings I won of you at betting' (2.1.90–1),[1] Pistol eventually offers him a deal: 'A noble thou shalt have, and present pay' (102). By checking the commentary we can learn that, unwilling to pay in full, Pistol is offering him six shillings and eightpence, discounting the sum owed by one-sixth for a cash deal, supplemented by the promise of 'liquor'. There is a system at work here that we can easily understand.

In that strange and hugely underrated tragedy *Timon of Athens*, something rather odder happens. Apart from some passing mentions of crowns and pieces, the standard form of currency being used in the play is a talent but there is considerable confusion about how much a talent is worth. In the first scene of the play it is clear that a talent is worth a considerable sum: Timon's reckless extravagance, his uncontrollable generosity is demonstrated by his willingness to pay five talents to release his friend Ventidius from prison (1.1.105) or by his giving three talents to his servant Lucilius as a dowry to match the three

From *Cahiers Élisabéthains* 60 (October 2001): 13–30. Copyright © 2001 by *Cahiers Élisabéthains*.

talents that the unnamed Old Athenian will bestow on his daughter (1.1.149). For those with even faint memories of the parable of the talents in the New Testament this seems an appropriate scale of value. Technically a talent was worth 6,000 drachmas and equivalent to more than 50 pounds weight of silver. But by Act 2 talents are clearly worth much less—as if the economy of Athens has collapsed—and Timon, sending out his servants to various seeming friends to borrow money, instructs them: 'Let the request be fifty talents' (2.2.189). Inflation bites quickly and a few lines later he tells Flavius to ask the senators to 'send o'th' instant / A thousand talents to me' (194–5). If three talents is a decent sized dowry, a dowry fit for the daughter of an Athenian gentleman, then a thousand talents is a wholly disproportionate sum. In Act three the playwright is totally confused: Flavius talks of fifty talents in 3.1, but in 3.2 the sums are carefully left vague and indeterminate as three times in the early part of the scene the precise sum is left out and the curious phrase 'so many talents' used: a servant tells Lucius, for example, that Timon is 'requesting your lordship to supply his instant use with so many talents' (36–7). Lucius's response is disbelief: 'I know his lordship is but merry with me. / He cannot want fifty five hundred talents' (38–9). 'Fifty-five hundred' is an odd phrase: it may represent an uncancelled correction, as if the author, having decided how many 'so many' should be, first wrote fifty and then five hundred and left them both in. In the last few years it has been strongly argued that *Timon of Athens* was not written by Shakespeare alone but instead that the play is a collaboration with Thomas Middleton and in a number of places in his other plays Middleton seems to be fond of the number fifty-five.[2] It looks as if the two authors forgot to agree about talents and Shakespeare had one value in mind when he was writing Act 1 while Middleton had a rather different value in mind when he was writing Act 3 scene 2. In other words, each dramatist was clear for himself but the two systems do not match up.[3]

I have pursued the problem of the sums of money as a prelude to thinking about ducats, for as the references to ducats proliferate in *The Merchant of Venice* they begin to suggest a coherent economic and fiscal system by which each sum of money can be weighed and valued, a system of difference and connection in which the sums take on a life of their own, as if money were a strangely creative force in the play. The play's economies, its systems of value are consistently measured against the coherence of the Venetian economy, a system where everyone has a clear idea of the worth of ducats. Apart from the bond of 3,000 ducats I want to concentrate on four other sums: 60,000, 36,000, 1,000 and 80.[4]

When the news reaches Belmont that Antonio could not pay his bond when it came due and that the pound of flesh is now forfeit, Salerio makes clear that Shylock will no longer accept the repayment of the sum: 'it should appear that if he had / The present money to discharge the Jew / He would not take it' (3.2.270–2). As Shylock himself makes clear in the trial scene, having the pound of Antonio's flesh is worth the loss of the sum of the bond: 'The pound of flesh which I demand of him / Is dearly bought' (4.1.98–9), the last phrase echoing Portia's valuation of Bassanio's love in relation to the gift she will make to him of money to settle Antonio's debts, 'Since you are dear bought, I will love you dear' (3.2.311). This pound of human meat would cost Shylock 3,000 ducats or 6,600 ducats per kilo.

Indeed it would not matter to Shylock if he were offered more. As Jessica tells the gathering at Belmont:

> I have heard him swear
> To Tubal and to Cush, his countrymen,
> That he would rather have Antonio's flesh
> Than twenty times the value of the sum
> That he did owe him ... (3.2.282–6)

So my first sum, 60,000, represents the limits of Shylock's imaginings, a fantastical excess of over-re-payment. Repaying the principal twenty times for a bond for three months represents an 8,000% base annual rate of interest, even though here, of course, it will not be an interest payment but a penalty payment. Crucially Shylock's bond has not been usurious and would have stood at no risk under English law, in particular the Statute of 1571 which defined English legal attitudes at the time of Shakespeare's writing *The Merchant of Venice*. Any bond which charged interest at more than 10% could automatically be nullified under this act and a number of subsequent cases tightened attempts to evade the statute but Shylock's bond would not have fallen foul of the statute or the case-law.[5]

Shakespeare has allowed the numbers 60 and 1,000 to appear earlier in the scene in Portia's extravagantly modest wish to be far fairer and richer, to be many times herself for Bassanio:

> yet for you
> I would be trebled twenty times myself,
> A thousand times more fair, ten thousand times more rich,
> That only to stand high in your account
> I might in virtues, beauties, livings, friends,
> Exceed account. (152–7)

But, though Portia's multiplication tables include wealth, it seems an abstracted conceptualisation of number, not something translatable into the

practice of Venetian or Belmontese economics. With Jessica's statement it is
newly grounded in the reality of Shylock's commitment to his bond.

Jessica makes her statement as forthrightly as she can but there seems to
be some problem in Portia's taking in the information. Perhaps she is simply
not listening to the account. Certainly Jessica's statement is not responded to
at all for the line which follows it, spoken by Portia, is addressed not to Jessica
but to Bassanio: 'Is it your dear friend that is thus in trouble?' (289) The hiatus
here between statements might be significant. There are many ways to play it: a
deliberate ignoring of the Jewess's words, a stunned silence at the absolute nature
of her information, a delivery of Jessica's speech to Lorenzo so that the others
do not quite hear it, a comment to her love triggered by Jessica's using Antonio's
name (284, 288). But, however it is played, the gap, the refusal of the normal
mechanism of dialogue—statement and response—needs noting and playing.
In that gap, the notion of the sum of money is translated into a definition of
social inter-relationship, the understanding of how Jewess and heiress interact.

When Portia does turn to the question of the sum, the riches of Belmont
become apparent. We have known from the first mention of her—by Bassanio to Antonio in the first scene—that Portia has been 'richly left' (1.1.161),
that she has inherited a considerable fortune from her father. That may have
been manifest in modern productions in the opulence of the set for Belmont.
Now, though, it becomes stated in terms of monetary value. Finding that the
debt is 3,000 ducats, Portia replies:

> What, no more?
> Pay him six thousand, and deface the bond.
> Double six thousand and then treble that,
> Before a friend of this description
> Shall lose a hair thorough Bassanio's fault. (296–300)

After the wedding is solemnised, then, even before it is consummated,
Portia suggests Bassanio rushes off to Venice: 'You shall have gold / To pay
the petty debt twenty times over' (304–5). I suppose it all depends what you
mean by petty. Portia finally offers Bassanio precisely the sum that Jessica
has already said Shylock will turn down. Where it was difficult for Antonio
to raise 3,000 ducats, where even Shylock says that he cannot, in his present
financial circumstances, lay his hands immediately on the money, 'I cannot
instantly raise up the gross / Of full three thousand ducats' (1.3.53–4), Portia has no hesitation in offering 60,000. 'Richly left' indeed.

Along the way, though, if the audience's mental arithmetic keeps up with
her lavishness, she offers a sum of 36,000—'Double six thousand, and then
treble that'—and the sum reappears in the trial scene. Bassanio offers Shylock

six thousand ducats, the first figure that Portia mooted as sufficient to 'deface the bond' and a sum he has presumably borrowed from Portia anticipating, foolishly, that it would be enough to assuage Shylock's demand for vengeance. If we have a notion of Bassanio as prodigal and wastrel, the spendthrift who has run through his fortune and is now dependent on the generosity of Antonio to go a-wiving in the style he thinks appropriate, then it is offset by a certain caution here or an assumption that his understanding of economics will indicate the sufficiency of 6,000 to appease Shylock's greed. Bassanio's notion of extravagance is, in this circumstance, quite circumspect, taking enough of his newly acquired wealth to do what he thinks is possible but unwilling now to go the whole way and use such a large figure, whatever it may be as a proportion of Portia's wealth, to deal with the Jew. But Shylock responds: 'If every ducat in six thousand ducats / Were in six parts, and every part a ducat, / I would not draw them' (4.1.84–6). The imaginary sums of ducats and the idea of what can be done with them now seem to multiply. The sums become creative and fertile, transferring from Belmont to Venice without any apparent means, magically transporting themselves from one place to another. Money as a concept is fluid and transient at exactly the point in the play in which, intransigent and intractable as he is at his most extreme, Shylock refuses to allow any transfer of sums at all. As the idea of what constitutes a lavish sum moves from Venice to Belmont and back to Venice so the money itself is tied up in Shylock's hatred and the operation of justice. It all depends now on Shylock's willingness to accept any sum, on his evaluation of the reasons to be merciful, given that there is no legal compulsion on him to accept the money. Indeed the law is as immovable as Shylock: Bassanio's suggestion that the law can be adjusted—'Wrest once the law to your authority. / To do a great right, do a little wrong . . .' (212–3)—seems to shock Portia: 'It must not be' (215).

Shylock's refusal continues the original agreement which locked the sum in an interest-free contract and defined the non-financial penalty for defaulting. Significantly, Shylock, typed and figured as the usurer by the Christians, did not charge Antonio interest on the loan. As a gesture of supposed friendship, he has offered the sum interest-free:

> I would be friends with you and have your love,
> Forget the shames that you have stained me with,
> Supply your present wants, and take no doit
> Of usance for my moneys; and you'll not hear me.
> This is kind I offer. (1.3.136–40)

Bassanio's reply picks up, perhaps suspiciously, on that crucial last word: 'This were kindness' (141). 'Kind' and 'kindness' are a common Shakespearean pun. Editors usually manage not to spell it out sufficiently clearly but Shylock means both that he will be benevolent and generous but also that he will be of Antonio's kind, like him in lending 'out money gratis', that the Jew is capable of and willing to behave like a Christian. Far from belonging to a necessarily other group, a subset of humanity or indeed a set of subhumanity, the group of Jews who are unable ever to be like Christians, Shylock offers something else, a form of integration, of effective assimilation into the dominant Venetian culture, through an acceptance of their business practices in this one offer at least. It is a notion keyed into this discussion through Shylock's elaborate description of the way Jacob made a fortune with the ewes, a process in which sex between rams and ewes becomes defined as natural, species-specific, 'the deed of kind' (84).

But there is a further problem, hinted at in Shylock's statement about where he will find the additional part of the 3,000 ducats that he does not have available: 'Tubal, a wealthy Hebrew of my tribe, / Will furnish me' (55–6). One of the crucial passages on usury is in Deuteronomy chapter 23, verses 19–20 and I quote from the Geneva Bible (1587), one of the translations Shakespeare is likely to have known:

> Thou shalt not give to usurie to thy brother: *as* usurie of money, usurie of meat, usurie of any thing that is put to usurie. Unto a stranger thou mayest lend upon usurie, but thou shalt not lend upon usurie unto thy brother, that the Lord thy God may bless thee in all that thou settest thine hand to, in the land whither thou goest to possesse it.

The marginal gloss in the Geneva Bible to the phrase about lending to a stranger reads 'This was permitted for a time for the hardnesse of their heart', a reminder of the depth of antagonism to usury even at a point where the Bible explicitly permits it. When Shylock borrows money from Tubal, a member of his tribe, a brother in the sense that the biblical phrase implies, Tubal would be unable to charge Shylock interest, even though the eventual destination of the money is Antonio—or properly Bassanio. Of course there will be nothing remotely like a legal agreement for that loan between Christians: it is a bargain between gentlemen, a gentleman's agreement, a loan without security which depends on the accuracy of Bassanio's aim with the arrows:

> In my schooldays, when I had lost one shaft,
> I shot his fellow of the selfsame flight
> The selfsame way with more advisèd watch,
> To find the other forth, and by adventuring both
> I oft found both. (1.1.140–4)

This image of Bassanio's is the only real economic justification or security he offers Antonio for Antonio's pouring yet more money into Bassanio's hands. The argument is doubly unconvincing: firstly it is simply an account of a frequent, but not consistent, solution ('I *oft* found both'); secondly, it is simply a false account of effective archery, for the schoolboy who mistakes his aim will be unable to replicate the mis-shot on any but the rarest of occasions.

Bassanio is doubly Antonio's debtor: 'To you, Antonio, / I owe the most in money and in love' (1.1.130–1). Bassanio is bound in love to Antonio; he needs to repay that love as well as the money. But some of his other debts have—he hints—a more substantial obligation:

> my chief care
> Is to come fairly off from the great debts
> Wherein my time, something too prodigal,
> Hath left me gaged. (127–30)

What happens to a Venetian gentleman like Bassanio, unlike a merchant such as Antonio, when he fails to meet the due date of his other debts is far from clear in the play. Gentlemen, especially gentlemen without other forms of income than their inherited wealth and with no intention of working for a living even by the trade of mercantile speculation, live on credit. Antonio's letter to Bassanio indicates that when a merchant falls on hard times, all credit is called in: 'my creditors grow cruel' (3.2.314) writes Antonio and we might reasonably assume that Shylock is the only Jew amongst them. Characteristically, however, the language of economics affects Bassanio's description to Antonio here, at the beginning of the play, about his style of living: he has showed

> a more swelling port
> Than my faint means would grant continuance,
> Nor do I now make moan to be abridged
> From such a noble rate. (1.1.124–7)

'Rate' is usually glossed as 'style' but the word also suggests a rate of expenditure: Shylock speaks of Antonio bringing down '[t]he rate of usance here with us in Venice' (1.3.42); Morocco wonders whether Portia is 'rated by thy estimation' (2.7.26); Bassanio, trying to explain his poverty to Portia, speaks of '[r]ating myself at nothing' (3.2.255). A word intrinsically bound up with finance is here appropriated by and appropriate to the nature of gentlemanly and gentile existence, living at 'a noble rate'. But the word spirals outwards, as so often with Shakespeare's language, for Antonio's attitude towards

Shylock is also a matter of 'rate': not long after he has spoken in aside about 'the rate of usance' Shylock uses both nouns again, separated more widely in a sentence,

> Signior Antonio, many a time and oft
> In the Rialto you have rated me
> About my moneys and my usances. (1.3.105–07)

Now the word 'rate', changed from noun to verb, carries the notion of opprobrium: Antonio berates Shylock for his rate of usance. One man's rate deserves another man's berating; Shylock's rate turns him into a loan shark or, to extend a pun that Shylock explores, a land-rat, a pirate.

Antonio's practice of loans without interest 'brings down / The rate of usance here with us in Venice', threatening the economic basis of Jewish income since Jews were more or less restricted to usury as a form of income, unable to make speculative investments in trade of the kind that Antonio so extravagantly has done in consigning his wealth to the ships heading across the world in different directions. Risky though such ventures could be, Antonio has been both extravagant and cautious. It may be that all his wealth is bound up in these ventures, that he has no liquidity, no monetary assets and indeed no assets sufficiently assured to enable others to use them as security for a loan. But he has chosen to spread the risk. As Shylock reminds Bassanio in the scene where the loan is set up, 'He hath an argosy bound to Tripolis, another to the Indies. I understand moreover upon the Rialto he hath a third at Mexico, a fourth for England, and other ventures he hath squandered abroad' (1.3.17–21) Squandering is significant: Shylock suggests that the ventures are a waste of money, a kind of venture that would be bound to lead to inevitable loss and catastrophe. Antonio, at this point, appears a little like Bassanio, another figure who has squandered his wealth incautiously. But such enterprises could produce phenomenal profits, a return on investment of many thousand per cent, far beyond anything that usury or the simple charging of non-usurious interest could expect. It may be something of a lottery but there were enough examples in England of merchants who had grown fantastically rich on the profits of a single such voyage. Venture capitalism in a context of mercantilist culture was the risky but often remarkably successful route to wealth.

Viewed in this way, Antonio's sending out his argosies to trade is remarkably like the reason that Bassanio needs to borrow the 3,000 ducats in the first place. The journey to Belmont is a sea-voyage, a speculative enterprise. Unlike Antonio who spreads the risk by having a whole series of different ships out at sea, a fleet of ventures, Bassanio will sink all his money in one last-ditch effort to extricate himself from debt. The journey to Belmont becomes, in Bassanio's first description of it, an epic quest, a voyage premised on the nature of Portia's hair:

> her sunny locks
> Hang on her temples like a golden fleece,
> Which makes her seat of Belmont Colchis' strand,
> And many Jasons come in quest of her. (1.1.169–72)

The risky voyage to Colchis undertaken by Jason and the argonauts to bring back the Golden Fleece objectifies Portia as a mythic object to be won; the Fleece becomes her hair and the temple where it was hanging becomes nothing more religious than a part of her head. When Bassanio chooses aright in the lottery (another speculative venture), Graziano comments 'We are the Jasons; we have won the fleece' (3.2.239) and the image returns. Perhaps it is a language that Bassanio would only use to Antonio, a kind of demeaning assessment of the meaning of his enterprise that he would never voice to Portia, but no such notion of tact inhibits Graziano.

But why does Bassanio need the money? There is a striking difference between the epic quest that Bassanio seems to be undertaking in venturing from Venice to Belmont and the kind of journey from Padua to Venice that Portia describes when instructing Balthasar to visit Bellario:

> look what notes and garments he doth give thee,
> Bring them, I pray thee, with imagined speed,
> Unto the traject, to the common ferry
> Which trades to Venice. (3.4.51–4)

There seems to be a regular public transport system around of traghetti, Italian ferries. Where Bassanio needs to be decked out at the right noble rate for this great questing journey, caparisoned in the style to which he has been accustomed and in which he hopes marriage to Portia will maintain him, Portia suggests a rather different way of navigating these ventures: one simply checks the timetable and catches the next ferry.[6] Bassanio's voyage, his stylish venture which will cost 3,000 ducats to set up, needs such extravagance not to impress Portia but to 'hold a rival place' (1.1.174) with the other Jasons. Once Bassanio has got the 3,000 ducats, we see him using it by instructing a servant to 'put the liveries to making' (2.2.110–11), ensuring his servants will represent his state properly at Belmont, so that his new servant Gobbo will have an especially ornamental outfit, 'a livery / More guarded than his fellows' (149–50). But Bassanio has other uses for the money: he will spend some of it on a 'supper', a party before the voyage at which he will 'feast tonight / My best-esteemed acquaintance' (165–6), a feast which will include a spectacle of a masque. Such extravagance among his fellows in Venice, like the proper appearance among his rivals in Belmont, is for Bassanio the right way of spending Antonio's loan. As far as he is concerned, this male rivalry is what matters and the expenditure of even such a large sum as this looks to him like 'thrift': 'I have a mind presages me such thrift / That I should questionless be fortunate' (1.1.175–6).

We will hear the word 'thrift' again later in the play and the cluster of meaning that surrounds it is another part of the play's revaluation of the language of money. Three of its occurrences will come from Shylock. In that powerful long aside about Antonio, 'How like a fawning publican he looks', he complains that Antonio rails 'On me, my bargains, and my well-won thrift' (1.3.48). He ends the long strange description of Jacob's tricking Laban, a passage which characterises the otherness of his linguistic register so strongly, with the statement 'thrift is blessing, if men steal it not' (87). Talking with Jessica, he lets the word appear in connection with another rather glib moral cliché: 'Fast bind, fast find—/ A proverb never stale in thrifty mind' (2.5.53–4). Making a profit is now a matter of thrift. Being careful with one's resources is a good lesson for anyone wanting to be thrifty. One meaning of thrift is being economical with one's assets: as Hamlet tells Horatio about the rapid sequence of his father's funeral and his mother's remarriage, 'Thrift, thrift, Horatio. The funeral baked meats / Did coldly furnish forth the marriage tables' (1.2.179–80). But that is not quite what Shylock means. 'Thrift' here in *The Merchant of Venice* is allowed to connect to its cognate verb, 'to thrive'. Where 'thrift' might suggest being frugal, 'thrive' might suggest to Bassanio being extravagant; certainly for Shylock it suggests being hugely successful. For Shylock the two may come together: as Shylock says of Jacob's stratagem, 'This was a way to thrive; and he was blest' (1.3.88). Like Bassanio's first use of 'thrift', thrifty thriving is a way to be 'fortunate'. Jacob's trick is a substantially profitable enterprise, a little like sharp practice perhaps in the way of persuading the ewes to generate more 'parti-coloured lambs' which would be Jacob's but a trick that the Old Testament and Shylock seem to approve of.

If you make the right—that is, thrifty—choice you should thrive but gold is not necessarily the way to thrift and thriving. A later appearance of the word is at the end of Morocco's speech of choice. He chooses the golden casket: 'Here do I choose, and thrive I as I may' (2.7.60). This choice, the reverse one might think of being thrifty, is no way to thrive. The meagre choice of lead, the thriftiest substance used in the manufacture of the caskets, proves to be the right way to thrive. Bassanio's journey will be thrifty in the sense that it will be profitable but the way to achieve it is, for Bassanio, to ensure that he continues to appear at the same 'noble rate' that had got him into financial trouble before.

There is here an ambiguity about how one uses one's resources that is central to the conflict of care and extravagance in the play. For Bassanio to be truly thrifty he must 'give and hazard all he hath' (2.7.16), venture everything to gain the golden fleece. It suggests the problem in the play's last use of thrift. Lorenzo teases—or taunts—Jessica that

> In such a night
> Did Jessica steal from the wealthy Jew,
> And with an unthrift love did run from Venice
> As far as Belmont. (5.1.14–17)

Lorenzo's language is disconcertingly ambiguous: does Jessica 'steal' away from Shylock or does she steal money from him? Is the 'unthrift love' Jessica's love for Lorenzo, her emotions and, as I shall suggest, financial practices that are not restricted by the habits of her father whose 'fast bind, fast find' is his form of thrift; or is the 'love' Lorenzo himself, a spendthrift like Bassanio who needs Jessica's wealth as much, or even more, than he needs Jessica?

But the financing of Bassanio's venture also affects another area of linguistic terminology, a value-system that Shylock suggests is connected with money. As Shylock, in conversation with Bassanio, considers whether Antonio is a reasonable risk, he comments to Bassanio 'Antonio is a good man' (1.3.12). Bassanio bridles at the suggestion that he might be anything else: 'Have you heard any imputation to the contrary?' (13–14). And Shylock has to spell out to this apparently unbusinesslike figure how the word 'good' is to be understood in this context:

> Ho, no, no, no, no! My meaning in saying he is a good man is to have you understand me that he is sufficient. Yet his means are in supposition. (15–17)

Being 'sufficient', the opposite of being prodigal, is to have sufficient sums available, to be solvent, not bankrupt like Bassanio, to be affluent, well-to-do. It is not only a question of Antonio's status but also whether he is a decent business risk. Morality, at least in the way that Bassanio hears the word 'good', is bound here to the language of business. Whether Antonio is moral or not, kind, generous, good-hearted or any other meaning of the word in conventional moral terms, is irrelevant to good business practices. Shylock is only concerned whether Antonio is good for the money's repayment.

Yet the bond is made without interest. Assimilation and acceptance by the gentile, gentle, aristocratic world of Venetian Christians will cost Shylock an entrance fee, the refusal of interest. He offers it as a gesture of being of the same kind, of belonging naturally to the group of humans, the social grouping on whose margins he exists: 'This kindness will I show' (142). Among people of the same kind there can be game-playing and even something as serious as a bond, a legal document that underpins the basis of the state as a just institution in which business can be properly conducted, can be the subject for 'a merry sport' (144), the condition which is attached to the bond by Shylock, the price of forfeiture at a pound of flesh. The aspiration for acceptance may of course be only a lie and Shylock's long aside, 'How like a fawning publican he looks' (39–50), belies the gesture of friendship.

But there are other ways of making money than mercantile speculation of trade or charging high rates of interest; one way is betting. Just before the threat posed by Shylock bursts into the restrained world of Belmont, Graziano suggests that fertility can be a way of making money fertile, making it as creative as the sexual activity he and Nerissa will enjoy as man and wife: 'We'll play with them the first boy for a thousand ducats' (3.2.213). Nerissa is hesitant about how the wager will be set up: 'What, and stake down?' (214). Her meaning, that the money would have to be laid on the table for the wager to be valid, is taken in a different way by her future husband: 'No, we shall ne'er win at that sport and stake down' (215). Typically Graziano turns her financial argument into a sexual pun, for he plays on the other meaning of 'stake down' as 'with a limp penis'. If he cannot get an erection the son will never be conceived. Making money in this context is an expression of masculinity, an extension to his virility. The more often his penis is hard, the more likely they are quickly to conceive a son worth a thousand ducats. A bet becomes a dirty joke, a bawdy pun on the sexual activity which is after all the subject of the bet. In the economy of Graziano's language such word-play, such creativity and multiplicity of language is fundamental—and in the infectious way his language operates I am left with the pun on 'fundamental' uncontrollably present.

In all kinds of ways there is nothing elsewhere in Shakespeare's drama quite like the end of this play but I find the fact that it gives its final lines to Graziano more than a little unnerving. No other Shakespearean comedy ends with such a direct and bawdy pun: 'Well, while I live I'll fear no other thing / So sore as keeping safe Nerissa's ring' (5.1.306–7). The play's most recent editor, Jay Halio in the Oxford edition, spells out for us what the pun means, both a piece of jewellery and Nerissa's vulva. The line is an allusion to an old joke, the assumption that the right way, indeed the only way, to keep one's wife faithful is not to keep her ring on one's finger but to keep a finger inserted in her vagina.

But when Halio suggests that 'the romantic comedy appropriately ends on another bit of bawdy punning' I have to disagree.[7] Graziano's pun is horribly reductive. The language of love has become the language of male fear of uncontrollable female sexual activity. Instead of allowing an unmediated focus on the rings that have moved from finger to finger throughout the later part of the play, Shakespeare instead requires that we become startlingly aware of Nerissa's genitals. Modern productions usually balk at the implications of this, preferring to leave the pun undefined and the attention of the audience looking at the ring now back on Graziano's finger but the pun is actively there, a threat to the kinds of emotions of love prevalent in the Portia–Bassanio relationship. In its salacious punning it demeans the romantic world of Belmont, a reminder of the laddish, loutish culture of Venice to which Graziano—and Bassanio—belong.

The movement of the women's rings serves to remind us of another ring in the play, another circle of prodigality and rejection of thrift, as well as providing a link to my last sum of ducats: 80. As Shylock laments the loss of his money and his daughter to Tubal, the latter passes on two pieces of news about Jessica's activities in Genoa that he has gathered. 'Your daughter spent in Genoa, as I heard, one night fourscore ducats.' Shylock is tormented by the news: 'Thou stick'st a dagger in me. I shall never see my gold again. Fourscore ducats at a sitting? Fourscore ducats?' (3.1.100–4). But worse is to follow: one of Antonio's creditors, while telling Tubal that Antonio is bound to go bankrupt, that 'he cannot choose but break' (106–7), showed him 'a ring that he had of your daughter for a monkey.'

> *Shylock.* Out upon her! Thou torturest me, Tubal. It was my
> turquoise. I had it of Leah when I was a bachelor. I would not
> have given it for a wilderness of monkeys. (110–14)

The two pieces of news seem to me strikingly different. The first is a simple mark of extravagance and of the impossibility of Shylock's ever recovering all his gold. He has lost money and jewels: one of the jewels, a diamond, 'cost me two thousand ducats in Frankfurt' (79).

This may be the moment finally to consider the value of money. A ducat was an Italian gold coin, first minted in 1284, and widely copied. As Fischer states, the reverse of some ducats showed Christ and may therefore be the source of Shylock's reported reference to his 'Christian ducats' (2.8.16).[8] There were Italian silver ducats in circulation worth in England at the end of the 16th century approximately 3s. 41/2d. (approximately 161/2p.) but the Venetian coins of *The Merchant of Venice* are almost certainly gold ducats, worth at this point, according to Fischer, approximately 9s. (45p).[9] In fact the exchange rate was not fixed: in 1436–40 it was worth 45p in Venice (as *pecunia praesens*) and 42p in London ('where it was *pecunia absens*').[10] By 1503–6 the rate was varying between 49p and 56p per ducat.[11] As Antonio Salutati commented in 1416 in a merchant's manual: 'He who deals in exchanges and he who deals in merchandise is always anxious and beset by worries. I will instead give you a recipe for lasagna and macaroni'.[12]

Shakespeare uses the term 'ducat(s)' 59 times in ten plays, though 33 of all occurrences occur in *The Merchant of Venice*. It is one of the units of currency in Illyria (*Twelfth Night*), Italy (e.g. *Cymbeline*), Denmark (*Hamlet*) and Ephesus (*Comedy of Errors*).[13] Unlike the kinds of problems with talents in *Timon of Athens*, Shakespeare seems to have maintained a consistent sense of its value, roughly equivalent to the exchange rate.

What the sum might mean in modern terms is much more difficult to calculate since calculations based on notions of inflation are always difficult as values shifted rapidly at certain periods during Shakespeare's working life and the relational value of individual items of expenditure alters substantially between the early modern period and the present. But the income of 3,000 ducats a year which Sir Andrew Aguecheek received represented a sum worthy of a gentleman (*Twelfth Night*, 1.3.20). As Wells points out,

> the salary paid to the Stratford schoolmaster in Shakespeare's youth ... was £20 a year, very much more than that of any of the wages stipulated by proclamation to be paid to members of the London companies in 1587—the highest paid were the brewers at £10 a year.[14]

If we multiply early values by about 200, it will serve as a reasonably cautious rule of thumb. Don John, in *Much Ado About Nothing*, pays Borachio a thousand ducats for his help in the plot against Hero (3.3.105–6) while the Courtesan in *The Comedy of Errors* is concerned that 'forty ducats is too much to lose' (4.3.96). At the time, Don John's reward would have been worth approximately £450 and the Courtesan was worrying about £18; in modern terms, the sums would have been approximately £90,000 and £3,600. In *The Merchant of Venice*, Antonio is borrowing a sum of about £270,000 to lend to Bassanio. Shylock refuses a repayment of £540,000; Portia offers extraordinary sums worth between £3.24 million and £5.4 million; Shylock's diamond cost about £180,000 and in one night at Genoa Jessica spent well over £7,200 on dinner.

I think such estimates of value are significant for our understanding of the meaning of the sums quoted: if the sums Portia offers seem to us extravagant they are seen in relation to other sums, the sums that belong to Venice as it were, that are large but not fantasticated. Portia's huge wealth does not therefore become a fairy-tale sum, even though it would put her on any list of the world's richest people. Jessica's expenditure of £7,200 must affect how we evaluate Shylock's reaction. If a ducat were worth considerably less, then Shylock's horror at the expenditure of fourscore in an evening would exemplify his stinginess. He could be accused of being not only a usurer but also a miser. But with these sums in mind the shock is unsurprising, almost reasonable: children, whether they have stolen the money from their parents or not, are not supposed to spend at 'such a noble rate'. This is expenditure in Bassanio's league. How Shylock reacts might be defined by our sense of Shylock's use of his money, as, for instance, typified by two performances of the role in Stratford. In 1978, at The Other Place, Patrick Stewart played Shylock in a production directed by John Barton. Three years later, Barton directed the play again, this time with David Suchet as Shylock. Both productions were set late: late 19th century for Stewart, 20th century for Suchet. Their readings of the role are encapsulated by what they smoked. Suchet puffed on a large fat cigar. As he faced Tubal across the table in this scene, both smoked large havanas so that the conversation was wreathed in cigar smoke. He wore a heavy overcoat and was expensively dressed, looking every inch the wealthy businessman, the affluent director of a multi-national bank, a modern Rothschild perhaps. Whatever else may have been true about this Shylock he clearly had no qualms about spending his money: being thrifty did not mean a refusal to spend anything. Here, by contrast, is Stewart's own description of his costume:

> A shabby black frock coat, torn at the hem and stained, a waistcoat dusted with cigarette ash, baggy black trousers, short in the leg, exposing down-at-heel old boots, and a collarless shirt yellowing with age.

In this production Antonio smoked cheroots, Tubal a havana and Shylock what Stewart called 'his mean little hand-rolled cigarettes, whose butt-ends were safely stored away for future use.'[15] For a man who was unwilling to spend anything on himself, for whom the acquisition of money was everything and the enjoyment to be found solely in the acquisition Jessica's extravagance must have been appalling. Hence, too, his horror at the moment when he comments, as much to himself as to Tubal, 'And I know not what's spent in the search', and Tubal pushes across the table to him the bill for his expenses. As Stewart comments in his account of the performance, the bill 'included, in writing just too small for the audience to read, a huge bar and restaurant bill for two nights at the Genoa Hilton'.[16]

For the playwright Arnold Wesker this was a particularly infuriating and indeed anti-semitic moment which occurred in both Barton's productions (he is actually describing the 1981 version) and was the kind of moment that led to his own adaptation of the play, variously titled *Shylock* and *The Merchant* in different states of revision, probably the finest rethinking of a Shakespeare play this century:

> canny old Tubal presents him with a bill. Ho! Ho! The audience
> laughed again to be reminded that not only do Jews suck dry
> Christian blood, they suck each other's as well! Of course! Jews
> are insensitive to each other's pain. A debt after all is a debt. Why
> wait till grief is past?[17]

But even for a Shylock willing to spend money, like Suchet, the sum of fourscore ducats that Jessica spent in a night must have seemed extravagant, far beyond even his comfortable life-style. Money has value; it exists in an exchange-system which ascribes value to it. Objects can have precise value as well. The meaning of the loss of diamond may be precisely and adequately expressed by its cost; its purchase price of two thousand ducats may be all we need to know about it. But we use another term for valuing the valueless or invaluable; we talk of objects having 'sentimental value' and, if sentimental is a word we are wary of, then in this context it may have a precise and deeply painful sense. Robbery reminds us of that which cannot be expressed in value, of the meanings we attach to objects in ways that insurance companies do not comprehend. Rings have an especial potency in this economic system of value and its denial. It is striking that in another play in which Shakespeare uses a monetary system based on ducats, *Cymbeline*, here too the problem is the value placed on a ring as Posthumus is drawn from prizing or pricing Imogen and the symbol of her, his ring, at 'More than the world enjoys' (1.4.77) into accepting that the ring—and hence Imogen—can have precise value, the wager with Iachimo of the ring against 10,000 ducats on Imogen's chastity (1.4.125).[18] When Portia, after the trial scene, tries to wheedle her ring out of Bassanio, he recognizes a distinction between its monetary worth and its meaning as a token of love in betrothal as well as an embodiment of the transfer of Portia's father's wealth to her husband: 'There's more depends on this than on the value' (4.1.431) since, earlier, when Portia had transferred it to him, she defined the full range of its potent meanings:

> This house, these servants, and this same myself
> Are yours, my lord's. I give them with this ring,
> Which when you part from, lose, or give away,

> Let it presage the ruin of your love
> And be my vantage to exclaim on you. (3.2.170–4)

Her sense of its future ('Let it *presage*') is as accurate as Bassanio's sense of his fortunate journey to Belmont: 'I have a mind *presages* me such thrift' (1.1.175). The ring signifies a transfer of wealth, of status, of love and, not least important, of Portia herself, a woman trapped, through the exchange processes of patriarchy, in the transition between father and husband, rescued, by Bassanio's choice of casket, from the limbo of being unattached to any man except the 'will of a dead father' (1.2.24). Hence, confronted by Portia's, or rather 'Balthasar's', pressing request, Bassanio offers instead 'The dearest ring in Venice will I give you, / And find it out by proclamation' (4.1.432–3). Money, here, is no object; he will spend anything but not pass over the ring. That he does so is in part to accede to Antonio's request in a precise expression of the relative value of two sides of Bassanio's life:

> My Lord Bassanio, let him have the ring.
> Let his deservings and my love withal
> Be valued 'gainst your wife's commandëment. (446–8)

Antonio carefully balances the deservings and love on the one hand and the orders of a wife on the other, a deliberately unequal equation.

At the climax of the trial scene, just as he is about to face Shylock's knife, Antonio had pointedly linked his farewell to his intrusion in Bassanio's relationship to Portia:

> Commend me to your honourable wife.
> Tell her the process of Antonio's end.
> Say how I loved you . . . (270–2)

The rhythm of the last line is tricky: is it an iambic instruction to describe the manner of the love ('Say how I loved you') or a non-iambic, trochaic emphasis that he should speak of Antonio's love for Bassanio rather than hers ('*Say* how *I* loved *you*')? Bassanio defines his response in terms of a theory of valueless value, an attitude to value that goes beyond anything that can be valued, something outside the exchange systems by which value is defined:

> Antonio, I am married to a wife
> Which is as dear to me as life itself,
> But life itself, my wife, and all the world

Are not with me esteemed above thy life.
I would lose all, ay, sacrifice them all
Here to this devil, to deliver you. (279–84)

Portia's list of the wealth embodied in the ring is precise and meaningful in a structure of exchange: 'This house, these servants, and this same myself'. Bassanio's is not. No wonder that Portia's response is a wry comment—usually, though for me unnecessarily—marked by editors as an aside:

Your wife would give you little thanks for that,
If she were by to hear you make the offer. (285–6)

The value Bassanio or Antonio might place on their relationship—however we read the degree of active homoerotic desire on either part between them—is one that could threaten Bassanio's marriage to Portia. In the eccentric and intriguing production by the American director Peter Sellars for the Goodman Theatre in Chicago in 1994, Portia did not at the end of the play hand over to Antonio a sealed letter announcing the safe return of three argosies—a moment of blatant artifice underlined by her comment 'You shall not know by what strange accident / I chancèd on this letter' (5.1.278–9). Instead she calmly wrote him out a large cheque, a clear indication that he should get out of her husband's life and stay out.

In a monetary system objects can be placed beyond value and that leads back, finally, to Jessica's theft of Shylock's ring. Shylock's distress at the loss of the turquoise has nothing to do with its monetary value. He does not price it. Instead he gives it a history, places it in relation to his life. Patrick Stewart described it as a 'simple gift, possibly a betrothal ring, from a woman to her lover'.[19] I would remove the hesitation over 'possibly'. The ring defines Shylock's wife's love for him and hence, in the value he attaches to it, his love for his wife. For Stewart much is contained in that word 'bachelor':

That word shatters our image of this man Shylock and we see the man that once was, a bachelor, ... Shakespeare doesn't need to write a prehistory of Shylock. Those two lines say it all.

It is striking how this lost youth points to the overwhelming sense of loss that surrounds Shylock. Leah, like many Shakespearean wives and mothers is invisible, unseen and largely unknown but it is difficult to hear in Shylock's lines anything other than love and pain, the two emotions captured together in the 'wilderness', the arid world inhabited only by chattering monkeys, those symbols of lust. Jessica's pet seems a peculiarly cruel substitute for the ring and the substitution itself, the choice of selling that ring, is a mark of her cruelty. For it is surely unlikely that Jessica did not know the meaning of that ring, the token of betrothal, the link between her parents.

I do not want to be reading too obsessively realistically but her act of theft is an act of vengeance, a response to the hell she finds her father's house to be. Much will depend on how the relationship between Shylock and Jessica is played in their scene together but Henry Irving, in his production in 1879, added a silent scene which epitomized what the loss of Jessica meant for Shylock. After an extravagant playing of her escape, complete with a gondola propelled across the stage, the curtain dropped quickly and then rose again. The sound was heard of Shylock's walking stick; he entered carrying a lantern and crossed the bridge over the canal. He knocked at the door of his house three times, for, it is worth remembering, he has trusted Jessica with his keys and he has no means of access to his own house without them (Elizabethan houses did not have spare sets of keys). The lack of response disturbed him and he knocked again. Then a look of dumb and complete despair came over his face. Ellen Terry, who played Portia in the production, wrote that '[f]or absolute pathos, achieved by absolute simplicity of means, I never saw anything in the theatre to compare with' it.[20]

Jessica exchanges her father for a husband, Lorenzo. Rather than being passed from one male hand to another she chooses to control her own act of betrothal mobility. Perhaps she deserves her Lorenzo, the man who, after Jessica has praised Portia to the skies, can only respond by praising himself: 'Even such a husband / Hast thou of me as she is for a wife' (3.5.78–9), a curiously tasteless piece of Venetian male arrogance. In the circulation of exchange in the play, the structures of value, Jessica makes a very specific intervention, claiming the kind of right that is not available to Portia or at least which Portia chooses not to accept as being within her control. Jessica controls the meaning and value of her acts, but, like the effect of her conversion on the price of bacon (in Lancelot Gobbo's account), the implications start to spin out beyond her control into the forms of social organization dependent on a fiscal economy. As, by the end of Act 4, the Jews vanish from the play, so only the ambivalence of Jessica is left, unclear whether she is Jew or Christian, left in a religious limbo of damnation, a token whose value is increasingly uncertain and whose position in the play is increasingly one of silence. By the end it is Portia who is controlling the activity, the play's final ring-master, until, that is, even she has to cede control back to the male view of female behaviour, a context within which rings no longer signify a value of ducats or a value beyond ducats but simply a value of sexual possession and male fear.

Notes

1. All quotations from Shakespeare are taken from William Shakespeare, *The Complete Works*, eds. Stanley Wells, Gary Taylor et al. (Oxford: Clarendon Press, 1986), unless otherwise stated.

2. See Stanley Wells and Gary Taylor et al., *William Shakespeare: A Textual Companion* (Oxford: Clarendon Press, 1987), p. 504.

3. Other explanations include the differing value of the talent in Plutarch and Lucian, the main sources for *Timon of Athens*. See T. J. B. Spencer, 'Shakespeare learns the value of money', *Shakespeare Survey* 6 (1953) pp. 75–8, the article that provided my title; Wells and Taylor, *Textual Companion* pp. 501–02; see also Richard Proudfoot, 'Shakespeare's Coinage' in M. T. Jones-Davies, ed., *Shakespeare et l'argent* (Paris: Les Belles Lettres, 1993 [Actes du Congrès, 1992, Société Française Shakespeare]), pp. 101–15.

4. On ducats in this play see also Stanley Wells, 'Money in Shakespeare's comedies', in M. T. Jones-Davies, ed., *Shakespeare et l'argent*, pp. 161–71. Much recent criticism of the play has explored exchange processes in the play (see, e.g., Karen Newman, 'Portia's Ring: Unruly Women and Structures of Exchange in *The Merchant of Venice*,' *Shakespeare Quarterly* 38 (1987), pp. 19–33), but no-one seems to have been especially interested in the ducats themselves.

5. On the statute, see Norman Jones, *God and the Moneylenders* (Oxford: Basil Blackwell, 1989); for a more general study of early modern attitudes to usury, see Sandra K. Fischer, *Econolingua: A Glossary of Coins and Economic Language in Renaissance Drama* (Newark, Del.: University of Delaware Press, 1985), appendix A, pp. 138–51.

6. It is, incidentally, an unnoticed characteristic of the exchange practices across classes of this play that Portia simply takes away her servant's name when choosing one for her disguise: she sends her Balthasar on a journey from Belmont to Padua to Venice and then when he arrives in Venice with the 'notes and garments' provided by Bellario he will somehow become unnamed as Portia takes on his identity.

7. William Shakespeare, *The Merchant of Venice*, ed. Jay Halio (Oxford: Oxford University Press, 1994) p. 227.

8. Fischer, p. 69. Fischer's analysis of usury also suggests a meaning for Shylock's accusation that Antonio 'was wont to lend money for a Christian courtesy' (3.1.45–6) that editors have never annotated, to my knowledge. Edward I's proclamation of 1290, one of the crucial steps leading to the expulsion of the Jews from England, complains that the Jews had 'maliciously' invented a new kind of usury known as 'courtesy', usually understood to mean an extra-contractual obligation to pay a fee or a gift for the loan of the money, thereby evading statutory controls on usury since, the 'courtesy' being non-contractual, 'it was beyond the law in both enforcement and punishment' (p. 143). Shylock is therefore complaining about the kind of courtesy that Antonio uses in his loans: a loan without interest, seeking, at most, gratitude in return.

9. Fischer, p. 69 and p. 152.

10. See Frederic C. Lane and Reinhold C. Mueller, *Money and Banking in Medieval and Renaissance Venice*, vol. 2, *The Venetian Money Market* (Baltimore, MD: The Johns Hopkins University Press, 1997), pp. 327–37.

11. Ibid., pp. 345–53.

12. Ibid., p. 355.

13. It is also referred to in *Two Gentlemen of Verona*, *Romeo and Juliet*, *Much Ado About Nothing*, *Measure for Measure* and *The Taming of the Shrew*.

14. Wells, 'Money in Shakespeare's Comedies', p. 168, quoting Fischer, p. 153. The figure for brewers included 'meat and drink'; by comparison, goldsmiths were to be paid £8 a year 'with meat and drink' but 6s a week (= £15.12s a year) 'without meat and drink' (Fischer, p. 154).

15. See Patrick Stewart, 'Shylock' in Philip Brockbank, ed., *Players of Shakespeare* (Cambridge: Cambridge University Press, 1985), p. 18, and see also John Barton, *Playing Shakespeare* (London: Methuen, 1984), chapter 10, 'Exploring a Character: Playing Shylock', pp. 169–80.

16. Stewart, p. 23.

17. Arnold Wesker, *The Merchant*, (London: Methuen, 1983), p. lii

18. Wells comments of the colossal sum Iachimo wagers that it 'should seem breathtaking in its self-confidence' (Wells, 'Money in Shakespeare's Comedies', p. 169).

19. Stewart, p. 23.

20. See Ellen Terry, *Ellen Terry's Memoirs*, ed. Edith Craig and Christopher St. John (London: Victor Gollancz Ltd, 1933), p. 146.

GRACE TIFFANY

Law and Self-Interest in
The Merchant of Venice

Shakespearean comedy is notable for the blitheness with which, in some latter acts, rulers overturn laws they have previously described as inexorable. In the first scene of *A Midsummer Night's Dream*, Duke Theseus tells the hapless Hermia she must acquiesce in her father's choice of husband for her, enter a nunnery, or die, since the Athenian law that gives Egeus the right to dispose of his daughter is one that the duke "by no means [. . .] may extenuate" (1.1.120).[1] Yet in act four Theseus discovers a means to change the law. He can simply do it. Encountering Hermia and Lysander outside the Athenian wood, the duke overrides the complaint of Egeus—who "beg[s] the law, the law, upon [the] head" of Lysander for stealing his daughter—announcing, "Egeus, I will overbear your will" (4.1.155, 179). A similar reversal occurs in *The Comedy of Errors*. There the Duke of Ephesus initially tells the captive merchant Egeon that though he "may pity" he may "not pardon" him for his illegal entry into Ephesus, a city at war with Egeon's city, Syracuse (1.1.97). Egeon must die unless someone buys his release. Yet in act five, the Duke waves away the bag of ducats Egeon's son tries to hand him as "pawn" for his father, saying breezily, "It shall not need; thy father hath his life" (5.1.390). Audiences never question the late-term rule-changes in these plays, since their causes are manifest in the comedies' conclusions. As romantic (rather than satiric humors) comedies, these plays' final scenes

From *Papers on Language and Literature* 42, no. 4 (Fall 2006): 384–400. Copyright © 2006 by the Board of Trustees, Southern Illinois University at Edwardsville.

are consecrated to celebrations of love, not law: family reunion, marital reconciliation, and above all erotic harmony. When facing the miraculous finding of lost relatives and amazing tales of spiritually restorative magical events, civic law may properly bow.

What I want to explore is the diminishment of romantic-comic fulfillment in a play in which law does not bow to love: where, in fact, the reverse occurs, and love conforms to law. *The Merchant of Venice* violates Shakespearean comic convention, by which eros nullifies or overrides rules. In *The Taming of the Shrew*, the law that makes it "death for anyone in Mantua / To come to Padua" is only a hoax Tranio invents to get a Mantuan to don disguise and help in a wooing scheme (4.2.81–82). In *Love's Labor's Lost*, the Navarran king's rules against men's fraternization with ladies do not survive the play's first scene. Even the contorted and troublesome conclusion of *Measure for Measure* depends, for its various marital pairings and formal reconciliations, on Duke Vincentio's pardoning of the play's sexual criminals, Angelo, Claudio, Lucio, and Juliet. Only in *The Merchant of Venice* are conflicts resolved through adherence to law rather than by law's suspension. Thus the comedy affords no romantic release from law's domain into the realm of love, where private selves are generously sacrificed to a larger, shared identity. Instead, the play proposes a generosity and sacrifice tempered by underlying rules that limit and curb those qualities and that ensure private selves and private property are kept safe. Put another way, since rules and laws in *The Merchant of Venice* concern the contractual safeguarding of things, their sway has an anti-comic because anti-erotic effect. *The Merchant of Venice* celebrates not characters' warm embrace of mutual identity, as in marriage, but their cold preservation or augmentation of what they legally own. (Certainly Shakespeare derived some skepticism regarding love's power to nullify self-interestedness from Marlowe's *The Jew of Malta*, a play wherein the "wind that bloweth all the world" is not eros but "[d]esire of gold" [*The Jew of Malta* 3.5.3–4].) Thus *The Merchant of Venice* dramatizes the sobering influence of a mercantile ethic, enshrined in law, on a romantic-comic economy.

Contractual laws, or rules, designed to keep property safe hold sway in *The Merchant of Venice* despite its Christians' protestations of absolute generosity. Throughout the comedy not only enemies, like Shylock and Antonio, but lovers and friends hedge their commitments to one another with rules, charges, directions, and laws safeguarding their interests. Things are not given, but loaned. Debts are incurred and are not dismissed. "To you, Antonio," Bassanio says in the play's first scene, "I owe the most in money and in love" (1.1.130–131). Bassanio's statement is not merely a poetic description of an emotional debt, but a literal account of a real financial problem in whose light the play's romantic plot will be launched. Bassanio owes Antonio money as well as love, and must repay it. His decision to woo Portia is thus seen to arise not from erotic impulse (as do, for example, Claudio's pursuit of Hero in *Much Ado about Nothing*, Lysander's of Hermia in *A Midsummer Night's Dream*, and Syracusan Antipholus's of Luciana in *The Comedy of Errors*). Bassanio's plan is instead a scheme "to get clear of all the debts [he] owe[s]" (1.1.133–134). Portia's eroticism is similarly chilled by the care with which she provides for her own interests while ostensibly surrendering them to Bassanio. Once he has won her, she eloquently pledges her house, servants, and self to him "with this ring," but provides a caveat that entitles her to revoke all gifts if he breaks the rules that govern the ring's disposition. Such violation of the rules will give her "vantage"—a financial term meaning "profit"—to "exclaim on," or legally arraign, Bassanio for the breach (3.2.170–174).[2] Presumably when that happens, all bets will be off.

Even the generous Antonio, like Portia, hedges his kindness with caveats. "My purse, my person, my extremest means / Lie all unlocked to your occasions," he tells Bassanio in the play's first scene (1.1.138–139). But subsequent scenes disclose that that purse and person have their price. In an exercise of what Barbara Correll has called "emotional usury"[3]—or, to quote Timon of Athens, "usuring kindness" (4.3.509)—Antonio will promise to clear Bassanio's debt to him "if [he] might but see [him] at [his] death" (3.2.319–320), and when Bassanio comes to witness, in the Venetian courtroom, what he thinks will be Antonio's death, he is charged with nurturing and promoting Antonio's claim on his own heart. "Commend me to your honorable wife," Antonio instructs him then,

> Tell her the process of Antonio's end,
> Say how I loved you, speak me fair in death;
> And when the tale is told, bid her be judge
> Whether Bassanio had not once a love. (4.1.273–277)

After the courtroom scene, Antonio further demands that Bassanio demonstrate that he values Antonio's love more than Bassanio's "wife's commandement" that he safeguard her ring (4.1.449–451). The language of loan, not of gift, marks Antonio's speech, as in his final description, in the play's last scene, of his prior transaction with Bassanio: "I once did lend my body for his wealth" (5.1.249). He does not say "I once did give my body for his love." Sylvan Barnet, editor of the Signet edition of this play, strives in a footnote to soften this crass reminder of the money relations among our heroes Portia, Bassanio, and Antonio, glossing "wealth" as "welfare" ("I once did lend my body for his welfare" [n249, 98]). But Shakespeare wrote "wealth." Out of that wealth, we remember, was to come repayment of Bassanio's original debt to Antonio. So Antonio's diction is apt. It reminds us that this play's plots have not been impelled by an impulse toward wild erotic self-surrender but by the regulated claims of property. *The Merchant of Venice's* celebrated darkness has much to do with the fact that in it, rules and laws concerning private ownership are never forgotten or departed from either in Belmont or in Venice, but instead preserved obsessively, even absurdly, to the very letter, by others besides Shylock.

It is not that the Venetians do not love, but that love—an impulse and commitment that upholds a shared rather than a private identity—is not the prime motivator of their actions. Many scholars have observed that among all this play's characters, money and emotional interests are inextricably mixed.[4] True to his promise—"we will resemble you" (3.1.68)—Shylock is like the Christians in his intermingling of private emotional *and* financial claims. He likes profit, but his chief charge against Antonio finally has little to do with money; he turns down twice the number of ducats Bassanio owes him because he has paid a higher emotional price for Antonio's flesh (it is "dearly bought, is mine, and I will have it," he threatens [4.1.100]). Both in soliloquy and conversation with Tubal, he has framed his desire to kill Antonio as a business decision ("were he out of Venice I can make what merchandise I will" [3.1.127–129]). But the scene in which his anguished reaction to Jessica's elopement is interwoven with his glee at Antonio's business losses shows a more complicated self-concern. That a Christian has invaded Shylock's family justifies his radical reach for financial security through harming a Christian, he seems to conclude.

As for Jessica, her love for Lorenzo is bound to the social advantage she imagines she will acquire by marrying him.[5] "[A]shamed to be [her] father's child," she will "end this strife" by "[b]ecom[ing] a Christian and [Lorenzo's] loving wife" (2.3.17, 20–21). Lorenzo's love for Jessica is expressed in terms that suggest his similarly mixed motives of love and private acquisitiveness. "She hath directed / How I shall take her from her father's house, / What gold and jewels she is furnished with" (2.4.29–31).[6] Although Jessica and Lorenzo break the law, stealing from Shylock to pad their pockets, their thievery is oddly validated by law in act four. After Shylock's claims on Antonio's person are thwarted in court, the Duke requires Shylock to "record a gift / Here in the court of all he dies possessed / Unto his son Lorenzo and his daughter" (4.1.388–390). This ruling both safeguards Shylock's property, or a portion of it, during his life and preserves Jessica's portion, implicitly and retrospectively reframing the theft of money and jewels as a lawful activity. Shylock must legally will his possessions to "the gentleman / That lately *stole* his daughter" (4.1.384–385). Here again, law is not suspended but called into service to support, not love, but financial security. For the apparently broke Lorenzo

and Jessica, who have squandered their cash and jewels at the gaming tables
of Genoa, this contractual promise of financial support will be "manna" for
"starved people" (5.1.294–295).

Superficially, Portia appears radically to contrast with those in the play
who, like Shylock, want what is legally theirs. The apparent possessor of limitless wealth, she offers it all to Bassanio: "Myself, and what is mine, to you and
yours/ Is now converted," she tells him.

> But now I was the lord
> Of this fair mansion, master of my servants,
> Queen o'er myself, and even now, but now,
> This house, these servants, and this same myself
> Are yours. [. . .] (3.2.166–171)

Yet, as I, and other scholars, have noted, Portia hedges her promise with
stipulations regarding the safeguarding of a ring, then works against that
ring's safeguarding by encouraging Bassanio to give it away, and in the play's
last scene re-presents the ring to him without renewing her generous pledge
of house, servants, and self. "[B]id him keep it better than the other," she
says briefly, to Antonio, the second time (5.1.255). She reminds Bassanio
that to secure his gain in her, he must conform to the rules with which she
regulates that gain.[7] Bassanio and his follower Gratiano are the "Jasons";
they have "won the Fleece" (3.2.241). Still, audiences may know that Jason
lost everything in the end for not respecting the rights of his wife.

Portia's final contract with Bassanio is the last expression of a proprietary attitude she has demonstrated throughout the play. Her concern to keep
what she owns is implied early by her anti-comic insistence on honoring her
father's will. Portia's free choice of a husband is not hampered by an angry
Egeus or even a benign Baptista, but by a piece of paper that pledges her
material estate to the suitor who wins the casket game. "[S]o is the will of a
living daughter curbed by the will of a dead father" (1.2.24–25), she sighs. That
Portia abides by her father's will indicates that she—a woman as unromantic
as are Bassanio and Lorenzo—is not willing both to marry and be penniless. Superficially her words to Bassanio upon his arrival in Belmont express
self-abandonment in pursuit of the larger self found in erotic relationship, yet
they also imply the same frustrated desire for control of property—including
control over herself—that she has expressed in the play's first scene. "One
half of me is yours, the other half yours," she tells her suitor. "Mine own, I
would say; but if mine, then yours, / And so all yours! O these naughty times
/ Puts bars between the owners and their rights" (3.2.16–19). But Portia finds
a means to squeeze between those bars. No less committed than Shylock to

the rules, she works within them to achieve not only the husband of her desire but the mastery of her fortune and her fortunes. While numerous scholars have suggested that Portia cheats and helps Bassanio win the wooing game,[8] she does not cheat but hints, thus upholding the letter if not the spirit of her father's law. Portia ensures that while Bassanio makes his choice, he is sung a song whose first three lines rhyme with the word "lead," the metal of which the right casket is made (3.2.63–65). Doubtless Portia stands by, supplying the "fair speechless messages" her eyes are wont to give Bassanio, as he has earlier bragged to Antonio (1.1.163–166). Thus she ensures his victory without breaking the rules.

Once he has won, despite her words of absolute committal of her wealth and person, she never stops exercising proprietary rights over her stuff, which now includes Bassanio, as Corinne Abate (292) and Sandra Logan have noted. It is Portia, not Bassanio, who offers money to redeem Antonio once the message concerning his wreck is brought (3.2.299). Even after their hasty marriage, she goes where she pleases and refers to her servants as "My people" (3.4.37). Bassanio may return to Venice after he obeys her instructions, which are, "First go with me to church and call me wife" (3.2.304). "*By your leave,* / I bid my very friends and countrymen, / Sweet Portia, welcome," Bassanio says meekly when his friends arrive from Venice (3.2.222–224; my emphasis). At the play's end, it is again Portia who dispenses gifts, including—mysteriously—the news that some of Antonio's ships have come safely to port (5.1.276–277). Her dispensation of the wealth underscores her commitment to controlling it. In Portia, as in Antonio, generosity co-exists with a firm insistence on private holdings.

"Commodity" is a word for the anti-erotic interest in private rights that Portia subtly and other *Merchant* characters overtly exhibit. The most famous Shakespearean reference to "commodity" occurs in *King John*, when the Bastard calls political commodity the "bawd," "broker," and "bias of the world" (2.1.582, 574). In *Merchant*, written perhaps the same year as *King John* (i.e., 1595), Shakespeare shows a fascination with the claims of commodity in a financial context. In Venice, known to Elizabethans as a thriving commercial center, citizens' own fiscal sufficiency depends on the city's protection of the private interests of official "strangers" like Shylock. It is ironically Antonio, the generous lender who stands to suffer most from law's demands, who insists on upholding Venetian law to preserve "commodity." The "play's committed legalist," in Samuel Ajzenstat's phrase, Antonio "considers the commercial law of Venice untouchable" (272). He willingly submits to the bond by which he must yield his own life to Shylock because the law safeguarding property interests—the law by which he himself lives—demands it. "The duke cannot deny the course of law," he tells Solanio,

For the commodity that strangers have
With us in Venice, if it be denied,
Will much impeach the justice of the state,
Since that the trade and profit of the city
Consisteth of all nations. (3.3.26–31)

As Janet Adelman writes, Antonio's speech "implies a political economy in which states exist to insure trade conditions among 'nations' conceived as political and economic units" (21). This politico-economic context gives meaning to his life. His subsequent words in court suggest that if he can no longer function within that context, he is better off dead. Therefore, though the enforcement of contract law in this case threatens to kill him, he welcomes the law because as a "bankrout" (4.1.122)—and the apparent loser in a contest for Bassanio's heart—he has nothing for *which* to live. In providing a legal means by which he may die, Fortune "shows herself [. . .] kind" to Antonio. Not only will she allow him to secure a posthumous claim to Bassanio's affections by dying for him, she will also not make him "outlive his wealth" (4.1.267, 269) in a city where not only Shylock but other, possibly Gentile, "creditors grow cruel" (3.2.316).

Antonio here aligns Fortune with law. Though Portia will prove more powerful than Fortune and will avert the fate that Antonio thinks dooms him, still, she will not—like the dukes of *A Midsummer Night's Dream* and *The Comedy of Errors*—overturn law. In fact, she, like Antonio himself, explicitly forbids the Duke to subvert the law in a conventional comic manner. Antonio has told Solanio that the "Duke cannot deny the course of law" in Antonio's case without alienating "strangers" on whom commerce depends. But this caveat is a caveat only. The Duke *can* deny the course of law if he is willing to put what we would call human rights above property rights. And in fact, the Duke seems ready to do this. "Upon my power I may dismiss this court," he says, after failing to elicit from Shylock voluntary mercy, "Unless Bellario, a learned doctor / Whom I have sent for to determine this / Come here today" (4.1.104–107). Bellario sends Balthazar, or Portia in disguise, who thus seems summoned as Shylock's advocate rather than Antonio's. Portia is brought to "stand [. . .] for law" like Shylock (4.1.142), and stand for law—the contract which secures Shylock's property rights—is exactly what she finally does. As she questions Shylock, Bassanio appeals to the higher authority of the Duke, begging him, "Wrest the law to your authority" (4.1.215). Before the Duke can answer, Portia stops him. "It must not be" (4.1.218). She claims that "There is no power in Venice / Can alter a decree established," but her next lines suggest that this claim is more an argument regarding the wisdom of overriding the law than a statement of fact. If the Duke does kick the case out of court, "'Twill be recorded for a precedent / And many an error by the same example / Will rush into the state" (4.1.218–222). A proper comic duke's response would be "Who cares? Court adjourned, forever." But this duke silently affirms Portia's anti-comic insistence that the commodity of strangers outweigh kindness.

That the legal commodity of strangers is distinct from kindness to strangers becomes plain when we examine strangers' treatment in both Venice and Belmont. Both realms are structured by adherence to laws that safeguard the commodities of residents and strangers who form complex networks of mutual social and financial obligations. Portia's world is thus in one sense a mirror of the Venice she penetrates.[9] In it, strangers are allowed to compete in a wooing contest because a legal document requires their admission to the game, but their welcome is severely qualified. Her father's rules demand that Portia open her doors to a Neapolitan, an Englishman, a Spaniard, a French-man, a Scotsman, a German, and a Moroccan, but she makes clear to Nerissa and to the audience that she does not like any of them (1.2).[10] Her warm welcome is saved for the "young Venetian," Bassanio (2.9.87, 3.2). In Venice, in its turn, commercial imperatives obligate the Duke to uphold "stranger cur" (1.3.118) Shylock's contract rather than to overturn it in comic mercy, but—deferring to Portia—the Duke honors legal claims rather than the claims of human kindness for Shylock as well as for Antonio. Thus the Duke allows Portia an absurdly literalist reading of the bond that prevents its execution and violates its spirit. Shylock may take a pound of flesh, but no blood, and may not let the flesh's weight exceed one pound by "the twenti[e]th part / Of one poor scruple" (4.1.325, 329–330), a stipulation whose exactness would put an end to all commerce if generally enforced. In addition, once Shylock has forsworn the bond, the Duke sits by as she unnecessarily invokes an anti-alien law that threatens to kill Shylock.

Shylock, of course, has asked for all this by assuming a literalist as well as a legalist stance with regard to the bond. Having introduced the contract as a joke—"a merry sport" (1.3.145)—he clings in court to its cruel letter. Shylock stands generally opposed to verbal figures that break the boundar-ies of the literal. (As Anne Barton has said, he is "distrustful of metaphor or figurative language" [251].) "You call me [...] cutthroat dog," he has told Antonio. "Hath a dog money?" (1.3.111, 121). There is, then, some comic jus-tice in Portia's demonstration to Shylock of the limits of literalism in law. Yet the play's critique of literalism is chastened by the self-serving uses to which Portia and the other Christians put metaphor. Antonio's calling Shylock "cur-rish" and "wolvish" (4.1.133, 138) is partly justified by his rage at Shylock's cruel treatment of his creditors ("I oft delivered from his forfeitures / Many that have at times made moan to me," Antonio says [3.3.22–23]). Though the canine metaphors are harsh, in Antonio they are at least partly aligned with a generous purpose. Not so for Bassanio, whose extravagant poetic description of himself as Jason in quest of the golden fleece is a mere pretty mask for the plain financial need that sends him to Belmont, to woo "a lady richly left," the phrase that first leaps to his lips as a description of Portia (1.1.161). Portia's elaborate verbal gift of herself to Bassanio is, as we have seen, a deceptive conceit undercut by rules limiting that gift, as well as by her subsequent behavior, which demonstrates her continued autonomy. Finally, in the courtroom, the kindness offered to strangers itself becomes a word-screen behind which private interests may be preserved.

We see this *faux* kindness in Portia's insistence that mercy towards Antonio be not mandated by the Duke but freely embraced by Shylock. When Shylock refuses, he is granted his bond under terms that guarantee his own decision not to enforce it. Likewise, Shylock's conversion is not, strictly speaking, "coerced," as it is generally called, but formally chosen as a means of safeguarding his wealth.[11] His choice to convert comes on the heels of Antonio's proposed modification of the Duke's decision to spare Shylock's life, leave him half his wealth minus a fine, and give the other half of his money to Antonio. Antonio interjects,

> So please my lord the Duke and all the court
> To quit the fine for one half of his goods,
> I am content; so he will let me have
> The other half in use, to render it
> Upon his death unto the gentleman
> That lately stole his daughter.
> Two things provided more: that for this favor
> He presently become a Christian;
> The other, that he do record a gift
> Here in the court of all he dies possessed
> Unto his son Lorenzo and his daughter. (4.1.380–390)

Antonio's bizarre proposition subverts Christ's instruction that to become his follower a rich man must "sell that [he] ha[th], and give it to the poor" (Matthew 19:21, Geneva). According to Antonio's caveat, Shylock will give up all he owns only if he *doesn't* formally follow Christ. Shakespeare here imaginatively reverses the popularly believed-in Venetian civic custom of appropriating the goods of Jewish converts. ("All their goods are confiscated as soon as they embrace Christianity," Thomas Coryate wrote of the Jews in 1610.) Conversion to Christianity is now, to the contrary, the only means by which Shylock may *keep* some of his goods during life. Conversion on these terms is, of course, a mockery of faith, but it is one framed by the Venetians in terms that support the play's overriding concern with the preservation of private property. Formally, if bitterly, accepting the proposal in order to stay in business—"I am content," Shylock says (4.1.394)—Shylock is merely participating in the anti-comic economy of property interests that structures the play.

Nor is Antonio selfless here. While several scholars have suggested that in the lines quoted above Antonio is proposing only to administer the half of Shylock's estate granted him "on Shylock's behalf,"[12] the sense of his words is surely otherwise. Superficially, the lines are confusing. Antonio says he is "content" for the Duke to remit a fine for Shylock and allow Shylock free use of half his own goods if Shylock "will let me have the other half in use." However, the first part of that statement is "precatory"—it has no legal bearing on the judgment just pronounced—and the second part is redundant. Antonio "has no power over, nor any interest in," the half of Shylock's wealth that was due the state before the Duke reduced that penalty, as Richard Weisberg says (15),[13] and as for the other half, he has already been granted it (and only it). He does not need to bargain for half of Shylock's wealth "in use." So what does he mean?

Joan Ozark Holmer argues that Antonio here pledges himself only to employ the interest, or "use," on Shylock's goods, and not to "touch the principal," but if this is so we see Antonio suddenly agreeing to profit from a business practice he has heretofore hated.[14] The more likely meaning is the obvious one: that Antonio, now that he is going to live in Venice after all, wants to *use* the money as though it were a lifetime loan from Shylock ("let me have / The other half in use"). To adapt Portia's phrase, one half of what's Shylock's—minus the court-mandated fine—is Shylock's, the other half, "Shylock's," though really Antonio's. At the end of Shylock's life—enough time, one would think, for Antonio to relaunch his hazardous business—the money will be converted, in the most punishing way, to the use of Shylock's hated son-in-law and daughter. Like the fake lifetime loan, the bequest will be a fake (but legal) "gift" from a fake Christian to a fake "son" and a daughter he has emotionally disowned. ("Clerk, draw a deed of gift" [4.1.394], Portia says to the fake clerk, Nerissa.) Shylock's choice to keep any of his money is thus made contingent on his official agreement to be financially kind to his bitterest enemies, Antonio, Jessica, and Lorenzo. Again, the appearance of generosity is made by law a mask for the property interests of everyone.

Samuel Ajzenstat has eloquently argued that the stress on private interests in *Merchant* makes the play not anti-comic, but a different kind of romantic comedy than most of Shakespeare's others. Perhaps, he suggests, with its "basic metaphor [of] the contract," the play is "meant to remind us that there was never a time when love and friendship did not have a hard time maintaining themselves against the necessities of nature and commerce even while depending on those necessities for support" (Ajzenstat 263, 277). Perhaps, though Shakespeare may also have meant to critique the commercial self-interestedness that debased human interaction in his own London, a place where, according to the late sixteenth-century pamphleteer Miles Mosse, "lending upon usury is grown so common and usual among men, as that free lending to the needy is utterly overthrown." What seems inarguable is that in *Merchant* Shakespeare's own interest lay in exploring how private interests, guarded by law, could challenge and taint the lawless but kind forces of erotic and filial love. In *The Comedy of Errors*, Antipholus of Ephesus, seeking his family, is like a dissolving

> drop of water,
> That in the ocean, seeks another drop,
> Who, falling there to find his fellow forth
> [. . .] confounds himself. (1.2.35–38)

In *Much Ado about Nothing* and *As You Like It*, characters embrace *the* danger of cuckoldry—the violation of masculine identity, in conventional terms—to embrace the mutuality of marriage. "The horn, the horn, the lusty horn / Is not a thing to laugh to scorn" sing the men of the Arden Forest (4.2.17–18).[15] In these as in most of Shakespeare's comedies, characters radically risk their private identities to engage the larger, shared selves found in familial or marital relationships. Laws that safeguard ownership—such as the law that upholds Egeon's rights to his daughter in *A Midsummer Night's Dream*—are done away with in celebration of these larger connections. Not so in *The Merchant of Venice*, which accomplishes the reverse. In this play, eros, friendship, and even mercy are managed so that each character keeps legal title at least to a portion of what he or she owns.

Notes

1. All quotations from Shakespeare's plays are from *The Riverside Shakespeare*.

2. "Vantage" and "Exclaim" are so defined in *The Compact Oxford English Dictionary*.

3. The term was used in a post-paper discussion at the 39th Kalamazoo Congress for Medieval Studies, 2004.

4. See, for example, Samuel Ajzenstat's "Contract in *The Merchant of Venice*" and Nancy Elizabeth Hodge's "Making Places at Belmont: 'You Are Welcome Notwithstanding.'"

5. Karoline Szatek comments on Jessica's "usury" in her marriage transaction in "*The Merchant of Venice* and the Politics of Commerce," in *The Merchant of Venice: New Critical Essays*, ed. John and Ellen McMahon, 338.

6. Michael Radford's film version of *The Merchant of Venice* (Sony Pictures Entertainment, 2004) brilliantly expresses the mixture of romantic and mercenary motives in the elopement in its interpretation of the scene wherein Lorenzo takes Jessica and the money from Shylock's house. In a gondola below her window he rhapsodically praises her beauty and virtues, but interrupts himself twice with "No!" as he sees her about to throw the casket of money and jewels from the window, out of fear that the loot will not land in the boat but sink in the canal.

7. As Ajzenstat writes, Portia implicitly tells Bassanio at the play's end, "my sexual fidelity is contingent on yours" (270).

8. See Bruce Erlich's "Queenly Shadows in Two Comedies" (*Shakespeare Survey* 335 [1982]: 65–77), S. F. Johnson's "How Many Ways Portia Informs Bassanio's Choice" (*Shakespeare's Universe: Renaissance Ideas and Conventions*. Ed. John M. Mucciolo. Aldershot: Scholar's Press, 1996. 144–147), Ajzenstat, and Michael Zuckert's "The New Medea: On Portia's Comic Triumph in *The Merchant of Venice*" (*Shakespeare's Political Pageant: Essays in Literature and Politics*. Eds. Joseph Aluis and Vickie Sullivan. Lanham, Maryland: Rowman and Littlefield Publishers, Inc., 1996), among others.

9. Adelman also makes this point (22).

10. Nancy Elizabeth Hodge points out that *déclassé* merchants are also not fully welcome at Belmont.

11. See James Shapiro's comment, "'Coerced' conversions were virtually unheard of in the various narratives circulating about Jews in sixteenth-century England" (131).

12. Lawrence Danson, *The Harmonies of* The Merchant of Venice, 164. See also Joan Ozark Holmer, who says that Antonio requests his half "in use" and "cannot touch the principal" (216), and thus appears "all the more generous" (217), and John Russell Brown, who says Antonio uses his money for Shylock. Hugh Short, among others, argues that Antonio will manage the money for the benefit of Lorenzo and Jessica (199).

13. As Peter J. Alscher writes, "Antonio's [. . .] disbursement of his half of Shylock's wealth with its two painful financial conditions" is unmerciful (25).

14. As Peter J. Alscher and Richard Weisberg note, Antonio's "'trust' arrangement practices a form of interest profiting which he [once] swore to Antonio's face he never engaged in" (204).

15. See the detailed discussion of the essentialness of the surrender of private holdings to mutuality in Grace Tiffany, *Erotic Beasts and Social Monsters: Shakespeare, Jonson, and Comic Androgyny*.

Works Cited

Abate, Corinne. "'Nerissa Teaches Me What To Believe': Portia's Wifely Empowerment in *The Merchant of Venice*." *The Merchant of Venice: New Critical Essays*. Ed. John and Ellen Mahon. New York: Routledge, 2002. 283–304.

Adelman, Janet. "Her Father's Blood: Race, Conversion, and Nation in *The Merchant of Venice*." *Representations* 81 (Winter 2003): 4–30.

Ajzenstat, Samuel. "Contract in *The Merchant of Venice*." *Philosophy and Literature* 21 (1997): 262–278.

Alscher, Peter J. "'I would be friends with you . . .': Staging Directions for a Balanced Resolution to 'The Merchant of Venice' Trial Scene." *Cardozo Studies in Law and Literature* 5.1 (Spring 1993): 1–33.

Alscher, Peter J., and Richard H. Weisberg. "King James and an Obsession with *The Merchant of Venice*." *Property Law in Renaissance Literature*. Ed. Daniela Carpi. New York: Peter Lang, 2005. 1–226.

Barnet, Sylvan, ed. *The Merchant of Venice*. By William Shakespeare. New York: New American Library, 1998.

Barton, Anne. Introduction. *The Merchant of Venice*. *The Riverside Shakespeare*. Ed. G. Blakemore Evans. Boston: Houghton-Mifflin, 1974. 250–253.

Brown, John Russell, ed. *The Merchant of Venice*. New York: Methuen, 1961.

Coryate, Thomas. *Coryate's Crudities*. London, 1611.

Danson, Lawrence. *The Harmonies of The Merchant of Venice*. New Haven: Yale UP, 1978.

The Geneva Bible, A Facsimile of the 1560 Edition. Madison: U of Wisconsin P, 1967.

Hodge, Nancy Elizabeth. "Making Places at Belmont: 'You Are Welcome Notwithstanding.'" *Shakespeare Studies* 21 (1993): 155–174.

Holmer, Joan Ozark. *The Merchant of Venice: Choice, Hazard, Consequences*. New York: St. Martin's Press, 1995.

Logan, Sandra. "'The Will of a Living Daughter': Letter and Spirit in *The Merchant of Venice*." Paper presented at the Ohio Shakespeare Conference, Toledo, October, 2005.

Marlowe, Christopher. *The Jew of Malta*. *Christopher Marlowe: The Complete Plays*. Ed. J. B. Steane. New York: 1986. 342–430.

Mosse, Miles. *The Arraignment and Conviction of Usury*. London, 1595.

Shakespeare, William. *The Riverside Shakespeare*. Ed. G. Blakemore Evans. Boston: Houghton-Mifflin, 1974.

Shapiro, James. *Shakespeare and the Jews*. New York: Columbia UP, 1996.

Short, Hugh. "Shylock Is Content." *The Merchant of Venice: New Critical Essays*. Ed. John and Ellen Mahon. New York: Routledge, 2002. 199–212.

Szatek, Karoline. "*The Merchant of Venice* and the Politics of Commerce." *The Merchant of Venice: New Critical Essays*. Ed. John and Ellen Mahon. New York: Routledge, 2002. 325–352.

Tiffany, Grace. *Erotic Beasts and Social Monsters: Shakespeare, Jonson, and Comic Androgyny*. Newark: U of Delaware P, 1995.

Weisberg, Richard. "Antonio's Legalistic Cruelty: Interdisciplinarity and 'The Merchant of Venice.'" *College Literature* 25.1 (Winter 1998): 12–20.

Chronology

1564	William Shakespeare christened at Stratford-on-Avon on April 26.
1582	Marries Anne Hathaway in November.
1583	Daughter Susanna born, baptized on May 26.
1585	Twins Hamnet and Judith born, baptized on February 2.
1587	Shakespeare goes to London, without family.
1589–90	*Henry VI, Part 1* written.
1590–91	*Henry VI, Part 2* and *Henry VI, Part 3* written.
1592–93	*Richard III* and *The Two Gentlemen of Verona* written.
1593	Publication of *Venus and Adonis*, dedicated to the Earl of Southampton; the *Sonnets* probably begun.
1593	*The Comedy of Errors* written.
1593–94	Publication of *The Rape of Lucrece*, also dedicated to the Earl of Southampton. *Titus Andronicus* and *The Taming of the Shrew* written.
1594–95	*Love's Labour's Lost*, *King John*, and *Richard II* written.
1595–96	*Romeo and Juliet* and *A Midsummer Night's Dream* written.
1596	Son Hamnet dies.

1596–97	*The Merchant of Venice* and *Henry IV, Part 1* written; purchases New Place in Stratford.
1597–98	*The Merry Wives of Windsor* and *Henry IV, Part 2* written.
1598–99	*Much Ado About Nothing* written.
1599	*Henry V, Julius Caesar,* and *As You Like It* written.
1600–01	*Hamlet* written.
1601	*The Phoenix and the Turtle* written; father dies.
1601–02	*Twelfth Night* and *Troilus and Cressida* written.
1602–03	*All's Well That Ends Well* written.
1603	Shakespeare's company becomes the King's Men.
1604	*Measure for Measure* and *Othello* written.
1605	*King Lear* written.
1606	*Macbeth* and *Antony and Cleopatra* written.
1607	Marriage of daughter Susanna on June 5.
1607–08	*Coriolanus, Timon of Athens,* and *Pericles* written.
1608	Mother dies.
1609	Publication, probably unauthorized, of the quarto edition of the *Sonnets.*
1609–10	*Cymbeline* written.
1610–11	*The Winter's Tale* written.
1611	*The Tempest* written. Shakespeare returns to Stratford, where he will live until his death.
1612	*A Funeral Elegy* written.
1612–13	*Henry VIII* written; The Globe Theatre destroyed by fire.
1613	*The Two Noble Kinsmen* written (with John Fletcher).
1616	Daughter Judith marries on February 10; Shakespeare dies April 23.
1623	Publication of the First Folio edition of Shakespeare's plays.

Contributors

HAROLD BLOOM is Sterling Professor of the Humanities at Yale University. Educated at Cornell and Yale universities, he is the author of more than 30 books, including *Shelley's Mythmaking* (1959), *The Visionary Company* (1961), *Blake's Apocalypse* (1963), *Yeats* (1970), *The Anxiety of Influence* (1973), *A Map of Misreading* (1975), *Kabbalah and Criticism* (1975), *Agon: Toward a Theory of Revisionism* (1982), *The American Religion* (1992), *The Western Canon* (1994), *Omens of Millennium: The Gnosis of Angels, Dreams, and Resurrection* (1996), *Shakespeare: The Invention of the Human* (1998), *How to Read and Why* (2000), *Genius: A Mosaic of One Hundred Exemplary Creative Minds* (2002), *Hamlet: Poem Unlimited* (2003), *Where Shall Wisdom Be Found?* (2004), and *Jesus and Yahweh: The Names Divine* (2005). In addition, he is the author of hundreds of articles, reviews, and editorial introductions. In 1999, Professor Bloom received the American Academy of Arts and Letters' Gold Medal for Criticism. He has also received the International Prize of Catalonia, the Alfonso Reyes Prize of Mexico, and the Hans Christian Andersen Bicentennial Prize of Denmark.

HARRY BERGER JR. is professor emeritus of literature and art history at the University of California, Santa Cruz, of which he also is a founding faculty member. He is the author of numerous books, among them *Imaginary Audition: Shakespeare on Stage and Page*.

COPPÉLIA KAHN is a professor of English and gender studies at Brown University and was president of the Shakespeare Association of America. Her work on Shakespeare includes *Roman Shakespeare: Warriors, Wounds, and Women* and *Man's Estate: Masculine Identity in Shakespeare*.

189

RICHARD A. LEVIN is a professor in the English department at the University of California, Davis. He has written *Shakespeare's Secret Schemers: The Study of an Early Modern Dramatic Device*.

ROBERT ORNSTEIN was a professor at Case Western Reserve University and a president of the Shakespeare Association of America. He wrote many books and articles on Shakespeare and other Renaissance dramatists, including the texts *A Kingdom for a Stage: The Achievement of Shakespeare's History Plays* and *The Moral Vision of Jacobean Tragedy*.

HARRY LEVIN was a professor of comparative literature at Harvard University and is considered one of the founders of the field of comparative literature in the United States. Some of his major works include *The Myth of the Golden Age in the Renaissance* and *Shakespeare and the Revolution of the Times*.

TONY TANNER was a professor at King's College, Cambridge. He edited the eight-volume Everyman edition of Shakespeare's works. Tanner's work also includes *Prefaces to Shakespeare* and many other titles that he wrote or edited.

W. H. AUDEN was a poet, essayist, playwright, editor, and librettist. He was Professor of Poetry at the University of Oxford and taught at several universities in the United States. He wrote many volumes of poetry and edited or co-edited many anthologies, including *Poets of the English Language*.

PETER D. HOLLAND is a professor of Shakespeare studies at the University of Notre Dame, where he also is chair of the department of film, television, and theatre. He is editor of *Shakespeare Survey*, associate general editor for the *Oxford Drama Library*, and co-editor of *From Script to Stage in Early Modern England*.

GRACE TIFFANY is a Shakespeare professor in the English department at Western Michigan University. She has written *Erotic Beasts and Social Monsters: Shakespeare, Jonson, and Comic Androgyny* and *Love's Pilgrimage: The Holy Journey in English Renaissance Literature*, as well as a novel based on *The Merchant of Venice* and two others about Shakespeare's family.

Bibliography

Adelman, Janet. "Her Father's Blood: Race, Conversion, and Nation in *The Merchant of Venice.*" *Representation* 81 (2003): 4–30.

Boehrer, Bruce. "Shylock and the Rise of the Household Pet: Thinking Social Exclusion in *The Merchant of Venice.*" *Shakespeare Quarterly* 50, no. 2 (1999): 152–170.

Bovilsky, Lara. *Barbarous Play: Race on the English Renaissance Stage.* Minneapolis: University of Minnesota Press, 2008.

Carroll, William C. *The Metamorphoses of Shakespearean Comedy.* Princeton, N.J.: Princeton University Press, 1985.

Cookson, Linda, and Bryan Loughrey, eds. The Merchant of Venice: *Longman Critical Essays.* Essex: Longman, 1992.

Critchley, Simon. "Universal Shylockery: Money and Morality in *The Merchant of Venice.*" *Diacritics: A Review of Contemporary Criticism* 34, no. 1 (Spring 2004): 3–17.

Danson, Lawrence. *The Harmonies of* The Merchant of Venice. New Haven: Yale University Press, 1978.

Forman, Valerie. *Tragicomic Redemptions: Global Economics and the Early Modern English Stage.* Philadelphia: University of Pennsylvania Press, 2008.

Freeman, Jane. "'Fair Terms and a Villain's Mind': Rhetorical Patterns in *The Merchant of Venice.*" *Rhetorica: A Journal of the History of Rhetoric* 20, no. 2 (Spring 2002): 149–172.

Frye, Northrop. *A Natural Perspective: The Development of Shakespearean Comedy and Romance.* New York: Columbia University Press, 1965.

Garber, Marjorie. *Shakespeare and Modern Culture.* New York: Pantheon, 2008.

Girard, René. "'To Entrap the Wisest': A Reading of *The Merchant of Venice*." In *Literature and Society*, ed. E. W. Said. Baltimore: Johns Hopkins University Press, 1980.

Gleckman, Jason. "*The Merchant of Venice*: Laws Written and Unwritten in Venice." *Critical Review* 41 (2001): 81–94.

Gross, John. *Shylock: A Legend and Its Legacy*. New York: Simon and Schuster, 1992.

Gross, Kenneth. *Shylock Is Shakespeare*. Chicago: University of Chicago Press, 2006.

Halio, Jay L. *Understanding* The Merchant of Venice: *A Student Casebook to Issues, Sources, and Historical Documents*. Westport, Conn.: Greenwood Press, 2000.

Halpern, Richard. *Shakespeare Among the Moderns*. Ithaca, N.Y.: Cornell University Press, 1997.

Holmer, Joan Ozark. The Merchant of Venice: *Choice, Hazard, Consequences*. New York: St. Martin's Press, 1995.

Honigmann, E. A. J. *British Academy Shakespeare Lectures 1980–89*. Oxford: Oxford University Press, 1993.

Huffman, Clifford Chalmers, ed. Love's Labor's Lost, A Midsummer Night's Dream, *and* The Merchant of Venice: *An Annotated Bibliography of Shakespeare Studies, 1888–1994*. Binghamton, N.Y.: Medieval & Renaissance Texts and Studies, 1995.

Hutson, Lorna. *The Usurer's Daughter: Male Friendship and Fictions of Women in Sixteenth-Century England*. New York: Routledge, 1994.

Janik, Vicki K. The Merchant of Venice: *A Guide to the Play*. Westport, Conn.: Greenwood Press, 2003.

Kitch, Aaron. "Shylock's Sacred Nation." *Shakespeare Quarterly* 59, no. 2 (Summer 2008): 131–155.

Lampert, Lisa. *Gender and Jewish Difference from Paul to Shakespeare*. Philadelphia: University of Pennsylvania Press, 2004.

Levin, Carole. *Shakespeare's Foreign Worlds: National and Transnational Identities in the Elizabethan Age*. Ithaca, N.Y.: Cornell University Press, 2009.

Lewis, Cynthia. *Particular Saints: Shakespeare's Four Antonios, Their Contexts, and Their Plays*. Newark: University of Delaware Press; London; Cranbury, N.J.: Associated University Presses, 1997.

Logan, Robert A. *Shakespeare's Marlowe: The Influence of Christopher Marlowe on Shakespeare's Artistry*. Aldershot, England; Burlington, Vt.: Ashgate, 2007.

Mahon, John W., and Ellen Macleod Mahon, ed. The Merchant of Venice: *New Critical Essays*. London, England: Routledge, 2002.

Majeske, Andrew, and Emily Detmer-Goebel, ed. *Justice, Women, and Power in English Renaissance Drama*. Madison, N.J.: Fairleigh Dickinson University Press, 2009.

McGinn, Colin. *Shakespeare's Philosophy: Discovering the Meaning Behind the Plays.* New York: HarperCollins, 2006.

McPherson, David C. *Shakespeare, Jonson, and the Myth of Venice.* Newark: University of Delaware Press; London; Cranbury, N.J.: Associated University Presses, 1990.

Newman, Karen. *Essaying Shakespeare.* Minneapolis: University of Minnesota Press, 2009.

———. "Portia's Ring: Unruly Women and the Structure of Exchange in *The Merchant of Venice.*" *Shakespeare Quarterly* 38, no. 1 (1987): 19–33.

———. *Shakespeare's Rhetoric of Comic Character: Dramatic Convention in Classical and Renaissance Comedy.* New York: Methuen, 1985.

Occhiogrosso, Frank, ed. *Shakespeare in Performance: A Collection of Essays.* Newark: University of Delaware Press, 2003.

Oz, Avraham. *The Yoke of Love: Prophetic Riddles in* The Merchant of Venice. Newark: University of Delaware Press; London: Associated University Presses, 1995.

Robinson, Elaine L. *Shakespeare Attacks Bigotry: A Close Reading of Six Plays.* Jefferson, N.C.: McFarland, 2009.

Roston, Murray. *Tradition and Subversion in Renaissance Literature: Studies in Shakespeare, Spenser, Jonson, and Donne.* Pittsburgh: Duquesne University Press, 2007.

Salinger, L. G. *Shakespeare and the Traditions of Comedy.* Cambridge: Cambridge University Press, 1974.

Schneider, Robert. *Shylock, The Roman: Unmasking Shakespeare's* The Merchant of Venice. Mill Valley, Calif.: Pulpless.com, 1999.

Schwartz, Regina M. "The Price of Justice and Love in *The Merchant of Venice.*" *TriQuarterly* 124 (2006): 225–241.

Shannon, Laurie. "Likenings: Rhetorical Husbandries and Portia's 'True Conceit' of Friendship." *Renaissance Drama* 31 (2002): 3–26.

Shapiro, James. *Shakespeare and the Jews.* New York: Columbia University Press, 1996.

Sherman, Anita Gilman. "Disowning Knowledge of Jessica, or Shylock's Skepticism." *Studies in English Literature, 1500–1900* 44, no. 2 (Spring 2004): 277–295.

Special Issue: Shakespeare's *The Merchant of Venice. Cithara: Essays in the Judaeo-Christian Tradition* 46, no. 1 (November 2006): 3–63.

Spiller, Elizabeth A. "From Imagination to Miscegenation: Race and Romance in Shakespeare's *The Merchant of Venice.*" *Renaissance Drama* 29 (1998): 137–164.

Turner, Henry S. "The Problem of the More-than-One: Friendship, Calculation, and Political Association in *The Merchant of Venice.*" *Shakespeare Quarterly* 57, no. 4 (Winter 2006): 413–442.

Weisberg, Richard H., ed. A Symposium Issue on *The Merchant of Venice*. *Cardozo Studies in Law and Literature* 5, no. 1 (Spring 1993).

Wells, Stanley, and Lena Cowen Orlin, ed. *Shakespeare: An Oxford Guide*. New York: Oxford University Press, 2003.

Wheeler, Thomas, ed. The Merchant of Venice: *Critical Essays*. New York: Garland, 1991.

Wilson, Richard. *Secret Shakespeare: Studies in Theatre, Religion, and Resistance*. Manchester, England: Manchester University Press, 2004.

Yachnin, Paul, and Patricia Badir, ed. *Shakespeare and the Cultures of Performance*. Aldershot, England; Burlington, Vt.: Ashgate, 2008.

Yaffe, Martin D. *Shylock and the Jewish Question*. Baltimore, Md.; London: Johns Hopkins University Press, 1997.

Acknowledgments

Harry Berger Jr., "Marriage and Mercifixion in *The Merchant of Venice*: The Casket Scene Revisited." From *Shakespeare Quarterly* vol. 32, no. 2 (Summer 1981): 155–62. Copyright © 1981 by the Folger Shakespeare Library.

Coppélia Kahn, "The Cuckoo's Note: Male Friendship and Cuckoldry in *The Merchant of Venice.*" From *Shakespeare's "Rough Magic": Renaissance Essays in Honor of C. L. Barber*, edited by Peter Erickson and Coppélia Kahn. Published by University of Delaware Press. Copyright © 1985 by Associated University Presses.

Richard A. Levin, "Portia's Belmont." From *Love and Society in Shakespearean Comedy: A Study of Dramatic Form and Content.* Published by University of Delaware Press. Copyright © 1985 by Associated University Presses.

Robert Ornstein, "*The Merchant of Venice.*" From *Shakespeare's Comedies: From Roman Farce to Romantic Mystery.* Published by University of Delaware Press. Copyright © 1986 by Associated University Presses.

Harry Levin, "A Garden in Belmont: *The Merchant of Venice*, 5.1." From *Shakespeare and Dramatic Tradition: Essays in Honor of S. F. Johnson*, edited by W. R. Elton and William B. Long. Published by University of Delaware Press. Copyright © 1989 by Associated University Presses.

Tony Tanner, "Which Is the Merchant Here? And Which the Jew?: The Venice of Shakespeare's *Merchant of Venice.*" From *Venetian Views, Venetian Blinds: Eng-*

195

lish Fantasies of Venice, edited by Manfred Pfister and Barbara Schaff. Copyright © 1999 by Editions Rodopi B.V.

W. H. Auden, *"The Merchant of Venice."* From *Lectures on Shakespeare*, reconstructed and edited by Arthur Kirsch. Copyright © 2000 by Arthur Kirsch for the notes and © 2000 by the estate of W. H. Auden for lectures and writings by Auden.

Peter D. Holland, *"The Merchant of Venice* and the Value of Money." From *Cahiers Élisabéthains* 60 (October 2001): 13–30. Copyright © 2001 by Cahiers Élisabéthains.

Grace Tiffany, "Law and Self-Interest in *The Merchant of Venice*." From *Papers on Language and Literature* vol. 42, no. 4 (Fall 2006): 384–400. Copyright © 2006 by the Board of Trustees, Southern Illinois University Edwardsville. Reprinted by permission.

Every effort has been made to contact the owners of copyrighted material and secure copyright permission. Articles appearing in this volume generally appear much as they did in their original publication with few or no editorial changes. In some cases, foreign language text has been removed from the original essay. Those interested in locating the original source will find the information cited above.

Index

197